Live with Flair
Seasons of Worship and Wonder

To Kerry

[signature]

Welcome! I'm so glad you are here.

You might be wondering what, exactly, you hold in your hands. As part memoir, part devotional, and part spiritual experiment, this book represents a five year journey of collecting beautiful moments of worship and wonder in ordinary days. What began as a blogging project to daily record *something extraordinary* in the most mundane things—whether acorns, cats, raspberries, or jump ropes—quickly became an all-encompassing paradigm shift. I learned a new philosophy of living. Through this challenge of locating and recording special moments, I became a different person. I experienced a deeper and more joyous kind of living. I began, as the poet William Wordsworth did as well, to "see into the life of things" and encounter a "sense sublime" in my surroundings.[1] After five years, and with the help of my friend Margaret Baker pointing this out, I noticed the seasonal patterns of worship and wonder and desired to cull my favorite 100 moments from each season over those years. My husband wondered how we might publish them altogether and keep them for our children. We wanted a book we might hold in our hands and pass on to grandchildren and great-grandchildren. I loved this idea since part of living with flair includes legacy-leaving and staying attuned to what we pass on as an everlasting witness to God's faithfulness.

The 100 moments in each season scatter across the pages like the acorns on my driveway. What unites these lessons more than chronological narrative or devotional themes is simply something random and astonishing that you weren't expecting to think about that day. You might read one a day throughout summer (and finish with 10 to spare), or sit with a hot mug of hot cocoa and a soft blanket in your favorite chair to read all of winter's lessons in one sitting. However you choose to enjoy this collection, I hope, by the end, you'll join me in realizing how precious each day is. Perhaps, like the poet Monique Duval wrote, you'll "swing your window open, the one with the fresh air and good eastern light, and watch for wings, edges, new beginnings."[2] I pray that you become so aware and so receptive to the wonder this day holds. Then, like me, you'll close your eyes and worship.

Special thanks to all the precious family and friends who have enriched the days recorded here. I offer my highest thanks to Jesus. This book is a deliverance song to God. May it be true, as the writer states in Psalm 105:33-35 that "I will sing to the Lord all my life. I will sing praise to my God as long as I live. May my meditation be pleasing to Him as I rejoice in the Lord."

Heather Holleman

Table of Contents

Winter

Spring

Summer

Autumn

Winter

Though the fig tree does not bud and there are no grapes on the vines, though the olive crop fails and the fields produce no food, though there are no sheep in the pen and no cattle in the stalls, yet I will rejoice in the Lord, I will be joyful in God my Savior. The Sovereign Lord is my strength; he makes my feet like the feet of a deer, he enables me to tread on the heights.

Habakkuk 3:17-19

Winter

1. Carefully Observed

As I prepare a writing lesson, I think about Mary Pipher's statement that "all animals, carefully observed, have things to teach us. So does every person we encounter."[1] On her chapter on diving into the writing process in her book, *Writing to Change the World*, she quotes Ernest Hemingway when he says, "If a writer stops observing he is finished. Experience is communicated by small details intimately observed."[2]

I've been observing the fat, fluffy cardinals that have discovered the four different feeders we placed in the backyard for them. They stay so close to this food source all day long. They lounge in the trees and enjoy the bounty. They don't leave. They just feed and rest, feed and rest.

That's the work of a winter in the heart. There's a season for staying so close to God—feed and rest, feed and rest—because the spring will come soon.

Besides observing the birds, I watch my kitten. Inside the warm house, I have a new kitten who can't stand to be alone. In the morning, he'll sit in the middle of the house and meow pitifully until my old cat comes to find him to play. Hearing him cry out like that, from the depths of his kitty self, and seeing the quick response of the older cat, teaches me something about crying out to God.

Feed and rest. Cry out. It's winter.

2. What You've Been Given

It's officially winter here.

Snow swirls up and settles, finally, on the land.

It's the worst kind of snow because there's not enough to do anything with it.

But the neighborhood children, despite the lack of significant snow accumulation, still coax sleds down hills all afternoon. They still make snowmen no matter how little they are given. In one child's front yard, I stop and notice she's made a mama and a baby snowman in miniature.

Lord, help me take what I've been given today and turn it into a beautiful thing.

Living with flair means I make something out of whatever I'm given.

3. Is There Such a Thing?

Today, my friend tells me I have the spiritual gift of "celebration." Is there such a thing? There must be! *Living with Flair* is all about celebration, especially in the stark, wintery times in life. Lord, help me continue to celebrate!

I want to remember to celebrate when I have long, boring days of work and chores and sadness and disappointment. There's *something* or *someone* to celebrate here. There's something to dance a jig about, slap a high-five for, squeal-with-my-hands-over-my-mouth for, perform little jumps in the air for, grab-my-friend's-shoulders-and-jiggle-and-jump-and-kiss-on-the-cheek about, pump my fist over, whoop and holler about, turn a cartwheel for, sing the Hallelujah chorus over, write a blog about. . . you get the idea. Living with flair means we're gonna celebrate. There's always *something*—or better yet, *Someone*—to celebrate. It might be anything—large or small, obvious or hidden—that's just waiting for us to observe and cheer over. Woo-hoo! Yahoo! Yeah!

4. What We're Meant For

Today I notice the Weeping Cherry, and the beautiful intricacy of the ice on her limbs captures my attention.

A swirling scaffolding of crystal sparkles in the late afternoon sun. It's so beautiful that I almost forget how terrible this weight is for my Weeping Cherry's fragile branches. She's not meant for it.

When I think about what I'm meant for, and when I start to desire that shimmer of fame or importance to capture attention, I remember this: God made the Weeping Cherry for its own unique kind of blossom and rich green foliage. Let everything else melt off and free her to be what she was meant to be. She'll bloom in time.

5. Beauty that Astounds

I learn something astounding about snowflakes today: the more hostile the environment, the more intricate the snowflake's shape. The bitter cold and wind encourage sharp tips and branching designs while warmer temperatures produce slow-growing, smooth, and simple patterns.

I'd rather have complex, sophisticated, and beautiful. I'd rather have unexpected and perplexing than smooth and simple.

I stand in my backyard as the storm swirls about me. I think of what it takes to make such beauty.

It's not easy; it's not warm and smooth. What's harsh in our environment right now shapes beautiful things in us. That kind of beauty—born from trial and thorn—truly astounds.

6. A Little Love Story

This morning, the little one plows into our bed and announces that she is about to lose her first loose tooth.

The world stops for a minute. A first lost tooth!

In our family, we let Dad do the tooth pulling. There's even a title assigned to this role. He pinches his thumb and forefinger together and calls his hand the "Extractor." The girls giggle and squeal as the Extractor approaches the loose tooth.

Meanwhile, my daughter's mouth contains exceptionally tiny teeth, and the Extractor can hardly get a hold of that one small front tooth.

I'm watching this dad—so large by comparison—bending low and peering inside that small mouth. He examines with great care that little tooth and suggests we try to pull it this evening since it's not quite ready. It seems so strange, so wonderful, as I observe this interaction.

Is there anything too small for this dad to care about—to know so well? Is there anything about his daughter that he wouldn't stop everything for, bend low, and examine and tend to?

God whispers in my heart from 1 John 3:1: "See what great love the Father has lavished on us, that we should be called children of God! And that is what we are!" I imagine myself as that daughter. Do I realize God knows everything about me? Can it be true, as the Psalmist says in Psalm 56, that our tears are on a scroll—part of God's record? Can it be true that, as Jesus himself proclaims in Matthew 10:30, "Even the very hairs of [our] head are all numbered. So don't be afraid. . . "?

A father knows—and cares deeply about—even a loose tooth. What can happen to me today that falls outside the knowledge and loving attention of the Father?

Living with flair means I realize that even tiny details about me are known, cared about, and tended to by God.

7. How You Know You're Getting Better

Do you remember the story of my one-eyed cat, Jack? We rescued this wounded kitty and brought him into our home. He couldn't even purr, he was that broken. But we knew his purr was in there somewhere.

We brushed him, fed him, bathed him, petted him, and loved and loved and loved him. And one day, he found his purr.

But he still had no voice; this kitty could not meow. We stuck with this messed up cat—despite the one eye, the injured mouth, and the tail that wouldn't hang right. We kept loving him.

And a year later, he stood tall and proud in the kitchen and let out his first squeaky meow. That cat found his voice. It took a year, but he learned to meow again.

A few months later, I discover that my wounded cat is serving another cat, holding her down and bathing her. Jack couldn't purr a year ago, and now he is taking care of others. I couldn't believe it.

Well, it gets better.

Last night, I'm reading books with my daughter in her bed, and Jack hops up on top of us and starts doing this strange dance. He presses his front paws in and then arches his back and presses his back paws into the blanket. He can hardly keep his balance, and he's tangling himself up in the sheets.

"What is Jack trying to do?" we laugh and ask each other. We stay very still and observe him. Then, we realize what is happening.

Jack is attempting a behavior that all domestic cats do (but Jack never did). He is kneading.

All cats, when they feel content and safe, press their front paws in and out like they're kneading bread. Some say that when cats do this, they remember their kitten days of pressing against their mother to get milk. Others claim that cats only enact this ritual when they feel at home. They knead a space to mark it as their bed, usually right next to their mother.

Jack never did this. It's like he had no memory of ever being a happy kitten or being at home. Maybe because he wasn't. But last night, Jack tries to knead. Kneading, however, represents a complex instinctual action. Cats alternatively flex each paw, press in, and then retract their claws as they lift each paw. Only the front paws knead.

Jack has no idea how to do it, but some kitty instinct kicks in. We watch Jack attempt to knead the bed. He starts, falls over, and then tries again with his back paws (all wrong!). Eventually, as he purrs loudly and rolls all over us, he gets it right. He presses his front paws in, alternating between left and right, before he curls up and falls asleep beside my daughter.

He found his purr. Then he found his voice. Then he found a way to serve despite his wounds. Then, he began to remember his true self—becoming fully alive and doing what he was meant to do. Finally safe, finally at home, Jack starts to act like a real cat in every way.

There's hope for us all, no matter how wounded.

8. Becoming an Adult

Getting small children ready to play in the snow requires patience. Change your agenda for the moment because this is going to take some time.

My child wriggles into her snowsuit and then reports that her jeans are bunched up by her knees. I pull each pant leg down, digging up underneath her snowsuit and repositioning her clothing.

We're almost there. Boots on, coat zipped up, hat secured, she stands by the door with her hands up and fingers splayed like she's just been arrested. She only needs her gloves. She can hardly move within that bundle of snow gear, but still she manages to hand me two pink gloves.

Carefully, I hold the glove's mouth open wide while she shoves each eager hand in.

We try again and again. Every finger has a slot—a place it belongs—and her task is to find it. I can direct her and inch her fingers just so far, but she needs to navigate the dark cave alone, journeying up until everything's in its place. She'll know when it feels right. Nobody can know it but her.

We try again, and this time, she's figured it out. I push open the door and stand to the side. I send her into the bright, white snow, where all the other children play, and she doesn't look back.

At some point (and it's a different point for everybody), I became the glove holder and the door opener. This is a good thing. Living with flair means adopting—with flair—my adulthood. It's not just parenting. It's embracing adulthood for all its work for those who come after us.

I'm a glove holder and a door opener. And then I sit back with my cup of coffee and watch with delight as children tumble down the hills—only a boot clinging to the sled.

Adulthood means I am more concerned with facilitating the joyous moment for others than I am living it for myself. I give myself away to a new agenda, serving with the strength God provides, and mysteriously—miraculously—find the deepest joy.

9. Belongingness

I learned last week about the word "belongingness." It's the human need to feel like we belong to a group and that we are part of something greater than ourselves. Right after the basic need for food, water, and shelter, belongingness ranks next in importance.[3]

I think we skip this need and move right onto the need for esteem and self-actualization. We abandon belongingness because it doesn't seem important. And yet, so many of us suffer from profound loneliness and the kind of isolation that drives us to despair. I've seen it with my own eyes.

My students often make comments that they felt like they really "belonged" in my classroom. Feeling like you belong—that you are in the right place, in the right situation, with the right people—might be one of the best feelings in the world. I labor towards this goal for my students; I learn about them, share about myself, and insist on ridiculous name games for the entire semester, long after we know each other.

Vibrant community—lived out in faith and love—fills the soul so deeply. I'm learning that it takes effort to build community. You have to do something: walk kids to school, launch fitness groups, host potlucks, inspire creative project nights, or arrange play dates for dads.

One day, you will all feel like you belong to each other. You'll never be the same when you look around you and feel belongingness.

Folks are suffering from a lack of where to belong. Living with flair means I gather as many folks as I can and help them find a place to belong. I don't wait for somebody else to do this work. And before I know it, my heart overflows.

10. A Beautiful Answer to Prayer

My daughter gives permission to share the following true story that just delights me:

I'm tucking my daughter in bed, and she opens up and starts crying about how nobody plays with her at recess. She spends the time walking alone around the school track with her head buried in her coat.

She's not athletic and still enjoys imagination games, and unfortunately, she can't find friends her age in those categories. And when she tries to join a group of girls, they are gossiping and using bad language. They don't let her in their circle.

"What can I do, Mom?" She feels so lonely and so rejected.

"How should we pray about it? What do you want to ask God for?" My heart aches, and I fight tears.

"Just one friend. Just one little girl who wants to be friends with me tomorrow." So we bow our heads and ask God to send a friend.

The next morning, I pray for my daughter. The Bible verse in Hebrews 1:9 comes to mind each time I start to ask God for help:

You have loved righteousness and hated wickedness;
  therefore God, your God, has set you above your companions
  by anointing you with the oil of joy.

I pray the whole morning that God would simply anoint my precious daughter with the oil of joy. Bring her joy. Bring her joy. Bring her joy.

That afternoon, she bursts out of the school doors and reports that a new little girl came to find her at recess. "She wants to become my friend, and we played the whole time!"

"What is her name?" I ask.

"Her name is Joy."

The Lord brought Joy indeed.

11. Be Soap

Before we leave to drive home from our holiday travels, we fear enduring the horrific smell in our minivan. On the trip down, both girls vomit all over the seats, the floor—everything in sight. Have you ever been in a situation that was so unpleasant that it becomes comical? Picture us pulling off of the highway, both girls vomiting, a snowstorm upon us, and no way to get the car clean. And we still have 6 hours of driving left.

It's hard to live with flair sometimes.

Once at our destination, we try everything to remove the smell, including all sorts of sprays and deodorizers. Nothing helps. Then, Grandpa tells us his tried and true way of removing any car odor. You simply take a bar of soap and put it under the seats.

As we pack up the car to drive home, I'm doubtful as I put that little bar of Irish Spring under the seat. I'm plugging my nose and hating everything about holiday traveling.

An hour later, we pile in, and we cannot smell the carsick odor. I keep smelling the air, skeptical.

It's completely gone. The carsick smell is gone! All day long, I'm thinking about a little bar of soap with the power to change a whole environment. I can't figure it out, but I know it's working. The soap somehow absorbs and neutralizes the offending smell.

Meanwhile, I have 10 hours of travel to consider my life. It occurs to me that I want to influence my environment like that little bar of soap. Can I somehow absorb and neutralize every terrible, offensive, negative thing—neutralize it—and in turn refresh whatever situation I'm in?

I want to absorb and neutralize. I want to counterbalance every attack with the good, the true, and the beautiful. And I can because of God within me. Might God use us all to change every toxic environment into a sweet smelling paradise? Even a small intervention—as small as soap tucked under a seat—can change everything.

12. Christmas Estuary

Yesterday, I read a book that mentions the word estuary. An estuary is the part of a river that nears the sea. In an estuary, salt water and fresh water mix. As one of the most curious habitats, estuaries house creatures that learn how to live in impossible contradiction; they must survive in overlapping environments—fresh and saline.

Salmon, for example. Salmon start their lives in freshwater, but they were made for the ocean. Something enables them to get there. I read about how when salmon transition between freshwater and the sea, the cellular structure of their gills changes. The gills learn to secrete salts (not absorb them) just like a normal salt water fish. The process has a name: osmoregulate.

A new verb! Osmoregulate means to maintain that perfect balance—that harmony—necessary to live in environments that threaten to either dilute or saturate the body. And in estuaries, salmon learn how. They slowly adapt themselves for what's ahead. Then, they journey on towards their lives in the great ocean.

How confusing that place must seem.

As I consider that journey, I can't help but think about *times of estuary*— impossible contradictions, places where life does not feel right. We've left but haven't arrived. We see the future but aren't ready to embrace it. It's as if we are left alone to adapt for what's ahead. We are becoming something.

Estuaries, because of their in-between status as both freshwater and saltwater, contain the best nutrients. Scientists tell me that estuaries are among the most productive habitats in the world. The swirl of confusion, as wild as the tide, ironically provides refuge and rest for marine life. They strengthen their ability to adapt and regulate in that estuary.

Life feels like an estuary when I consider the miraculous Christmas claim that I'm meant for another world. And, by design, I find myself *here*, becoming something for *there*.

Living with flair means I don't despair when I'm not at my destination. I'm osmoregulating in my perfect estuary for what's ahead.

13. Under New Management

I'm driving home from North Carolina, and I see an old restaurant with a dangling sign, half-lit. It says, "Come In! We're Under New Management!"

Something about that sign grips me and won't let me go. It's hope. I know it like I know my own hands typing on this keyboard. The broken-down restaurant gets a fresh start—a new dream—under new management.

The old has gone, the new has come. This will be our best year yet. We're under the new management of a Great God. We're surrendered, strong, and steady. Under new management means whatever was left broken down, hurting, and hopeless gets a makeover. Renovated, restored, renewed.

Living with flair means I'm under new management. I'm sorry, Old Self. I'm under new management.

14. The Rich Club

Last night a dear neighbor and I were talking about our fascination with birds. I'm seriously thinking about joining a Pennsylvania birding club. In the woods behind my home, I can find snowy owls, barn owls, woodpeckers, and even eagles. By my kitchen window, the northern cardinals dance about all day.

I'd love a great camera with one of those zoom lenses. I want to take photographs like my friend over at Pollywog Creek who takes photos of the most beautiful birds.

As my neighbor and I share a moment of wonder over birds, I remark that God didn't have to make birds.

"And he didn't have to make them sing, either," she says. They seem placed here for such delight I can hardly bear it.

Then, my wise neighbor reminds me of the riches of it all. "You never have to worry about being rich," she says. "You have the riches of nature always available to you."

Yes!

I think about the birding club and the riches of friendship. I think about my wonderful neighbor and the riches of wisdom. I think about my backyard feeder and the riches of winter cardinals robed in deep red. I think of the riches of family, laughter, vivid verbs, and blogging friends like Mark and Stephanie or Elaine. I think of Judy Gordon Morrow who mailed me her wonderful book of devotions last month.

Today I'm rich in snowflakes, dark coffee, and fuzzy slippers. I'm rich in icy ponds and crackling icicles that make the houses seem swallowed in great jaws. I'm rich in poetry books, old dusty journals, Bibles, new novels buried inside me, and Penn State students who write so honestly I sometimes cry when I grade their papers.

I'm rich in professors who have lunch with me even though we only have 45 minutes once a week. I'm rich in neighborhood moms and dads who are raising children alongside my awesome husband and me.

I'm rich in Italian Mamas.

God has poured out all these riches all over me as if knowing Him weren't enough. He wasn't lying when He said in John 10:10, "I have come that you might have life and have it abundantly."

15. Downcast and Disturbed? A New Question to Ask

I've realized something new about idolatry. As I read the scriptures, I see that David connects being downcast and disturbed with somehow not hoping fully in God. He writes in Psalm 43:5, "Why so downcast, o my soul? Why so disturbed within me? Put your hope in God."

For most of my Christian life, I've come to understand idolatry as something you love more than God, something that captures your heart more than God, or something you give your time and attention to most of all. Yet this week, I've been thinking about idolatry differently.

Idolatry is when I turn aside to false gods that promise to do what God says He will do. This person or thing circumvents, counterfeits, or even counteracts what God has said about His character.

For example, we know several clear and distinct names of God: God is our banner of victory (Jehovah Nissi), our shepherd to care for us (Jehovah-Raah), our healer (Jehovah Rapha), our provider (Jehovah Jirah), our sanctifier (Jehovah Mekoddishkem), and our peace (Jehovah Shalom).

I realized this week that idolatry takes root in the heart when I prevent God from being God in my life because I choose another avenue of victory, care, provision, healing, and peace. If I'm trusting in something or someone as the ultimate source of provision, I'm preempting God's provision. If I'm taking responsibility for my own care—through various well-intentioned means—I might be thwarting God's plan for my care.

It reminds me of the time my husband was traveling, and I asked for prayer for protection. I felt like my protector was gone. My friend reminded me that God was my Protector. It reminds me, too, of how I respond when I receive rejections from publishers. I imagine that book contract would be such a source of financial provision! Publishing isn't my provision. God is my provision. Or when I raise the banner of achievement or fruitfulness as my victory, I must remember that God's banner over me declares His love (anything I may write on that banner isn't the truth about me) as my victory. Finally, what about trusting in my own obedience or ability to change? God is the sanctifier, not me.

When I am downcast and disturbed, I ask this question: Where have I turned aside to a false god that masquerades as promising something declared within the character of God? That's a new question for me, and I'm so glad I asked it.

16. Much Later in Life

As I keep to the writing task, both fiction and nonfiction, my daughter reminds me that our favorite *Little House* book series was not published until Laura Ingalls Wilder was well into her sixties.

There's a whole group of late-blooming writers! On my bedside table, I have the lovely book, *Watership Down* that Richard Adams wrote in his fifties. Frank McCourt wrote *Angela's Ashes* in his mid-sixties. Wallace Stevens, one of my favorite poets, wrote most of his poems in his late thirties.[4]

I'm so glad they didn't quit writing because they felt old or irrelevant to the culture. I'm so glad they didn't give up in discouragement. Each writer had something vital to say—at just the right time.

With each passing year, I remember that some of the best things in life happen much later. My older and wiser friends testify that wonderful things happen past middle age. Some of the best writing and thinking happen much later. Some of the best, richest, and rewarding friendships even happen later. Why are we in such a rush, thinking life has passed us by?

Some great stories bloom late. This is just the right time for them.

17. I Refuse to Wear My Coat

Every single winter, my daughter insists she doesn't need to wear her winter coat. You'd be amazed at the resistance to outerwear from the children in my family.

Today, I decide to just let her go. She rushes outside in a tank top, shoes with no socks, and a flimsy sweater. There's snow on the ground from flurries; it's that cold. "See! I told you I didn't need a coat! I'm fine! I'm fine!"

A few minutes later, she returns to me, freezing.

Does God just let me go sometimes so I finally feel the effects of my own wandering? He stands there by the door, coat in hand, waiting for me to feel it and return.

18. Some Things Are Just For Now

We're driving down a country road, and the winter moon hangs low and buttery yellow in the deep black of night. "Pull off the road!" I cry. "I want to photograph it!"

He pulls off into the dirt of a farm, and I roll down the window to try to capture the moon.

You can't do it; the moon never photographs well, at least with the kind of camera I have. I look out at that moon and wish I had a record. I wish I had the film to prove it, to share it.

He holds my hand and says, "Some things are just for now."

Some things, I learn, you don't need to always blog about. You don't need to capture them at all. They are just for now.

19. Unlikely Success

Today, Jack alerts me to a beautiful bird in the Weeping Cherry.

He talks to the bird with that strange broken meowing sound, moving his jaw rapidly. I've wondered for years why cats make this sound when they look at birds.

My husband tells me that cats imagine eating the bird and therefore make munching sounds with their mouths.

Jack's on the hunt, imagining success. Would a cat ever capture a bird like this? Unlikely. Would a cat with one eye, indoors, catch a bird like this?

Never.

Still, the cat munches. Still, he visualizes success.

Maybe one day. The confidence of my One-Eyed Cat inspires me. The bird flies from the tree, uncaught, and Jack, undaunted, settles under the lights of the Christmas tree.

Maybe, in his mind, he simply let the bird go.

20. Secrets of the Wandering Albatross

Last night, my daughter wins a book about winged creatures at the school's winter Bingo Night. We read all about butterflies, bats, hummingbirds, flying squirrels, bees, and ladybugs. Then, I turn the page and learn about the magnificent Wandering Albatross.[5]

I learn that the Wandering Albatross stays in flight for *months* without landing.

I stare, stunned at the page, as I consider the lonely, distant travels of this bird who never finds a secure place to land. And even when she does, the awkward bird tumbles over her own feet, crash-landing into the others, and somersaulting several times before finally standing.

She prefers the flight to the landing.

I have to check my facts this morning. Is it true that this bird stays aloft for months? How is this even possible?

I discover that the Wandering Albatross has the largest wingspan of any living bird. I also uncover the bird's secret: she knows how to sharply swing into air currents to let the wind blow her to great heights. She lets the wind do the work for her.

As I consider the Wandering Albatross today, I realize how often it feels as if we wander—for months—unsure of where to land. As lonely travelers, we struggle to stay aloft. And we must. Our survival depends upon our ability to soar in the midst of our wandering. Sometimes, there's no land in sight.

You spread wide your arms, turn sharply into the wind, and you let it carry you to great heights. I think about a life lived with God's power. I think, too, about adversity being a stronger air current. I throw myself against it, leaning hard against the Lord. What a magnificent flight!

21. If You Were an Explorer

This morning I learn about the exploration goals of the 3rd and 4th graders. If they could be explorers—anywhere—where would they go and why?

My daughter says, "I would explore the ocean depths to find sea glass, coral, and dolphins." Her friend agrees, but he suggests that they explore the Bermuda Triangle for these things because you can always discover the lost city of Atlantis along the way.

I follow along, hands in my pockets, listening as the children describe, in specific detail, this exploratory trip. They will need underwater cameras and a submarine, obviously. I hear the children talk about sea glass and how you never know what kind of object that glass came from. "It could have been on the Titanic, you know!"

Anything is possible.

Everyone walks much faster when we have these conversations. Nobody notices the freezing cold, and nobody complains about the slippery trek uphill. When we access the explorer in us, something changes.

The world, vast and unexplored, lies before me. I transform myself into an explorer: one who travels into unknown or less understood regions—physical, emotional, or spiritual regions.

I learn to inquire, take notes, preserve artifacts. Like a child dreaming of the depths of the sea, I experience the thrill of discovery. Anything is possible today.

22. Count Your Whorls

I learn this morning that you can tell the age of a pine tree by its number of "whorls." One child stops in the woods on the walk to school, and she counts the circles of branches that shoot out from a tiny pine tree. The top layer of branches is one whorl and represents one year of growth. The next layer represents another. This baby pine tree boasts seven whorls, so it's been growing for seven years. It stands as tall as my daughter.

"Next year, they'll be eight whorls!" The children, wide-eyed, pause and look down upon the tree.

I'm struck by the slow growth of this little pine that's witnessed our journey to school all these years. Now, we witness the pine tree, mark its age, and incorporate that growth into the whole system of things that grow and change about us.

These things matter so much to children. Just last night, at Neighborhood Fitness Group, the children always gather to record their growth on my kitchen wall. They inevitably check, every single week, if they've grown even a little bit.

They record each other's heights, and they claim they've really grown each week. The wall, smeared and nearly illegible, tempts me every Saturday morning as I stand beside it with my cleaning bucket. I just can't clean the wall.

We have to count our whorls. And, even though I'm no longer getting taller, I want to count my own growth somehow—*visibly, publicly*. Am I growing kinder? More patient? More wise?

Let me retain that child-like quality of marking my own growth. There's something to celebrate; there's something to note here.

Living with flair means I count whorls. We're growing—changing—and we must witness it.

23. What You Stir Up

Today, for some odd reason, I think about how many times I stir throughout the day. I stir my coffee or tea; I stir the oatmeal; I stir the batter; I stir the juice; I stir the sauce as it simmers. Stir, stir, stir. Maybe it's the Italian Mama rubbing off on me, but I have a spoon in my hand most of the day.

I stir because the good stuff settles at the depths, and my quick spoon riles it up and mixes it back in.

I'm in church, praying that God would stir up good things in me. I want passion stirred, hope stirred, and the kind of faith that moves mountains stirred. It's in there, settled at my depths. Stir me!

Later, I go home to look up that beautiful verb. Unfortunately, it's often associated with negative ideas. We stir up dissent, controversy, and drama. We stir up anger, bitterness, and jealousy. In the book of Proverbs, I find that every single use of the verb *stir* warns against rousing up these negative traits.

I don't want to be a person who stirs up the wrong sorts of things.

I want to stir up goodness. I want to leave a wake of peace, joy, hope, and faith. Once you spend time with me, I want to have stirred up love and happiness in you—not conflict or anger.

Living with flair means I trust God to stir up good things, and I, too, stir my environment to mix in every wonderful element I might.

24. Our Uncommon Uses

While cleaning my home today, I notice two of my favorite objects: a flowerpot and a serving dish. We received them as wedding gifts over ten years ago, and they were both too beautiful not to use.

But I don't grow flowers inside in pots, and I rarely transfer our dinner onto serving platters (and this one seemed too small for my family). I couldn't keep these things hidden away! Instead, I found uncommon uses for both the pot and the platter.

The pot became my cooking utensil holder.

The platter became our key tray.

I realized that the pot can hold more than soil; the platter can carry more than a meal.

As I think about all my specific plans and dreams—the things I know I was made for—I have to pause and ask about the uncommon uses for my skills.

Over the years, I have been so busy telling the Potter what I am really made for, and He's already using me for broader, more interesting, and more useful things. Things I hadn't imagined. Immeasurably more!

Sometimes we emerge into the world on unusual paths, using our gifts and talents in uncommon but wonderful ways. Living with flair means I allow it. We are too beautiful—too loved—to be kept hidden away.

25. How to Increase Your Capacity

Today, I read this quote from E. Stanley Jones: "An organism expends as much as it receives and no more; therefore, receptivity is the first law of life."[6]

Receptivity: the willingness and readiness to receive.

I wonder how we might receive from God, draw life and energy, and then expend. Otherwise, we find ourselves in unnatural and impossible deficits, exhausted by our lives.

All day long, I think about how much we expend as we go about our days. I've mastered the art of expending, but I want to learn the art of receptivity. I receive from God through prayer and the scriptures, and I receive from others as I let them care for me when I'm in need. What makes this so hard every day?

My husband reminds me that, in terms of biochemistry, certain drugs block the receptor sites of a cell so they cannot receive. In our lives, what would block our receptor sites so we cannot truly receive from God?

We both know the answer as soon as we ask the question. It's pride; it's our own self-sufficiency and our belief that we can control and direct our own lives. My supreme busyness reflects that deeply embedded pride. I must go and go and not ever sit and receive.

Not today. I need to receive.

As I position my heart to receive, I find that God sends strange offers my way: a ride home, a friend delivering a meal, a moment alone to read my Bible, an unexpected treatment offered by a doctor. I relax into this day and open every receptor site I have. I find peace soothing my soul. I let God fill me, and then, I have the capacity to expend.

26. The Only Way to Make It

The driveway and sidewalks—every path we try—stretches out black and shiny, smooth as glass, and treacherous. Ten of us set out for school, and by the time we reach the corner, we've fallen down six times (some of us twice).

The danger is real, and I'm nervous.

"Hold on to me!" I cry to the little ones. We find another mitten to grab or another arm to link through, and we suddenly stabilize. When one starts to slide and fall, the others catch him, find a new balance, and press on.

Instead of falling on our backs, our sliding on ice resembles smooth acrobatics: our legs shoot out from under us, but then someone has our back and we bend forward and backward. Arms flail and clutch, yet *we do not fall.*

Every child laughs. Even I can't help but enjoy this treachery. It's now an adventure, a pleasure.

I think about the strength in numbers. I think about finding others to balance us as we flail and clutch the air. Holding hands and shoulders, we approach the crossing guard who warns us of an upcoming stretch of ice to avoid. We walk a wide circle around it, arm in arm.

Safe at school, I recall what it takes to get here. The danger was real, but we overcame together. Nobody can make it alone.

27. What You Alone Can See

Walking to school, we notice how everything drips. It's nearly 35 degrees (a warm day!), and we're jubilant as we slosh along the sidewalk.

I observe the water droplets on the branches and winterberries, and it suddenly occurs to me that not one other living creature sees what I see at this exact moment.

The droplets fall to the earth, and I know that never again—not even once in a million years—will that exact configuration of molecules exist on this limb.

I observe them, behold their passing, and consider the sublime fact that I took note of what nobody else could see. In this enormous earth, filled with billions of people, no one—not even one!—saw that droplet reflecting the neighbor's pine tree in its orb.

My day bursts with wonder. I'm seeing what no one else sees. I'm documenting a beauty that would be otherwise lost.

You see things in your world that I do not see and will never see. You notice what a billion people will not ever behold.

Living with flair means we erupt with wonder—with worship—at these things around us. No other creature looks at what we are seeing, in the way we are seeing it.

We experience beauty that God places before us, and living with flair means we proclaim it.

28. **From Cowardly to Courageous**

My little cat, Jack, advances even further in the direction of being fully alive. Once wounded, this now strong kitty first relearns how to purr. Then he figures out how to meow again. Then, he moves past his wounds and chooses to love and serve others. Finally, he begins to master basic feline behaviors like kneading.

My daughter asks me, "Mom, what else will Jack do as he becomes more and more like a healthy cat?" I have no idea. But we wait and we watch.

Recently, a friend delivers a gift to our three cats. It's a huge, fluffy cat bed to sit by my rocking chair. But we have three cats. Who will get this soft bed? Jack has no chance, especially with that one cat (Louie, alpha male) who dominates every household scene. Normally, Jack cowers around the others. The three cats stand there, observing this amazing bed.

Then it happens. Jack moves forward and claims the bed for his own. He transforms from cowardly to courageous right before our eyes. He kneads the bed, turns a few circles, and has slept there ever since.

I watch that little cat, and I remember God's work as Healer.

On our way to recovering from whatever wounds us, we suddenly realize the plans in store for us. One day, we find we have the courage to move forward, claim our dreams, and stand up to those who threaten us. We discover our place. We find we are so healthy that nobody even remembers where we came from or how we were wounded.

We find we are fully alive, doing all the things we were meant to do. Nothing holds us back.

29. **Surrendering**

This morning after breakfast, we take the girls sledding. We travel behind the house, past the forest, and into a wide clearing. All I see is space—so much of it that I actually want to breathe a little more deeply and stretch my arms out. I understand why folks from the city want to visit for a while and send their children to experience a rural life for a month.

I never thought I could survive in a town like this. I had to surrender to God and believe I belonged here. But what would we do all day long?

Right now, we are learning the rhythms of winter. We aren't diminished at all by whatever storm assaults us.

The storm just means we grab our sleds and ride. There's a good thing to experience here, and so we launch ourselves out, gain momentum, and surrender.

It's so great that we do it again and again. Sure I'm sore. But it's worth it. Surrender always is.

30. These Aren't Interruptions

I'm in the university library to find the article I want on neuroscience and writing. I'm suddenly interrupted by the pull of the juvenile fiction section on the 5th floor where I remember they have all the P. D. Eastman books that my youngest daughter still loves (*Go, Dog. Go!, Sam and the Firefly, The Best Nest*).

I spend all my time there, and for once, it doesn't feel like I'm just getting through some kid's library event on my way to what I really want to be doing.

Many times over the years of being a mother, I've felt like I'm just trying to get through something. I'd think to myself: I just have to get through this night waking, this potty training, this noise at the dinner table, this driving everywhere, this laundry, this cleaning, this bedtime routine. I need to get through these interruptions in order to arrive at what I really want to be doing.

I believed some clever lie that kept me from embracing motherhood fully. Motherhood was something to endure, and this made me so deeply troubled and ashamed that the dark days of depression stole half a decade of my life.

My doctor told me one afternoon that "my children are not interruptions" to the life I want to have. They are my life. Exactly how God designed it.

That's what I remembered last night: It's 3:15 AM, and my youngest wakes me up needing a drink and a snuggle. We've been training her for months to stay in her bed, but still she comes, a wandering little soul wanting me in the night. I gather her to me, and when I tiptoe into the cold kitchen to get her a cup of water, I notice the fresh snow in the moonlight.

This isn't an interruption. This is worship and wonder at 3:15 AM. I don't sleep after that; I listen to my daughter breathing and can hear the icy whisper of snow falling outside. I don't have to get through this. This isn't pain to endure on the way to what I'd rather be doing.

There's wonder and worship here—every day—no matter how sticky, loud, or sleep deprived this day seems. Our days are not something to get through as we endure interruptions to our real life. This is our life: wonderful, beautiful, and just right for us. And as I hear snow falling, I remember that sometimes we have to listen harder to comprehend that truth.

31. A Great Cloud of Witnesses

This morning, my friends and I huddle by the school entrance, making conversation with other parents and school administrators. As we notice the line of cars pulling up to drop off children, I'm overcome with the desire to run up to the car doors, open them wide, and greet each child like he or she were a celebrity.

I imagine each car to be a long black limousine. I even include fashion commentary like we're on the Red Carpet for some premiere.

My friend and I laugh about making this our community job each morning. We wonder what it might feel like to arrive at school and have folks open your car door, celebrate your arrival, and compliment your outfit. What if we even brought paparazzi to our morning Red Carpet event? What if we really did announce a child's arrival? *You've arrived! Welcome to school you beautiful, wonderful person! You are very important to us!*

Walking home from the school, I feel like I've touched upon something eternal in that moment of opening a car door and celebrating a child's arrival. Something about that act seems to echo in eternity.

All of us parents, surrounding those youngest members of our community—celebrating them like that, protecting their journey from car to school entrance—represents a spiritual reality for me: I too am surrounded by that love and protection at all times. I have cheerleaders in the heavens.

Doesn't scripture teach in Hebrews 12 that we are "surrounded by a great cloud of witnesses" who cheer us on, helping us "run with perseverance the race marked out for us?" We cannot see the saints and angels, but aren't they surely there in some unseen realm about me?

Later, I ride in my minivan across town. As I unfasten my seat belt and turn to touch the door handle, I imagine them all there outside my van. My Red Carpet Moment unfolds as I walk into the cold, bright day, surrounded by my cloud of witnesses.

They cheer about me, celebrating and protecting.

32. Make Yourself That Somebody

For months, my friend and I travel by this one treacherous patch of sidewalk on our walk to school—the place that dips down towards a jagged ravine of rocks and icy water—and say, "Somebody should really put a fence up."

We rescue kids as they slide off the sidewalk, shake our heads and say again, "Somebody should really put a fence up."

As the months go on, we realize how much we say, "Somebody should really..."—whether referring to cleaning the house, fixing something, or generally improving the world.

We laugh about this expression: somebody should really. . .

Who is this Somebody person? Can I meet her?

It occurs to us that we are the Somebody. We stop saying, "Somebody should really put a fence up," and we decide to make ourselves that somebody.

I don't know where to start, so I ask someone at the school who tells me I should "call the county." (I didn't realize you can call people in your county and get help with things your community needs. You can!) I look up in my phonebook the name of my township and call the number there. A man answers the phone, and I explain that children are slipping off the sidewalk and falling into a ditch on the way to school. Can we put a fence up?

"Yes," he says. "Let me check who owns that property, and I'll send a crew out today. We'll take care of it."

I even ask the man if he could make it a *nice* fence, a *charming* fence, and not some metal thing with orange mesh reserved for danger zones.

He sends out his crew and builds our fence.

Now, on the walk to school, my friend and I look at that charming wooden fence and remember to make ourselves that somebody.

She says, "Somebody should really write a book with that title."

Somebody should. If you make yourself that somebody, you can really change something.

In fact, what initiates my friend's 100 pound weight loss last year is a t-shirt she sees that says, "Somebody should really do something about how fat I am."

She decides to make herself that somebody.

I want to make myself that Somebody.

33. A Disaster Waiting to Happen

This morning, fog cloaks the neighborhood. I pull out of my driveway and cannot even see the house next door.

Every instinct I have makes the situation worse: High beams? No! Their light reflects off the fog and blinds me. Brake and swerve? No! Sudden movements mean cars pile up behind me or I hit the thing beside me. Drive up close to the car in front? No! No, no, no!

I read later about a "visibility expert" at Virginia Tech (Ron Gibbons) who devotes his life to the study of how to ensure visibility in fog, snow, or rain. Most every instinct we have when we experience low visibility endangers us. Instead, we must use low beams, tap our breaks as we ease off the accelerator, make no sudden movements, and pull over if we need to.

And, perhaps most importantly, choose not to drive at all.

All day, I think about things in my future I cannot yet discern. With that horrible visibility, I'm tempted to trust my instincts and react on impulse. I'm tempted to engineer my circumstances (swerving, braking) and stay in charge of my life. Really, I'm just a disaster waiting to happen.

What if I slowed down, pulled over, left the car and trusted a Visibility Expert? When God obscures my path, I need not worry. I just trust something deeper than instinct, deeper than my own control.

I pull over. I rest. I resist my frantic instincts.

34. A Very Public Failure for My Daughter

Yesterday, Barnes and Noble slates my daughter to perform a piano piece as part of a winter fundraiser for the Music Academy. Neighbors come, cameras focus, and parents beam.

But when it is her turn to perform, my daughter bursts into tears and freezes. She cannot even approach the piano.

Instead of forcing her onto the piano bench, we gather up her blue puffy coat and the sheet music in her red tote bag and travel home as fast as we can.

She slumps into the house and says over and over again, "I couldn't do it!" She cries and falls onto the couch. She writes apology notes to the neighbors and her piano teacher.

And then something beautiful happens. The neighbors send messages that they went to the event to support her, and it didn't matter whether she performed or not. She could turn away from a thousand stages, and they'd still come every time. My daughter, not her performance, mattered.

Her piano teacher calls to tell her that learning the piano isn't about performance. She tells my daughter that she can choose when, if, and why she wants to perform at all. Learning the piano has intrinsic value as an end in itself. The goal was never public applause, flashing camera bulbs, and bragging parents.

Nobody is disappointed.

My daughter nods with understanding. She wipes her face and remembers that she loves to make music. And I remember the gospel truth with every comforting phone call: it was never about performance. God's love and favor are never dependent on my good performances. The sooner children learn this, the more they might relax into the freedom that comes with being unconditionally loved, accepted, and valued.

I ask my daughter for permission to tell her story. She says, "Sure, Mom!" It doesn't bother her anymore. She knows now that it's never about performance. And it isn't a public failure after all.

35. Keeping Hope Alive

Yesterday, my youngest brings home a homemade winter bird feeder. She announces that the bagel was "a rotten one, left over from her teacher's kitchen," and the birdseed and spread cannot be eaten by humans.

Noted.

We hang the bird feeder on the Winterberry bush. And we wait.

And we wait.

We wait, wait, and wait some more.

I read somewhere that it takes backyard birds a few days to find a new feeder.

All day today, we stop every few minutes and glance out the kitchen window just in case a bird has arrived. We talk about who might be the first to catch sight of that first little bird.

No birds yet. But the desiring of them, the wait, delights us.

We remember another wait, last April, for a hibernating turtle to emerge from underneath our deck. It feels just like that, this waiting, and we love it.

I want to construct more apparatuses designed to teach me the beauty of hope. A backyard bird feeder reminds me to hope today. I wait patiently with my daughters, peer into the landscape ahead, and keep our longing alive. Tomorrow might be the day!

36. Every Problem We Have Is Related to Our View of God

Today, I remember this quote that I read almost 15 years ago in a little book called, *Disciples are Made not Born*, by Walter Henrichsen and Howard Hendricks. The authors claim that "every problem we have is related to our view of God."[7] It was the kind of sentence a person underlines and then rewrites in her favorite journal by her bed.

It's the kind of quote to repeat to yourself when you're thinking about everything that's going wrong in your life.

I remember it because I have received multiple emails from the English Department entitled: EMERGENCY MEETING! to "update us on the financial situation." The budget crisis affects all of our jobs, and I have no doubt that the purpose of this meeting will confirm our fears.

I look at these emails and ponder the meaning of the words "emergency" and "crisis." Then, I restate the truth: Every problem I have is related to my view of God.

Can this really be true? The quote argues that if we have a big God, we have small problems. If we have a small God, we have big problems.

What kind of God do I have?

Do I view God in such a way that what the world sees as an "emergency" or a "crisis," I now see dissolving into a peaceful opportunity to see the work of God displayed? What do I need to believe about God to live with the kind of flair that smiles in the face of bad news? The Psalmist in Psalm 112 (a wonderful acrostic poem) proclaims that those who know God will "never be shaken." He writes, "They will have no fear of bad news; their hearts are steadfast, trusting in the Lord. Their hearts are secure, they will have no fear."

Living with flair means our hearts stay steadfast, trusting, unshaken, and fearless. We have a very big God.

37. Licking the Blender Whisk

It's a snow day in our county, and the children and I make cookies to frost. The girls crowd around me and eagerly reach for the blender whisks after I've made the vanilla frosting.

I hand the whisks down, and I purposefully arrange some extra frosting on each one.

A child licking the blender whisks reminds me of Henry David Thoreau's famous quote about sucking the marrow out of life. Back in July, I wrote about how the "Live with Flair" blog was my way to "live deep and suck all the marrow out of life."[8]

When my daughter licks the blender whisk, I see her searching out every last drop. When she hands it back, it's as if it's been cleaned in the dishwasher.

I want to search out the beauty in this day, relishing every part. God hands me the whisk, and I sit back and enjoy it.

38. What Good Is This?

Today I attempt to make "Ginger Beets." This means I can roast in my kitchen, warming the house against the winter winds.

I've never roasted beets before. I scrub off the dirt, chop off the stems, and roast them for an hour. When cooled, the beets slip right out of their skin. I slice them in quarters, toss them with fresh ginger and olive oil, and finally sprinkle a dash of salt.

Beautiful! Delicious!

I'm amazed that roots, buried deep in the darkness, can produce such vibrant color. That deep red paints everything: my fingers, the counter tops, and the kitchen sink. This winter kitchen has bright red flair! One would never know, just by looking at those old roots, what a beet can do.

No other vegetable has such color. I learn that, at first, the leaves were the only parts of a beet considered edible. The roots, tossed aside and wasted, weren't enjoyed as they are today.

But now we know differently. The beet root, beautiful and vibrant, nourishes.

The parts of us we toss aside—viewed as waste—or bury deep await God's use: beautiful, vibrant, nourishing to others.

39. Secret Agent Life

This morning, I read about how a businessman responds to a doctor's order to go to a train station and "look for someone who needs help."[9] The doctor believed that if the businessman practiced doing something for another person every day, that man would begin to feel better about his life.

He did. It worked.

I wonder about the direction to "look for someone who needs help." What if that mission shaped this dreary winter day? I wonder what it means to live a life that anticipates, on a daily basis, how I might serve another person.

Someone we'll encounter today will need something (a hug, a word, a ride, a lunch). What if God wanted to use us to meet that particular need? What if each day we were on a special assignment to care for somebody in our path?

But we will not know who, where, or when this person might appear. We just know that it will, most certainly, happen. So we keep our eyes open, waiting for our special assignment.

I tell God I'm available. But I'm nervous about what shape the day will take.

The day transforms into an action-adventure film. I'm the one scanning the train station platform, looking for the helpless. But it's not the train station; it's my own street, my own neighborhood, my own office.

I feel like a secret agent on a mission from God. I feel like this covert operation changes the focus, the purpose, and the meaning of what it means to be alive today.

Living with flair means I'm available for secret missions to care for anyone and everyone, stranger or friend, who enters my life today.

40. When Your Scars Leak

Yesterday, my daughter cries out that Jack's scar is leaking.

Remember Jack? Our one-eyed cat, over this past year, seemed fully recovered from the day we rescued him: he learned to purr again; he discovered his lost meow; he started caring for other cats; then he learned to stand up for himself against the other cats; and finally, he learned how to knead the bed like normal kitties do.

He was fully alive, fully cat.

We hardly notice the scar anymore. It's only when other folks come over and comment that we remember.

But the wound where his eye once was becomes infected. The vet says the infection is so great, so deep, that it has to burst out of the scar.

We hold Jack all evening. We care for the infection, treat it with medicine, and give special attention to him.

I remember that sometimes wounds leak. Even after a year of healing, the old scar can ooze. Just because we don't notice the wound, one day, it bursts back into our lives and threatens us with that discouraging reminder.

But we aren't discouraged. We go back to the basics. We hold him, love him, and treat him. We aren't shocked or repulsed. It's part of his journey, and we're right here with him.

Living with flair means I'm in this with you. Even when the old wounds leak out, we go back to the basics, take care of one another, and let the healing begin again.

41. Going to the Bottom of the Well

In winter, conversations go deeper. Just this week, a dear friend of mine describes herself as "holding on to the edge for dear life so she doesn't fall to the bottom of the well."

You grip the well's ledge, keep your chin up, and refuse to fall.

It's a haunting image of a life lived in fear of surrender. My tight grip on the ledge represents a picture of what I cannot face on the road to personal transformation, freedom, and joy. I'm afraid of what's down there if I journey deeper into places of brokenness. Can't I just stay up here, white knuckled, with my jaw clenched, fighting?

All day, I consider how I need to let go of my tight grip on my life, trying to hold everything together in that desperate and clenched way that drains out the life and hope.

A friend looks her straight between the eyes and says, "You need to let go and fall to the bottom of the well." That's the way to begin to heal.

But what happens when she lets go? What fearful thing awaits? She cannot do this alone.

Another friend says, "I'll fall to the bottom with you."

And another, days later, adds: "God is at the bottom of the well."

We release our grip, surrender to the work of healing God wants in our lives, and look around. We aren't alone: Friends journey down into the darkness with us, and God himself embraces us at the moment we let go.

It is scary. That's OK. Go straight into what needs to heal. Go straight into the fear, straight into the dark thing, and straight into the unknown. Once you do, you'll find yourself free. You'll find your hands—which once clutched your life so tightly in that controlled half-life—are now open wide to receive a new kind of glorious life.

42. A Picture of the Friend I Want to Be

A local photographer arrives for a photo shoot in my home. I need a professional head shot for my writing, and I have the worst time looking natural and being myself. I never look nice in pictures! But I have a secret weapon today: I invite a friend over who I know tells the truth and helps me be myself.

We're knee deep in snow, and the photographer asks my friend to assist her by holding the "reflector." It's freezing outside, and I'm standing by my favorite Winterberry bush. My friend positions herself beside me and holds up the circular shade. She accomplishes two tasks: she reflects the light toward me (so light bounces off her shade towards me), and she diffuses the harsh sunlight that's overpowering the shot.

Imagine the snow, the wind, the freezing cold, us shivering, and plain me trying to look like someone important.

I'm smiling at my friend, suddenly feeling just like myself. I can't stop looking at her and what she's doing to me.

I want to be a friend like this. I want to reflect the light towards her, and I want to diffuse whatever attempts to overpower her.

Living with flair means I'm a reflector and a diffuser.

43. And There Was Light!

We're slumped upon the kitchen table. One daughter labors over math homework while the other colors slowly on paper. I'm answering an email, sighing. The day feels sluggish and old, dark and spent.

Then, light invades through the kitchen window.

A hallelujah chorus of dappled light dances all around us. For days—months, really—we've been in the dark shadow of winter. The sky looks more like a sidewalk.

But not now. Not for this one glorious moment when light breaks through. The forest sparkles with it. The sky has never seemed so blue, so wide, so clear.

We bask in it.

To bask means to derive great pleasure from something. As I open wide the door and feel the sun on my face, I realize what makes this moment so pleasurable.

It's because it's been so very dark, so very grey.

I'm thankful for contrast in my life. I realize that's the only way I learn to bask. The hot showers I love because I've known the freezing ones; the deep breath of air I relish because I battled congestion for a month; the authentic community I cherish in my neighborhood because I've walked the road of loneliness; the joy rising up in my heart, so precious, because I once knew the despairing days of depression.

The beauty of contrast: what we bask in because we've seen its absence. A blessing, a mystery.

44. Visualize This

Just now, we return from attending our first college gymnastics meet. At the uneven parallel bars, the gymnasts perform extraordinary movements that, when seen live and up close, actually terrify me. I squeeze the arm of the neighbor sitting next to me with every rotation and every dismount. I'm certain these gymnasts will crash-land into the floor.

As I watch, I notice the coach (suit and tie, arms crossed firmly) at the sidelines. As soon as one of his gymnasts begins a difficult and dangerous sequence, the coach plants himself directly under his gymnast, holds both hands out as if to catch her, and waits for her to complete her performance. And how that coach cheers!

Within one routine, he darts in and out from underneath the bars many times, ready to assist and catch in the exact moment of possible danger or difficulty.

Oh, what I would risk if I knew I wouldn't fall! What things might I attempt if I knew someone stood beneath me, arms ready to catch or cheer?

This uneven life, running parallel to spiritual realities, offers chances I cannot possibly attempt (out of fear, out of danger). But with One beneath me? I swing out into new directions, and I visualize the firm stance and wide arms of a God who will not let me fall.

45. Larger Hearts and Wilder Yearnings

I read a quote from Jens Peter Jacobson (the Danish poet and novelist) as the snow falls this morning.

He writes, "Know ye not that. . .people there are who by natural constitution have been given a different nature and disposition than the others; that have a larger heart and a swifter blood, that wish and demand more, have stronger desires and a yearning which is wilder and more ardent than that of the common herd. They are fleet as children over whose birth good fairies have presided; their eyes are opened wider; their senses are more subtle in all their perceptions. The gladness and joy of life, they drink with the roots of their heart, while the others merely grasp them with coarse hands."[10]

Surely, these artists suffer more, but they also live more fully.

I, too, want to have a larger heart and swifter blood. I want to wish and demand more, with stronger desires and wilder yearnings.

I want to live out of the roots of my heart and drink up all the gladness and joy there is to be found right here.

And then, of course, to recount it all to others.

46. When Your Candle Won't Light During the Christmas Eve Service

My candle won't light. Everyone leans over to help me; wax falls everywhere, and it's becoming distracting. Every time someone tries to light my little candle, it burns for a moment and then flickers out.

Come on little candle. Come on flame. Shine bright, girl. Do it!

Nope.

Finally, from out of nowhere, a complete stranger hands me a huge, new candle. "There's no hope in yours. Take this one."

I'm standing there with two candles (one hopeless, one Glorious) singing *Silent Night*. Looking down at that strong, bright flame, I realize that my own candle indeed has no hope. I need Someone Else's.

I need an exchanged life. I need the Light of the World because there's no hope in me.

I take it, Lord!

Merry Christmas: Jesus comes down for the Great Exchange; He takes on our flesh, our sin, our hopelessness, and in return, hands us a new life and a new light.

47. **Out There Alone**

On two separate afternoons, I watch my youngest bundle up and go outside to play in the snow alone.

Later, I find that she's examining the snow, looking for animal tracks, and making her own sledding paths.

Alone.

She's an extrovert, yet she has stuff to do out there by herself.

I remember all those days I played alone in my backyard. I remember the white expanse of snow and my small self waving snow angels in it.

When you're alone out there in nature, something happens to you. You connect with yourself, with God, and with nature, and you grow up a little. You think about things and maintain the pure satisfaction that the whole experience was between you and God. Nobody saw what you saw. Nobody felt what you felt or thought your thoughts. You become a *you*—without anyone's commentary on what you're doing.

Sometimes we need to go out there alone for awhile.

48. **Build Your Life Around It**

I'm reading Rainer Maria Rilke's *Letters to a Young Poet,* and I love his advice about writing. He tells the young man to essentially figure out if he *must* write. And if he *must*, then he should "build his life according to this necessity."[11]

So I write.

Living with flair means you know what you *must* do, and you build your life around that necessity. You write, no matter what. You write as dinner cooks. You write with a baby in one arm. You write on the bus or at stoplights.

I wrote my first novel with a 3 year old and a colicky newborn right there in the room. I don't know why, but I *had* to.

You do what you do—whether it's writing or something else entirely—because you *must.*

Your life becomes a sign and a testimony to what God made you to do.

49. "Your Path is Following You."

I'm reading an advice column from E. Jean, and a reader asks her, "How can I find my passion?"

E. Jean responds, "Here's the way: Run down as many paths—straight, winding, high, wide, narrow—as you can. Get going, my girl! Run! Fly! Try them all! Take them all! One day, you'll look down and see that your path is following you."[12]

I'm reminded of that simple truth in scripture in Isaiah that promises this: "Whether you turn to the left or the right, you'll find a voice behind you saying, 'this is the way; walk in it'." There's something so true about the voice behind us—the path that follows us—whispering the way and reminding us what we're made for.

There's also the great advice to get going: Run! Fly! Try!

No matter what I do, God leaves those little breadcrumbs that, like in the fairytale, always lead home.

50. Always a Portal

I stand under a darkening sky this afternoon. We notice a pinhole of blue sky that looks like a portal. There's even a little lamppost beneath it to remind me of Narnia.

It just seems like a message in the clouds: *There's always a way out or in. No matter what we're going through, there's a way out. No matter what we're wanting, there's a way in.*

Portals have everything to do with faith and imagination and hope and whimsy. Look up and find that little blue tunnel, that lamppost, that rabbit hole, that closet, that train platform, that moving staircase. There's a parallel world, and we might enter if we choose.

51. I Always Forget

It only takes a few thoughts to fall into a pit of delusional thinking. It happens so quickly: Suddenly, we feel like everything depends on our ability to think the right thoughts, do the right things, and be the right kind of people.

But it's only God in us.

I always forget this.

I always forget that this is what Christianity is: Christ in us, the hope of glory—transforming us, renewing us, and making us new creations.

I always forget that all my efforts to improve myself aren't really improvements at all. When I rely on God to accomplish what He wants in my life—when I cooperate with that movement of His Spirit—real change happens.

It feels very weak. I love that the Lord says to Paul, "My grace is sufficient for you, for my power is made perfect in weakness" (2 Corinthians 12:9).

52. Ready to Drip Diamonds

We wake up to early morning icy rain. The Winterberry Bush and Weeping Cherry look adorned with dangles of diamonds and crystals.

All that bleak autumn dreariness was worth it. The stripping down, the emptiness, the stark reality of it become the canvas for a glorious display.

It's all fine-cut crystal now. The empty season that brings on this new thing—that's required to showcase it—shows me how when God strips away, empties us out, and brings on something stark and dreary, it's because He's getting ready to drip diamonds.

53. Through My Being With You

Today I read in Philippians 2:25 Paul's reasons for continuing in ministry even though he just wanted to depart to be with Jesus. He writes, "I know that I will remain, and I will continue with all of you for your progress and joy in the faith, so that through my being with you again your joy in Christ Jesus will overflow on account of me."

His words turn into the prayer of my heart; I want to be the kind of woman who causes your joy in Christ Jesus to overflow.

Imagine!

I fear this isn't always the case. Lord, make it so that—on account of me—joy in Christ Jesus overflows. I wonder about the kind of person about which this statement could be true. Does this person display weakness so God's power is obvious in her? Does this person rejoice and proclaim with her mouth about God's wonders?

I'm thinking about this. I'm praying about being the kind of person who enables others' joy in Christ Jesus to overflow.

54. I Went to Meet a Tree

I learn from the Italian Mama about an oak tree in our neighborhood that's over 200 years old. It's a ten minute stroll from my house, and I've never seen it. This is why every neighborhood needs an Italian Mama who knows the secrets. She's the one who told me where to find the hidden vernal pond. She's the one who knows this land.

I'm thinking about the oak tree all morning. I have to see it; I have to touch it; I have to thank it for being here all this time, witnessing lives lived right here. My friend and I see the bare oak tree's arms raised above the houses, and she takes off running. "There it is! It's right here!" she cheers and points. I run behind her, full of joy and awe. (Every neighborhood also needs the kind of friend who not only agrees to walk with you to meet a tree, but who also runs with joy at the sight of it.)

We're going to meet a tree!

With those wide branches, it feels like the arms of God bestowing a blessing upon my head.

You have to dance around a bit when you stand next to something this big. You have to step way back to capture the whole thing.

But you also have to lean in close and run your fingers along the veins and wrinkles of its skin.

I love ancient things. I love the physical evidence that time passes and that new generations come and old ones die. In 200 years, another woman and her friend will run and dance around this old oak tree. I'm aware, suddenly, of my own mortality. But I'm equally aware of one thing:

I'm here right now.

Psalm 90 requests, "Teach us to number our days, that we may gain a heart of wisdom." As I touch the old oak, I know my days here are numbered. The tree makes me step back.

I number the days, anticipating and recording the wonder of God, as sturdy and expansive as the oldest oak in our town. I'm full of joy as I stand with my friend, and I can't wait to tell the Italian Mama what it felt like to see the tree.

Once again, I learn that living with flair has nothing to do with fame, prestige, or wealth. It has everything to do with beauty in community.

55. The Single Moment

This week, I find a quote from Argentine writer Jorge Luis Borges.

Borges states, "Every destiny, however long and complicated, essentially boils down to a single moment — the moment when a man knows, once and for all, who he is."[13]

In a few weeks, I'll begin to teach memoir writing again, and I'm asking myself and my students if the statement rings true. Can we remember falling upon our own identities in a single moment?

I know it sounds silly, but I remember the single moment when I looked out my front door and longed to be part of a neighborhood. I remember calling people I didn't really know to invite parents and their children to ride bikes and jump rope in the front yard.

In that moment, I felt a calling: I was to devote myself to building a neighborhood.

It would mean walking to school with neighbors, Neighborhood Fitness Group, Potlucks, Play Dates for Dads, and Creative Women Nights. It would mean not going anywhere but *here*, not leaving my street, not seeking all those things I've always wanted in my life that involved fame, wealth, and prestige.

It would mean putting down roots right here in Central Pennsylvania. It would mean blogging about it, even through the bitter winter.

It would mean realizing that community—real community—met a need in me I didn't know I had.

So my moment came in my own front yard when I wanted to build a neighborhood.

56. Places You Can't Reach Alone

Today I observe the way cats bathe each other.

Cats know that some places you just can't reach alone: behind the neck, way down the back, the shoulder blades. So one bathes the other.

I'm watching Jack and Snowflake, and I realize that some places in my own heart I just can't reach alone. I think about the beauty of good counselors, wise friends, skilled teachers, and discerning pastors. I think about spouses and children. I'm not meant to reach some places alone, and God sends understanding people to journey there with me.

I once heard a translation of Proverbs 20:4 that reads, "A person's thoughts are like water in a deep well, but someone with insight can draw them out." When I don't know what I'm feeling, and when I don't understand myself, I find someone with insight.

Cats know that some places you can't reach alone. Living with flair means knowing we aren't meant to. We find people to journey with us to the deepest places in our own hearts.

57. The Best Way to Wake Up: Pretend You're Six Again

This morning—before my eyes open, before the cats clamor and fuss for food, and even before coffee—my daughters bounce and squeal on the bed.

"You won't believe it! You won't believe it!" they giggle, urging me out of bed. "It snowed!"

They run to the window with eyes big. Their little bare feet jump up and down.

Oh, to be a child again! *I* envision a day of shoveling snow, negotiating with the ice, and battling the traffic. *They* envision a day of sledding, snowmen, hot chocolate, and snow angels. Of course you wake up happy when you see the hope and possibility of it.

I sit up in bed, and I suddenly remember this truth: that little child still lives in me and in us all. Today, I'm going to have hot chocolate and make the world's plumpest and tallest snow angel in my backyard. I'm going to sled down the big hill at the park, and I'll go faster because of my size. I'll bring the carrot for the snowman. You bring the hat.

58. Where You Return

I remember an author who shaped my spirituality in my mid-twenties. During that deepest darkness of despair—when you've lost hope—certain written voices bring you home. Henri Nouwen's *Return of the Prodigal Son* will always stand as that book that led the way Home.

I pull the old book off the shelf and see the places I've underlined. It's been over a decade. Back then, far from God and far from even myself, I read of Nouwen's own search for both.

Nouwen describes a particular movement towards God in this way: "It is the movement from the glory that seduces one into an ever greater search for wealth and popularity to the glory that is hidden in the human soul and surpasses death." He tells his reader that "[We] are called to enter into the inner sanctuary of [our] own beings where God has chosen to dwell. The only way to that place is prayer, unceasing prayer."[14] In that sanctuary, we encounter Jesus and—not surprisingly—the very self we've lost along the way.

It sometimes takes years to realize that wealth and popularity do not bring one Home. The more hidden and more sparse a thing is, the more glory it reveals. The counterfeit glory shines so brightly, but it cannot compare to the illumination within when I die to myself.

59. When All Else Fails, Bring Chocolate

Sometimes I find myself having to attend meetings I don't want to attend with people I don't know. Sometimes I have to enter into hostile classroom settings with students who scowl about grades or class assignments. Sometimes I find myself at odds with a neighbor.

As I prepare for a meeting today, I turn to Proverbs 18. Here, the wise man says, "A gift opens the way and ushers the giver into the presence of the great." Some translations say a gift enlarges the way of the giver. Others claim the gift opens closed doors and connects you to people.

I know what I need to do.

I buy chocolate. Really good chocolate. I enter the room with an armload of it. "I brought chocolate!" I exclaim. The gift never fails in classrooms, meetings, and even between friends with hurt feelings. You stand on the doorstep, ring the doorbell, and just hand over the chocolate.

I remember the story of a little girl who had her first fight with her best friend. Days pass. Finally, one of them sulks over, still mad, knocks on the door and says, "My mom wants to know if you want some chocolate."

The other girl, angry and frowning says, "Of course I do." She then smiles and says, "Come in and let's play."

When all else fails and you don't know what to do, bring chocolate.

60. Seeing Inside Your Knot

I'm trying to untie a jumbled mass of a thin gold necklace from my daughter's jewelry box. A tangled knot on the chain challenges me to the point of frustration. Finally, I put the chain down and find the tip of a pencil to loosen the knot.

I don't even know where to begin; I just dig around inside that knot until I see the tiniest bit of space.

With even that small bit of space, the knot starts to unravel. The chain releases its tension, and I can see inside the trouble. Strand by strand, the whole thing relaxes into order.

I start thinking that this is what great teachers do. This is what mothers and fathers and spouses do. This is what friends do, especially those friends who know the exact verse of Scripture for every problem.

They help us unravel what's so tied up in us. They loosen us up enough to see inside the knot.

I want to be a pencil tip in a knot.

61. "You Keep Glancing"

This morning, I enter the elementary school's gym to retrieve my daughter for her dentist appointment. It falls right in the middle of her very first band practice. I sneak in, and I'm overcome with the scene.

The fourth and fifth graders—at their first band practice—do the best they can. It's loud, squeaky, but actually beautiful. It's orderly. My daughter holds her flute with the other flautists, and as I watch her play, it seems like she's truly separate from me now, truly her own girl.

I never played a musical instrument. I never once read a piece of music or obeyed the ethereal dance of a conductor's hands.

Now the conductor holds his baton in a particular way, and the children stop their music. Before I motion for my daughter, I hear this:

"You have to watch me so closely that you'll know if I'm telling you to stop or go, quicken or slow. I won't use words, so you have to watch my hands so closely so you'll know what to do."

I'm standing there, full of delight, thinking about the ways God directs the tempo and sound of my life. When He doesn't speak, I watch for the hand of God and that ethereal dance that tells me to stop or go, quicken or slow. The Holy Spirit always seemed musical anyway, a Conductor indeed.

Later, on the way to the dentist, I ask my daughter how she manages to look at her music and the conductor at the same time. What an impossible focus on two things at once!

"You learn," she says. "You keep glancing."

I keep glancing: the music and the Music. I want to be part of this grand performance. I want to notice and obey the gestures of a God who leads.

62. Under Occlusion

Right about this time of year, my hands inevitably crack and bleed. The knuckles, red and leathery, reveal winter fissures that make me wince.

Nearly every part of my skin, if not already chapped, is vulnerable to the bitter cold winter air.

And right about this time of year, I wear gloves everywhere. I even wear them to bed. I especially wear rubber gloves when I'm doing housework. These tender hands need a barrier of protection against the elements.

My doctor friend says to put my hands "under occlusion" (covered with gloves) after using lotion to keep the moisture from evaporating. Under occlusion, my hands have a chance to heal. Occlude means to cover, block, or close, and I've decided it's a great winter verb.

My whole day becomes about protecting these little bleeding knuckles! My skin isn't as tough as I thought! I'm putting these hands under occlusion!

I realize that sometimes that's the season I'm in: vulnerable. So I pull back, go inward, and rest more. I'm under occlusion, and that's right and good. When I'm in a tender place emotionally, spiritually, or physically, that's exactly when it's appropriate and necessary to produce an extra layer of protection from whatever comes against me.

My extra layer? It might be more sleep, more prayer, more nourishment, more fellowship, more laughter. It's that kind of season, and we aren't as tough as we thought. We go under occlusion, and we'll be ourselves again soon.

63. Finding the Right Vein

I'm sitting in the doctor's office, and the nurse enters to draw my blood to check my thyroid. She's been practicing phlebotomy for over 10 years (I never knew the name for it!). A skilled phlebotomist, she tells me, trains one finger to locate the perfect vein.

"How do you find it?" I ask.

Venipuncture—the process of gaining intravenous access—isn't easy.

"I've taught this one finger to feel the bounce of the vein against it when I tap it. When I feel that bounce, I know."

I sit back, close my eyes, and let her tap my arm. Then, she pierces swiftly and confidently; she's gained access, and within a few seconds, she's finished.

A phlebotomist gains access to that hidden life force, that secret current, by instructing herself to feel what locations allow access to it. I want to gain access to life-giving places, places where God's Spirit leads, places of rich and deep flowing. I want to pierce life swiftly and confidently and enter in, straight to the heart of God. Maybe, when I'm not accessing abundant life, it's because I'm hitting the wrong vein.

64. I Can't Tell You

I'm eating dinner with my six year old, and she announces that she has the world's best math teacher. For a little girl who has struggled in school, her report amazes me.

"She doesn't tell us the answer, Mom. She lets us learn. Do you know the difference between telling and learning?"

I feel the flair coming on, and I put down my fork and look her right in the eyes.

"*Telling* means you just get the answer from the teacher. *Learning* means you have to figure it out. And then you know it. And then you can solve any problem because you know it."

She tilts her little chin up in the air, proud and confident. "I can probably solve any math problem now," she reasons.

This, of course, explains why God doesn't always tell me the answer. He's letting me figure something out so I know it. Oh, the problems I will be able to solve one day!

65. Scratch Life Anywhere

This morning, I read the quote, "Scratch life anywhere, and you find a witness to the Way."[15] It's E. Stanley Jones again, talking about how life always bears witness to Jesus.

I stop and ponder. Hasn't it been true as I've scratched the day, looking for evidence of Something Beautiful, that God's principles appear in acorns, snowflakes, one blade of grass, Lady Slipper Orchids, and even a cat with one eye?

That's what I'm doing: I'm scratching life anywhere—everywhere—and finding God's glory.

66. Hide the Things You Don't Like Inside the Things You Do

I'm starting to think that flaxseed can solve many problems. We've decided to use a few teaspoons a day in things like smoothies, sauces, and even mashed potatoes. Nobody knows the difference, but I promise that everything works more smoothly with flaxseed around. Maybe it's the fiber, or maybe it's the omega 3's or the lignans.

Whatever it is about flaxseed, my children have more energy and better moods.

So I hide it in the smoothies. And with blueberry smoothies, you can put in a handful of spinach (it doesn't show up against the deep blue color of the berries) and children drink it down lickity-split. My sister calls these kinds of smoothies

"Sneaky Smoothies," and her children have one every day. They did not have one sick day last fall.

I realize that when you hide the things you don't like inside the things you do, you can stomach almost anything. I'm coupling exercising with friendship, folding laundry with chatting on the phone, scrubbing floors with new music downloads, and completing stressful writing projects with homemade lattes.

And consuming flaxseed and spinach with berry smoothies.

Hide the thing you don't like inside the thing you love. That's helping me.

67. Little Cabin in the Woods

Solitude and silence both require faith.

You sit down for the day in a cozy little cabin by a big mountain, and you have to believe certain things:

You must have faith that stillness constitutes its own form of productivity.

You must have faith that the real you—and all her honest and unspoken thoughts—won't terrify you when you meet her. God can handle this unruly woman.

You also have to trust that God will help you find your way out of the dark woods when you walk up towards the mountain.

He will.

68. Once You Know, You Can't Unknow

It occurs to me again this morning that some things you can never go back from. Some things you just can't undo. Learning to read, for example, forever dooms you to a life of reading. You have no choice but to read the bumper sticker in front of you, the advertisement on the bus, the message in front of the church, or the billboard by the car wash.

Try as you might, you have no choice but to read once you know how. The brain makes reading like breathing—involuntary—so you see letters and make the words without really thinking about it.

Just try and not read this sentence. What a beautiful and inescapable outcome of learning to read!

I thought of other things I can't undo. When I heard the story of God's love for me, I couldn't go back from it. I couldn't undo that truth, and it changed how I read everything around me. Once I knew, I couldn't unknow, and now each moment becomes filtered through Jesus's love.

Do you wish I could undo it because it offends? I can't.

I'm doomed in the best possible way. The inescapable outcomes of a life of faith mean you'll learn things you cannot go back from. It's that powerful and that complete.

69. While Falling, You're Caught

My husband and I walk in the woods in search of icicles.

I've always been enchanted by icicles. They possess a strange beauty.

Icicles form because the warm sun melts the snow, but then that water freezes as it encounters the lower temperatures below. With each attempt to melt, the icicle simply grows longer and more beautiful.

Little by little, drop by drop, the structure forms. Just when the water above thaws, freeing it, the cold air below paralyzes it again.

Sometimes, we stay suspended just when we think we're finally free. We attempt and fail, attempt and fail. But in it, we grow more and more beautiful. Conditions aren't right just yet. We hang on, letting the process work.

Winter won't last forever.

70. Essence

My daughter wants to make real perfume from nature for her science project this year. I'm learning that she wants to discover the essence of things.

She researches ways to get the fragrance out of the flowers and into little vials for students to guess the essence she's extracted. She wants rose, grass, orange, cocoa, and lily to start. It's the middle of winter, but we venture to flower shops. We learn that you can, in fact, capture the essence of something. You can distill it by creating steam (which picks up the essential oil of the flower) and cooling the steam (which then you can catch in a bowl). The bowl of cooled steam, in theory, will contain water and the oil from the rose. The oil will separate from the water in the bowl, and we can use that oil for our perfume.

"Will this work?" we ask my husband. He's the one with the graduate degree in chemistry.

"Yes," he tells us. I'm so excited! I'm filled with wonder at the thought of seeing the essential oils. I'm amazed that you can actually distill a fragrance out of something.

My daughter fills the pot with rose petals, and we place a brick inside the pot to elevate our collecting bowl.

Then, we let the rose petals simmer on the stove with a bowl of ice sitting on top of the pot. When the steam hits the icy bowl, it condenses and falls back into our collecting bowl.

This way, we capture the essential oil in the condensed water.

A few hours later, we pour out the collecting bowl. The top layer of water is oil! I can't believe it! We captured the essence of the rose!

We can make perfume, potpourri, soap, bubble bath, or anything we want with that wonderful smell of rose. We immediately move on to capture orange oil.

I'm amazed at the process of capturing essence. Distill means to purify—to separate out—that thing I wanted, *that one true thing*. It requires such extremes of heat and cold. In my own heart, I think about the extreme places of pain and joy, sorrow and rejoicing. I think about times of instability and unrest. In the midst of this dramatic process, God distills some essential thing.

He does it because that fragrance released can bless a hurting world.

71. A Million Ways to Prosper

I'm reading Psalm 1 (where it says whatever we do will prosper), and I notice all the things I wanted God to "prosper" in my life. I've scribbled down everything from boyfriends to book contracts in that narrow margin.

This particular Bible was given to me by my great friend, Elizabeth, back in 1995. I therefore have 17 years worth of hopes and dreams written in the margin of this Bible.

I notice something as I look at all the things that didn't ever seem to work out.

The promise in Psalm 1 is this:

Blessed is the man
  who does not walk in the counsel of the wicked
or stand in the way of sinners
  or sit in the seat of mockers.
But his delight is in the law of the Lord,
  and on his law he meditates day and night.
He is like a tree planted by streams of water,
  which yields its fruit in season
and whose leaf does not wither.
  Whatever he does prospers.

I wonder for the first time what that verb "prosper" really means. Very few of my dreams in the margin came true, but does that mean they did not prosper? In the midst of failure, broken dreams, disappointments, and unanswered prayers, did I nevertheless thrive? Did I nevertheless meet God? Did God not use it somehow?

Whatever I do, God prospers it. He makes it succeed and thrive in a million incomprehensible ways.

I might not see it until 17 years later. I might not ever see it, but the promise in Psalm 1 is that whatever I do prospers in some way.

Whatever we do today will prosper.

72. Nothing Hides Here

The cats alert me that something's outside the window. They pace nervously, meowing and pawing at the glass.

It's a little bird.

I peer outside and notice the tangle of branches against the morning sky. I've looked out this same window for seven years. I used to wait for the most glorious morning when the Weeping Cherry blooms for those precious few days in the spring. That's the thing to see. But this morning, I love the skeletal branches, the deep shadows, the dim winter light, and the pale browns. I love that, like this, one can see the birds. They have no foliage in which to hide.

God reminds me that there's something to experience and rejoice in no matter how bare the landscape appears. Nothing hides here.

I think of Psalm 65:

The whole earth is filled with awe at your wonders;
where morning dawns, where evening fades
you call forth songs of joy.

73. In a Single Night

When I was in 6th grade, my teacher, Mrs. Kaiser, told the class what Christmas was like for her as a child.

She went to her grandparents' farmhouse out in the country. All the aunts and uncles and cousins gathered for Christmas Eve. What was strange was that nobody decorated for Christmas. No lights, no tree, no sweets, no presents. Christmas had not arrived.

That Christmas Eve, all the children slept in the basement. They went to bed in a normal farmhouse that had no evidence of Christmas at all.

Sometime in the night, the entire house transformed. Every surface was covered with garlands of pine, lights, and Christmas decorations. In the night, an enormous Christmas tree somehow arrived, decorated with the most beautiful ornaments. Presents burst from under the tree and went up the stairs of that farmhouse. Kitchen counters magically filled with cookies and pies. The table erupted with food.

In this family, Christmas came all at once, in a single night. My teacher explained that the magical transformation—so thorough and complete— brought so much wonder and joy to her heart. In a single night, everything changed.

I thought about this story for years. I imagined the faces of those children as they crept up the basement stairs. I imagined the wonder, the disbelief, the awe, and the mystery. But how? When? Who?

In a single night, everything changed.

That is Christmas: a little baby born one night. In a single night, the whole world was set free by something so wonderful and so mysterious as God coming down to us.

We creep up the basement stairs, open the door, and let the light of Christmas flood our hearts.

In a single night, everything changes.

74. Oh, So Ugly

We have a stubborn oak tree that won't drop her leaves.

She just won't!

These leaves endure snow, sleet, ice, and rain. They survive harsh winter winds, and they refuse to drop. It's nearly Christmas, and they still hang on.

They sit there in all their crispy brown mess, blocking my view. Ugly!

I've wondered about this ugly mass of leaves for 7 years now. I learn today the reason why this oak tree hangs on to her leaves. There's even a name for it: marcescence.

Holding on to the dead leaves (marcescence) protects the branches from hungry deer and bear who eat the bark. The leaves also trap snow which helps water the roots. Some theorize that the leaves stay to warm new buds and twigs and drop only when it's an ideal time to fertilize in the spring. If the leaves dropped in fall, they'd decompose before spring, and this is when the tree needs the nutrients of the decomposing leaves the most.

The apparent refusal to do what all the other trees do—at the time they do it—actually signifies something smart and adaptive. Trees that manifest marcescence are the smartest and best!

So if our timing's all wrong and we feel behind all the others, let's remember my sturdy oak tree. Having a different schedule might just mean we're doing what we need to do to protect and nourish ourselves and others.

I slow down, hold on to plans for now, and smile up at my lovely caramel oak leaves. How marvelous they are!

Isn't it funny how when you understand something, you suddenly find beauty in what was once ugly?

75. No Matter What Happens

Some mornings, I wake up and say, "No matter what happens today, God, I belong to you."

It's something I like to remember especially if I have fear and anxiety in my heart.

I can easily overwhelm myself if I think about accidents, failures, illness, or crime. If you battle any type of anxiety, you know the feeling that you're not safe or that something terrible is just about to happen.

When I say, "No matter what happens today, God, I belong to you," I'm affirming that the Lord holds me in the palm of His mighty hand and can take care of me.

76. You Need Only to Be Still

As I walk to my classroom today, I feel overwhelmed with various situations and dilemmas.

I'm praying and asking God for the wisdom I need. What immediately comes to mind is the verse in Exodus 14:14:

The Lord will fight for you; you need only to be still.

Here, Moses tells the people of Israel that they do not need to be afraid.

They could stand firm. They could stay calm.

Moses says to the terrified people, "See the deliverance the Lord will bring you today."

Be still. See.

77. The Other Abundant Life

I have a list in my head of what constitutes the "abundant life" Jesus describes in John 10. His promise is that "[He] has come so that we might have life and have it abundantly," so naturally, I imagine all sorts of wonderful things that could come about in my life.

This morning, however, I wonder if I've really surrendered to God's idea of what abundant life means for me. Am I willing to receive the abundant life He offers (and not the one I'm devising in my mind)?

I feel a strange and wonderful freedom—most moments of true surrender feel strange and wonderful at the same time—because I'm allowing God to build my life and bring all the abundance He's planned.

I cease blocking this abundance by my own effort to craft what I think abundance means. Does it mean more friends, more money, more house, more success, more. . . anything?

It doesn't matter what I think about it. I can let that go and invite God to shape my abundant life which will be better and brighter than anything I could make happen on my own.

Oh, the joy of surrendering even this.

78. "Epiphanies cannot be scheduled, but they can be invited."[16]

I'm teaching from a chapter in *Writing to Change the World* that talks about "orchestrating moments" to experience awe and realize the hope and beauty of the world. At their root, I think of these moments as worship and connection to God where I'm growing as a person.[17]

I begin to think of how I might invite epiphanies—those spiritual and emotional breakthroughs—that foster real change.

Last week, I watched the way my daughter sat outside alone in the snow as the sun set behind the trees. As I finished dinner preparations, I saw, out of the corner of my eye, how she fell back into the snow and just stared up into the sky. She stayed that way for a long time. She closed her eyes and the snowflakes fell on her cheeks. As the darkness settled onto the backyard, she remained there, just thinking.

Stillness in nature, solitude, and quiet allow for a special kind of reflection into the life of things. Most of my life-changing moments have come in natural settings, when I'm alone, and when I'm finally listening. Although I can't schedule epiphanies, I can invite them.

I'm not sure what my daughter thought about in the snow, but I know that when I was a little girl staring up into a snow-filled sky, I began my education in wonder.

79. Not My Problem

I recently heard my husband describing an interview he heard with the late Bill Bright. When asked about some of the biggest problems he had faced in his life, Dr. Bright replied that he didn't have any problems.[18]

When the interviewer pressed him on it—surely Dr. Bright had problems!—the man insisted that he had no problems.

The interviewer kept asking him over and over again because he just couldn't believe that a man's life couldn't have any problems.

At this, Dr. Bright explained that he didn't say his life didn't have problems. He said that they weren't *his* problems. They were *God's* problems. Dr. Bright said that he had no problems because he transferred ownership of his life to Jesus and therefore any problems were really God's problems.

Bill Bright later restated that if his only concern is what the Master wants, then his life could be problem free.

Today, I throw my hands in the air with relief. This is not my problem. It's God's problem, and He can handle it.

80. Whether by Many or by Few: A Different Way to Think About Your Platform

There's a great little Bible verse in 1 Samuel 14:6 where Jonathan claims that "the Lord will accomplish His purposes, whether by many or by few." Some translations say, "Nothing can hinder the Lord; He can win a battle with many warriors or just a few."

The phrase "just a few" resonates with me this week as I encourage fellow bloggers, book writers, community builders, and speakers. We're increasingly expected to produce proof of our influence though followers, retweets, shares, event attendance, mentions, and of course, book deals. Bigger is always better in social networking circles.

But is that God's way to think about influence? What about the few that we care for? What about the few that God calls us to love and influence?

I'm driving home from teaching my small class of students. Just 24 in each class, 48 altogether. In the world of influence and big numbers—of platform and importance—I am woefully inadequate. I'm a joke to publishers and conference teams.

I'm nobody. Even my blog doesn't rank high enough to mean anything.

But *you* read it. And I love you and am thankful for you. I'm not trying to measure influence anymore; one really can't. Jesus didn't employ performance metrics in his ministry on earth. He turned away from big crowds and invested in the few.

I'm realizing how much I love the few.

God accomplishes His purposes whether by many or by few. Maybe it shouldn't matter to us either.

81. My Day Is Not My Own

Today, nothing goes according to plan. With a school closure and all my dreams for solitary writing dashed, I prepare for the exact opposite: boisterous little girls and a whole day of activity. My quiet, uninterrupted day becomes loud, busy, and very messy.

My day is not my own. When God changes the plan, I'm learning to go with it.

Besides, I know that one day I'll give anything to have a house full of little girls who need a mom to stir brownie mix, attend to crafts, make lunches, and supervise makeovers. On this day, what was supposed to happen did happen.

Solitude can wait; there's a dance party to join in my basement.

82. A Nest Filled with Snow

The sun explodes onto the backyard this morning. We shade our eyes from the snow's reflection of her. The whole scene sparkles and shimmers.

My youngest stands by the window to watch all the winter birds at the feeder. The Northern Cardinals, in particular, feast and then fly about the yard. We count seven birds that scatter when we pull on our boots to try to capture a photo.

The Northern Cardinal still stands devoted to that Winterberry bush. We talk about that old nest—the one the birds either add to or rebuild each year—that's now filled with snow. That poor nest! A nest filled with snow and not baby birds!

That's just what this season means. Our hearts are open nests for growing things, but maybe now's the time to fatten up spiritually and strengthen ourselves emotionally as we get ready for spring.

Meanwhile, I wait in the kitchen and will try again tomorrow to take photos of these beautiful winter birds.

83. Better Than You Found It

I'm talking about oath taking in my advanced writing course. We're reading the Hippocratic Oath for health professionals and asking ourselves what a professional oath might look like in our diverse fields.[19]

I remember my husband reciting for me the Boy Scout Oath and adding on that you always want to leave a place "better than you found it." For him, this isn't just about camp sites; it's for grocery stores, restaurants, and even gas stations. Although technically not a Scout law, from the time he was a young boy, he pledged to leave places—and now people—better than he found them. This might mean picking up garbage. This might mean encouraging an employee. This might mean helping someone with a task.[20]

What if we all left places and people better than we found them? Every encounter becomes an opportunity to add beauty and order. We leave a blessing wherever we go.

84. A Different Metaphor

Today, I consider the metaphors that come to mind when I think about myself as a teacher, wife, mother, and friend. In my professional development class, we're reading Parker Palmer's "Good Talk About Good Teaching."[21] He recommends a simple exercise to help us uncover strengths and weaknesses about our practice as teachers. I find so many applications to my whole life.

We fill in the blank:

"As a teacher, I think I'm a _____."

Some see themselves as coaches, orchestra conductors, cartographers, translators, circus ringmasters, lightning rods, or even fishmongers. Many see themselves as performers.

Then, we talk about certain teaching situations and ask how one might respond differently based on whichever metaphor governs the situation. If something difficult happens, a coach responds differently from a conductor. A performer will respond one way while a circus ringmaster responds another. A drill sergeant would handle a situation one way while a gardener would do something else.

Sometimes, the way we see ourselves limits our responses. We might need to be more like orchestra conductors perhaps.

I fill in the blank for myself as a mother, and the first thing that comes to mind is the word, "Cheerleader." As a mother, I think I'm a cheerleader. Well, no wonder I'm exhausted trying to keep everyone happy and enthused. No wonder I become discouraged when the energy level sinks in the house. What if, instead, I saw a mother as a sweeper on a soccer team?

Maybe a mother is a spotlight or a gardener or a bridge.

Maybe a teacher is a warm fire to come sit by, an umbrella, a stick of glue, or a travel guide.

Perhaps, if things aren't feeling right in my various roles, it's because my metaphor isn't quite right.

85. Robust and Hardy: Capable of Enduring Difficult Conditions

Lately, I've been praying for God to strengthen me. I'm too fussy. I'm too addicted to my comforts. What would happen if I were thrust into truly difficult conditions?

Over the years, I've learned to adapt, to find beauty, to think positively, and to rejoice through various trials, but I still have a long way to go.

I would like—in a few years—to be able to describe myself as hardy and robust.

I look out my window and see the Weeping Cherry patiently bearing the weight of winter. Experts claim the Weeping Cherry is hardy and robust. They endure harsh conditions. They richly bloom every spring despite whatever kind of winter they've had.

86. "Find New Folks Each Time Around."

I take some girls ice skating today, and we're having the best time holding hands as we all go around the rink. But then, an official looking skater approaches us and tells us that we "can only hold hands with one other person."

Apparently, our long chain of hilarious bliss hinders other skaters. Our great little group blocks, distracts, and endangers others.

"Break apart!" I call out. "Mix up it! Find different partners each time around!"

Suddenly, I recall a conversation I had with a woman who still—after all these years—feels hurt by various cliques in her community. I see it visually: people holding hands, forming little groups of hilarious bliss, that, in all their fun and joy, end up hindering, distracting, and even endangering others. They end up oblivious to the journey others are on right beside them.

"It's a good lesson, girls."

Don't hold so tightly to a little group that you hurt the flow of community. Mix it up. Find new folks each time around.

87. What They Don't Deserve

Sometimes I just want to punish students for asking me for recommendations last minute. I want to close my office door when they come by to get class notes because they overslept for class. I think about withholding all my good will and servant mindset because they just don't deserve it.

But neither do I.

I don't deserve any of the goodness and blessing of God, and yet He bestows it freely. I think about this theological truth and change my heart towards the people in my path today. Neighbors, children, students, and colleagues: their good (or terrible) behavior shouldn't change my opinion of them. I freely extend the grace God shows me.

Living with flair means we stop punishing people because they don't deserve good things. Neither do we.

88. Singleness of Heart and Action

It all starts again next week. This time, I teach juniors and seniors for the winter. We begin with professional materials that include résumés, cover letters, and personal mission statements.

I love personal mission statements for their particular simplicity; they state in a concise sentence or two what a person devotes herself to in her field or future career. Flowing from this devotion comes attitudes, behaviors, and goals.

Beyond our professional lives, I consider what it means to have a mission statement for marriages and families.

It's actually very difficult. Students tell me that this particular sentence might be the hardest one they write in their lives. It's the hardest but perhaps the most vital. When you narrow things down to a single mission, it suddenly becomes so easy to make choices. You don't live a scattered life. You don't live out of control. You live purposefully, intentionally, and easily.

In the book of Jeremiah, I learn that God gives singleness of heart and action. Some translations refer to a unified lifestyle—one heart and one way—that I've always thought sounded so freeing and beautiful.

I want to live purposely, intentionally, and easily. I want a singleness of heart and action that determines my attitudes, behaviors, and goals.

89. God's Mercy—In Whatever Form It Takes

I've always thought that God simply cannot resist us when we appeal to His tender mercy.

We cry out. He answers. He loves to show us His great mercy.

I read over and over again about this "God who is rich in mercy" (Ephesians 2) and how the Psalmist prays that God's "mercy [will come] quickly to meet us, for we are in great need" (Psalm 79). I read in Isaiah 63, even, that: "In all their distress He too was distressed, and the angel of His presence saved them. In His love and mercy He redeemed them; He lifted them up and carried them."

I know that we have a merciful, wonderful God. When I pray for mercy, however, it often comes in the form I do not expect or want. But I think I know what it should look like.

It suddenly occurs to me to pray, "God, I want to receive your mercy today, in whatever form it may take." I don't want to limit God or imagine what mercy looks like. I want to look through the lens that it's all His great, tender mercy today.

90. Too Good to Be True

I place my bird feeder outside, and within minutes the Northern Cardinals come.

They spy on the banquet: doubting, cautious, suspicious.

It's too good to be true. A feast? Here? Now? Just when all the winterberries are gone. Just when we wondered if we'd make it.

I stand by the window and watch them finally—after much hesitation and much fuss—dare to feast.

The whole scene calls out to me: Yes, there's a feast—Here! Now!—and you are welcome to it. Cease the doubt, the caution, the suspicion. Stop fussing, come out of hiding, and just feast.

(And there's even more. I have a whole bag of food inside, waiting for you.)

Psalm 36:8 "They feast on the abundance of your house; you give them drink from your river of delights. For with you is the fountain of life; in your light we see light."

91. "Believing They'd Already Died"

Today, my students discuss suffering and loss in the context of Japanese haiku. Various writers suggest that we suffer so much because we're so attached to certain outcomes. Releasing these expectations provides a coping mechanism that helps us enjoy life more.

A student raises his hand to tell us about his historical research about soldiers in wartime. He reports that "they went into war believing they'd already died. They were grateful for anything that happened to them that day because they weren't expecting to be alive at all."

They'd already surrendered their lives. They'd already assumed they would die, and that made them endure. They moved ahead without fear.

I think about this conversation all day long. I mull it over in my office and think of those soldiers on the walk across campus to my car. What must it feel like to surrender so deeply that anything that happens is a pure gift from heaven? What does it mean to receive what comes each day as a miracle because you expected nothing but death?

Enduring indeed.

I remember Galatians 2:20: "I have been crucified with Christ, and I no longer live but Christ lives in me. The life I live in the body I live by faith in the son of God who loved me and gave himself for me." I've already died; anything that happens now is a pure gift and a pure miracle.

92. It Must Be a Place of Rest

As I clean my home today, I realize that whatever I set on the ground (blankets, coats, pillows, duvets), my cats assume it's a place of rest.

Even when I sit down, they assume my lap is a resting place. It's funny that they actually believe I'm walking around for the express purpose of creating resting places for them. And they don't discriminate; a bumpy backpack suits as well as a fluffy feathered duvet.

Here's another place to rest. And another. Oh, look, there's another!

Psalm 23 resonates in my mind that God does perhaps move about with the express purpose of creating resting places. God says to come to Him and He "gives rest." I'm told our hearts are "at rest in His presence" and that God provides "undisturbed places of rest."

I look down at those cats who quickly, gladly, and indiscriminately receive places of rest. Whatever strange burden is flung across their path, their immediate response is to use that obstacle as a place of rest.

If God is in the business of leading me to resting places, then might I see my own blocked path differently?

This obstacle—this strange burden on the path—just might be my resting place if I let it, if I receive it as such.

93. Exactly What You Should Never Do

Driving into campus today on the icy, snow-covered roads, I find myself skidding.

I remember my Driver's Education teacher's words:

"Do exactly the opposite of what your instincts demand; turn in the direction of the spin and accelerate."

What? Go faster? In the direction of the spin? Surely, you must be kidding.

It's true. The car rights itself this way. I accelerate and turn where the car skids, and I find I'm free of the danger.

What if God wants me to move in the direction of my greatest fear—accelerating towards the very thing that frightens me—in order to right myself?

I turn into the spin and pick up speed. I face it and find myself free.

94. Take Your Seat

Last night, I study Ephesians 2:6 with graduate students who always enlighten me. I can't take my eyes or mind off the simple word, "seated." The verse claims that "God raised us up with Christ and seated us with him in the heavenly realms."

We talk about being seated. So much of our lives is a clamor and competition to get a seat at the table. We want to be recognized, approved of, and applauded. Much of what we do is for the sole purpose of impressing.

Why? Why impress? Simply to feel like we belong at some great party with the coolest and most clever, the sought after and the important?

I ask God to help me stop trying to impress. I realize the greatest truth that I'm already seated at the table. I'm already included, recognized, approved of, and applauded by God himself.

So I'm not going to impress you anymore; I don't have to.

95. The Strength and Courage You Need

This morning, I note the repetition of God's command to "be strong and courageous" in Joshua 1. Five times in just one chapter!

I'm not sure what each day will bring; nobody can know for certain. I do know, however, that when moving into new territory, we require special strength and courage like Joshua and the people of Israel. God gives this strength and courage!

Perhaps it's strength and courage to try something new, mend a hurting relationship, teach a new class, parent in a different way, or attempt a new physical, mental, or social challenge. What would we do if we had all the strength and courage we needed?

We do. All the resources of heaven are available to us.

96. All My False Rests

Today I find an obscure and rare little document written in 1650 by R. Wilkinson, a member of the British army. He composed an 81 page paper entitled, *The Saint's Travel to the Land of Canaan: Wherein are Discovered Seventeen False Rests.* [22]

The university library happens to have the images of this old text, and although it's hard to read, I find myself fascinated by Wilkinson's list of where the soul is tempted to "rest" apart from Christ alone. His language is much more beautiful and complicated than my notes, but essentially, Wilkinson warns the Christian of the "false rests" we base our hope, peace, and joy upon.

These false rests include feeling superior to others, our obedience, our spiritual gifting, our right theology, our mystical experiences, our feeling of special deliverance, our skills, our large and thriving ministry, our shame or regret over sin, or even our application of certain biblical promises for Israel that were never meant for individuals. In these things, we often find a false security and a counterfeit peace.

(Wilkinson, by the way, influenced Hannah Whitall Smith who adds to this list such false rests as reputation, knowledge, and wealth.)

In the end, I'm challenged to think about from where my rest actually comes. I need not work for it or manufacture it. Instead I remember Psalm 62:5 and how "My soul finds rest in God alone; my hope comes from him." Or I note how, in

Isaiah 63:14, the people "were given rest by the Spirit of the Lord." Even more specifically, I apply Matthew 11:28 where Jesus says, "Come to me all who are weary and heavy-laden, and I will give you rest." Finally, in Hebrews, we're told to enter "his rest" repeatedly.

So there you have it: I enter in and receive it.

97. "The Number of Things One Can Do Without"

Today I read that Tolstoy's definition of wealth was "the number of things one can do without."[23]

Yes.

Wouldn't it be wonderful to grow into the kind of maturity where we found contentment in every situation, especially those devoid of all the usual accessories?

98. The Song Your Heart Will Sing One Day

I read this morning a Psalm that meant so much to me during my darkest days. In Psalm 30, David writes, "Weeping may remain for a night, but rejoicing comes in the morning."

Later, David proclaims to the Lord: "You turned my wailing into dancing; you removed my sackcloth and clothed me with joy, that my heart may sing to you and not be silent."

That my heart may sing to you . . .

I wonder about what my own heart sings to the Lord.

A few Psalms later, I learn that David knows God is his "hiding place" who protects him from trouble. He announces, "God will surround me with songs of deliverance." These kinds of songs must be wonderful indeed.

As I study more, I find that most of the Psalms are actually *deliverance songs*.

This is the song. This is the song my heart will sing: Deliverance. The songs our hearts will sing to the Lord are the songs of rescue and freedom. I consider that deliverance songs—the song my heart is singing and will sing—are part of this life's purpose.

I have been delivered. I am being delivered. I will be delivered.
This is a beautiful song.

99. The Well-Ordered Day

Today I remember that Jesus ordered his day around the Father's exact
instructions.

No more, no less.

Jesus says "yes" to what he's supposed to say "yes" to. He declines what he must
decline. He travels here and there under divine order.

It's supernatural. It's freeing.

I read in John 14 where Jesus says, "I will not say much more to you, for the
prince of this world is coming. He has no hold over me, but he comes so the
world may know that I love the Father and do exactly what my Father has
commanded me. Come now; let us leave."

When I look closer, I see that Jesus knows when to stop talking and when to
speak. He knows when to get up and leave, and he knows when to stay.

He does exactly what he's supposed to do.

Just a few verses later, we learn that we can do exactly what Jesus instructs
because the Holy Spirit teaches us "all things" and "reminds" us of everything
we've been taught.

If the Holy Spirit teaches us all things, can't we ask God for specific instructions
for our day? We pray and ask, and then we order our day exactly.

When to say *yes* or *no*. When to stay or leave. When to speak or stay silent.

I pray for a well-ordered, Spirit-led day.

100. In Case You Wondered If You Should Write it Down

As students work on personal essays over the next few weeks, we consider what
we might pass on. We offer our life experience to others—the pain, the beauty,
the joy, the despair—to *provide insight*.

Mary Pipher explains that "with personal essays, we turn our own lives into teachable moments for others."[24]

As I age, I realize how important this is. Whether I like it or not, whether I want it or not, folk perceive me as older and wiser. I have things God wants me to pass on.

Why shouldn't we do this work? Why shouldn't this become part of our spiritual practice, as important as prayer or reading the Bible or worship?

I consider how in Psalm 78:3-5, the poet writes:

Things we have heard and known,
* things our ancestors have told us.*
We will not hide them from their descendants;
* we will tell the next generation*
the praiseworthy deeds of the Lord,
* his power, and the wonders he has done.*

Or in Psalm 102:18, we know the reason for writing it down:

Let this be written for a future generation, that a people not yet created may praise the Lord.

What if we decided we will not hide our stories? What if we wrote down the deeds, the power, and the wonders God has accomplished and displayed in our own lives (because they were never just for us alone anyway)?

We will go and write, so it can be an everlasting witness.

Spring

Forget the former things; do not dwell on the past. See, I am doing a new thing! Now it springs up; do you not perceive it? I am making a way in the wilderness and streams in the wasteland.

Isaiah 43:18-19

Spring

1. I Hear Things Melting

All morning at my desk, I hear the drip, drip, dripping of melting snow and ice. We're thawing, folks. Water trickles down the gutters and flows into great puddles.

It's a beautiful sound.

I love to hear the work of thawing. Those icicles and snow banks stand no chance against this bright March sun.

I turn my face to that sun and bask a bit. I find myself asking God to thaw me, too. Just this morning, my friend, Nature Girl, tells me to "take my cues from nature today." She's the same friend who tells me to remember that things "just take time." She reminds me that what nature does, perhaps I should do today.

I think about this all morning. Well, nature's defrosting today. Maybe that's what I need.

In Psalm 147:17, I read that "He sends his word and melts them; he stirs up his breezes, and the waters flow." Today, I want God to thaw any icy, hardened thing in me. I want to stay soft and flowing and sensitive to the Spirit.

So I keep my whole face to the sun and bask some more.

2. Luring the Turtle

Today I tried to lure a hibernating turtle out from underneath my back porch. I actually devised an elaborate plan. Coaxing turtles into the open isn't necessarily extraordinary, but why I did it felt like flair.

My elaborate plan involves calling to our turtle and leaving fruit around the yard. I realize this is ridiculous. But still.

I know he's in there. Last fall, I fed him tiny slices of fruits and vegetables. Then, in a bombardment of freezing rain, winter came early. The turtle burrowed deep somewhere in my yard, and, since we couldn't find evidence of digging, we assumed he went where it was warmest: under the porch near the house.

Spring is here. Let the turtle emerge!

Today, I circled the yard, looking for that beautiful box turtle. As I walked among all the green shoots in the garden, I knew in my mind that the hunt was completely useless. Our turtle most likely departed for the woods long ago.

Chances are slim he's anywhere near my yard. He might be in another state by now.

But my heart—and the glimmer of childhood left in me—focused my eyes to spy any hint of that brown and yellow mosaic turtle shell. No turtle. But I'll wake up tomorrow wondering if today's the day I'll be drying dishes at the kitchen sink, look out across my back yard, and see him lumbering towards the apple slice I've left for him.

I'll circle the yard tomorrow, too. It's good for my soul.

Living with flair means I hunt, despite the odds, for what might be.

3. So You'd Get What You Really Needed

I've been researching how to best preserve my lilac bouquets in the house. It turns out that you can add some sugar, some lemon juice, and some bleach to your glass vase, and you'll have many days of fragrant blooms in your home.

While I'm researching, I discover that the lilac stem is *so tough* and *so thick* that it's nearly impossible for those stems to draw up their life-sustaining nutrients in a vase. They wilt and expire within one day.

I learn that you must crush and split the stems to soften them and provide many points of entry for the lilacs to suck up all the water.

I'm standing in my kitchen, damaging those stems—literally breaking them open with a knife—(in order to save them!), and I realize the tender hand of God in my own heart that crushes in order to provide a special and rapid access to what I really need: Him, the Living Water.

The tough, thick me softens so I can get what I've wanted and needed all along. This was the crushing and cutting that saved me.

4. The Double Dutch Challenge

I learned Double Dutch with the neighborhood children.

I did it. Seriously, I did.

It was a community effort. One mom bought the jump ropes at a sporting goods store, one mom offered her vague memories of how to do it, and one mom agreed to turn the ropes with me.

We read an instruction booklet first.

So there we stood, us moms and dads, with all these children around us, rising to our newest neighborhood flair challenge: Learn Double Dutch jump rope.

It's a terrific game to learn. Think about the fact that two ropes are turning in opposite directions, fast, and some child (or adult) jumps over these ropes in a sequence that resembles running in place or else doing little hops to avoid getting tangled up. We practiced turning the ropes (that's a sport in itself), we sang traditional jump rope songs (something about candy), and soon, 6 children learned this skill. We cheered each time. We slapped high-fives. We celebrated like we were at the Olympic Games.

And then it was my turn.

I am an older woman, remember. Put it this way: I jiggle in places and need support in more ways than one. But I always wanted to learn Double Dutch, and for whatever reason, I never took the opportunity.

Well, now. If I'm going to live with flair, I can't let this be.

It took me two tries, and I did it. I maybe jumped 5 times in total, and I didn't get tangled up in ropes or anything. It's actually not that hard once you learn to jump really fast. Now I'm moving on to performing Michael Jackson's "Beat It" moves while I Double-Dutch (thanks for the suggestion, friends).

What made it an overwhelming flair moment? Double Dutch represented the best of community organizing. We set a goal, we divided tasks, we gathered to accomplish our goal, and then we celebrated. As I teach my family about community service, I instill the value of building a neighborhood. We are learning how to gather people together around common goals.

Our neighborhood values physical fitness and raising children with the skills they need for life-long health. We can't do this alone. We need the group.

Something about this shared task of learning Double Dutch felt truly authentic. I'm not sure how to define it other than to tell you that authentic community involves jump ropes. I keep them in my minivan at all times.

Besides, life is hard. Some days I feel like I'm trying to jump over ropes going in opposite directions with out-of-control schedules, sick children, working, and just living. But then I look up, see my community with their hands on the ropes, steadying me, encouraging me, looking me straight in the eyes and saying: You can do this, Heather! Ready, Set, Go! And the ropes turn, and the neighbors cheer, and then I'm doing it! I'm doing this impossible thing that I couldn't do just yesterday!

Having a neighborhood that comes out to play after dinner is community flair. We value exercise, and now, we value it with flair. Living with flair means keeping jump ropes in the back of your minivan just in case the neighbors come.

5. 15 Minutes of Flair

So far, finding daily flair hasn't been too hard (thank you Michael Jackson, seashells, doughnuts, crab teething rings, and worms), but today seemed profoundly flairless. I walked to school, taught classes, held office hours. All good things, but nothing extraordinary stood out. I did see someone wearing the brightest blue shirt I've ever seen—it was practically glowing—and I thought about stopping him, taking a picture, and asking if he minded appearing in my flair blog.

But then, my cell phone rang. My husband was picking me up from campus, and he'd be 15 minutes late. I stood on the curb, wondering what in the world I could do with 15 minutes. What can anyone do with just 15 minutes? It's exactly the sort of time increment worth wasting away doing absolutely nothing.

Instead, I called my friend (I knew her office was across the street from the coffee shop).

"Hey," I said.
"Hey," she said.
"I have 15 minutes," I said.
"Where are you?" she asked.
"By the coffee shop," I said.
"I'm coming," she said.

For exactly 15 minutes, I drank a skinny mocha (I put that in just in case my Weight Watchers friends are reading), sat outside of the coffee shop, and had a wonderful conversation. In 15 minutes, we covered the topics of men, teaching, clothing accessories, children, procrastination, spirituality, over-committing, class presentations, sandwiches, and, finally, my husband's new glasses.

This friend knows how to create conversation flair. She knows the art of asking great questions to draw me out quickly. I've noticed that she asks about my day, but she'll do so in a way that encourages me to tell a story about it. She'll say, "Tell, me more," or "What was that like for you," or "What is that making you think about?". She'll mention things she's observing about my life by saying, "I noticed this about your daughters," or "You seem to really enjoy this about teaching." And then I ask questions and make observations of her in return. We laugh together, express sadness with each other, and most of all, celebrate our day. We talk deeply, with flair, for 15 minutes, exchange a quick hug, and then I am off to deal with groceries, grading, play dates, and laundry.

Living with flair means I turn any moment into a worthwhile one. It means spending time building relationships through meaningful conversation whether I have 15 minutes or 15 hours. Deliberate questions, connecting deeply. That's flair.

6. Wormy Joy

On the day marking a triumphant entry of a King into Jerusalem, this Palm Sunday started out drizzly and bitter cold. Rain in the forecast again. As I sat behind the registration table in the foyer of my church, welcoming families and their children, I noticed the palm branches limply splayed on a bench nearby.

Not so joyful of a Sunday, I thought. Even the palm branches can't find anything to be excited about. Nevertheless, I greeted each child and asked how her or she was doing. Most said, "Fine, thank you," and moved on. But one little boy, maybe nine years old, leaned over my table, his hands in excited little fists. "I'm doing awesome!" He smiled so big, squishing his freckles into one another.

Since I don't hear that response very often, unless it involves a Disney vacation, I asked him what made him so happy on such a depressing, rainy day.

"I love the rain! I love the rain because it makes the worms come out, and then I can catch them!" He continued to smile and he even jumped up and down in anticipation. And then, before I could say another word, he turned and ran towards his family, leaving behind a trail of flair.

As he left, I thought about finding flair in the inconvenient, bitter cold rain. Come to think of it, most of life seems inconvenient and bitter. Our plans change. Our dreams die. We get sick. Loved ones pass away. Natural disasters strike nations. Children suffer. We suffer. Life doesn't often give us the luxury of living with flair in the midst of suffering.

But this little boy somehow saw past the rain. He knew that bad weather "makes the worms come out." Living with flair means I think beyond the inconvenient circumstance or the suffering to what it might make "come out." What beauty, what compassion, what goodness, what secret treasure? I can dread the rain, or I can dig deep into it, find the joy, and let it squiggle across my palm.

7. **Becoming an Umbrella**

Flair opened early this morning on the dreary mile walk to school. It was drizzling (drizzle is the worst: it's indecisive and taunting with its half rain / half fog constitution) and remarkably chilly for March.

I have a huge bright blue and white umbrella. I like to spin it and do a little Gene Kelly dance as soon as I open it. And then, I'm driven by pure instinct to invite anyone near me in, to stand close, cuddle up, and stay warm. With my arm around a child or my head pressed to a friend's cheek, I feel like it is a sacred space. It feels like flair.

And it's no wonder I feel this way. Nearly every culture recognizes the important role of umbrellas and the treasures they protect. The umbrella's rich history reflects how communities use umbrellas to shield their most holy objects, to announce sacred ceremonies, and to signal the presence of royalty. In Egypt, the figures of gods are covered by umbrellas, in the Roman Catholic liturgy, the umbrella covers the Most Holy Sacrament, and in the ancient Chinese book of ceremonies, the umbrella always covered imperial carriages.

What sacred treasures, what dignitaries were underneath my umbrella? Was that child, picking a nose and stooping to fix a sock that had inched its way down her foot, a treasure?

I imagine that the umbrella doesn't discriminate. I imagine the honor the umbrella feels to partake in the ceremony of walking to school.

What if I acted more like an umbrella? Living with flair means I open my arms wide to point out and protect what is sacred and of supreme worth in everybody around me.

This morning it felt like I walked to school with royalty. And I did.

Living with flair means I am an umbrella today.

8. **Learning the "Beat It" Moves**

This morning, my neighbor and I learned the choreography for Michael Jackson's "Beat It."[1] We had my laptop propped for maximum visibility and water glasses filled for potential dehydration. We adjusted our workout clothes so they wouldn't inhibit our moves.

We learned the whole dance from a YouTube video. This is no small thing.

I'm not sayin' I can do it well, or in any way resembling MJ, but I did learn it.

Why did we do it? I have no idea. But it counts as my flair for the day.

Living with flair means I'm doing something a little ridiculous, a little "out there," a little beyond what's expected or appropriate every day. Something about dancing this morning reminded me that joy often lies dormant, waiting to be unearthed and brought forth. What made learning dance moves so joyful? What is it about the spontaneous, the supremely useless, and the silly that lets the joy in?

Whatever it was, I needed it.

Flair signals embellishment. I want to embellish the day; I want to celebrate it and set it in the right light. Doing my MJ moves (the thrusts, the snaps, the round kicks) made things shimmer this morning. But it really wasn't, in terms of productivity or market value, useful.

But the day felt hopeful, not because I scrubbed a kitchen floor, but because I danced on it, hard, for no reason at all. And then I told all the neighbors about it.

Flair needs company. Dancing with my friend, banging into her when I mirrored the moves incorrectly, made us giggle like preschoolers. We weren't talking about anything. We weren't processing all the dysfunction in our lives or in the world. We were just trying to learn this dance. . . together. And we did it. We participated, somehow, in some larger dance: we are wives and mothers, aging and aching often both internally and externally, with enormous amounts to accomplish in any given day. Who has time to learn a dance from the 1980's?

And yet, we danced.

9. Prepare for Flair

There's this trick I use to help me prepare for flair. I assume I'm going to be amazed by anyone or anything. It could happen at any time: when I'm frying an egg, putting on socks, or standing in line somewhere. If anything, I'm learning the obvious truth that things aren't what they seem.

I keep needing to learn this.

The semester ended today. I gathered final papers, shook hands, agreed to write recommendations, and voiced all the usual blessings a college professor might give. Mostly, though, I recalled how much this particular group of students surprised me.

Living with flair means I throw out the stereotypes. I abandon presuppositions. I used to scan a room of people and determine, in advance, what sort of students they'd be: the fraternity boys would be late every morning; the tattooed and pierced would be angry and defiant; the military students would be prompt and tidy; the athletes would be ambitious but average as writers; the quiet girls in the back wouldn't engage with me all semester.

I know stereotypes exist for a reason. They might be generally true. But this semester, I discovered every single exception to the rules of how types of people behave. Nobody acted like they were supposed to. The soldiers came late, and the fraternity boys wrote the most compelling papers, on time, and with flair. The tattooed and pierced were the most loving and compliant of all. The athletes were the best writers. The shy girls provided ongoing humorous commentary.

I've learned to assume nothing. This prepares me to receive the extraordinary moment when it comes. When I tell that thing or that person what it represents—without giving it a chance to amaze—I'm sabotaging all the flair.

I've been hanging out with strangers all day (hence the late blog post). I'm in a wedding party with lots of folks I've never met. When I met each new person, I prepared for flair by imagining how great this person must be, anticipating all the wisdom and inspiration they possess, and doing all I could to draw it out. That's the secret to friendship, teaching, marriage, parenting, and even my relationship to myself. No need for stereotypes. No need for judgments.

I just want to prepare for flair.

10. From the Bottom Looking Up

For Mother's Day, my dear family takes me to Ricketts Glen State Park so we can hike and view amazing waterfalls.

I explain to my daughters that a "glen" is a narrow valley. The whole drive to the park, I think about how we're going down into a deep, dark, narrow valley. I think of the "valley of the shadow of death" from Psalm 23.

How different from last summer when I was hiking in the highest possible Alpine Tundra in the Rocky Mountains. I've been *very high up* in this world, but today, I'm going to a valley instead. I think about the spiritual metaphor of "mountaintop experiences (all joy and peace and beauty) as opposed to the "dark valley" experiences of hard times (despair and hopelessness and confusion).

As we hike to see the magnificent waterfalls, I think about how the valley experiences allow for a particularly important phenomenon:

You experience *power* there.

I stand at the base of those waterfalls, and I know that it's a much different experience from when you're at the top looking down. At the base, you *know the power*. You feel the rumble, the wind, and the spray of water. You see the way the water cuts right into the heart of rock.

It cuts even the rock.

You're put in your place; you're humbled and a little scared.

I would describe the early years of motherhood as the lowest valley of my life. Yet there, I knew God's power. I was right where I needed to be for God to cut and smooth me into something beautiful.

There are some things you can only learn deep in the dark, narrow valley.

11. How to Survive Rejection

There's a way to handle rejection with flair. I always come back to the same three truths to survive it.

When it comes—that awful companion, Rejection—and says no, I realize what the *No!* signals.

It signals that I put myself out there. It means I risked something. It means I offered myself. These are good things. These are *really good* things.

But it doesn't make us feel any better in the face of a friend who spurns us, a company that jettisons our resume, a publisher who turns down our novel, or a family member who forsakes us. It doesn't soothe the hurt that comes from hoping for something that doesn't come about because somebody—or just circumstance—delivers that awful *No!*

But three things do soothe. Or at least they helped me this morning when I read another email rejection about a book proposal. I want to live with flair, after all. What does it look like to endure rejection with flair?

1. We do what we do because it's our calling—our unique way to offer a gift to the world. We do this whether or not it ever receives approval or recognition. We keep doing it because we serve others, because we want to make a contribution for love, not for money or prestige or even anybody loving it back. Phew! Aren't you so glad your doing is not dependent on our loving it? I had a student who didn't get a call-back for an audition for a major network singing competition. But this guy was born to sing. Did a rejection stop him? That week, we asked him to sing for us in class. He stood up, sang the most amazing renditions of various songs, and we cheered and hollered like crazy. He's not going to Vegas, but he delighted us. For that day, at that time, it was enough. Somebody, somewhere, wants to receive the gift we offer.

2. Every "no" is an opportunity for a "yes" somewhere else. I think this applies to break-ups, schools that reject us, and jobs that fire us. My dream school turned me down for graduate school. I wept and wouldn't leave my dorm room. I went to Michigan instead, certain I was doomed never to meet my Southern Gentleman. My Southern Gentleman also got into Michigan. You know the rest.

3. If I believe in a divine plan (which I do), I know that God does not withhold good things from his children. If I don't get the thing I want, it means it wasn't good for me (at least at this time). If it's good, and part of God's plan for me, then I can chill out and enjoy the wait.

Rejection is good for me because it brings me back to reality. It reminds me that I do things (write, teach, plan new projects) because I love to do these things. That's the reward—not any prestige or wealth or even anybody loving it back. And there's a divine mystery to the order of a life. *The no is also a yes somewhere.* I can rest in the timing and the plan of the yes.

Rejection is a beautiful and terrible thing. It's awful in the truest sense of the word. Awful: to inspire awe and deep reverence. I respect rejection. I'm thankful for what it reminds me of and how it helps me live with flair.

Living with flair means to respect the rejection. It reminds me why I do what I do.

12. How to Gather in Your Life

I hate that feeling of being scattered. I'm beginning to think that if I'm not careful, I will always tend towards an out-of-control life.

To scatter means to disperse in different directions. When I'm scattered, it means I'm investing energy in multiple, often opposing, directions.

The opposite of scatter is to gather in.

Today, I considered the difference between a scattered life and a life that's gathered in. Last semester, I was frazzled every single day. I was involved in 4 major campus projects including teaching 3 different courses and directing an unrelated project for another program. Besides this, I was freelance writing, meeting with graduate students, parenting, trying to be a great wife, serving my church, relating to my neighbors, and attempting to keep a clean house while preparing nutritious meals. And exercising. And remembering to do the laundry.

I lost it. I was angry and very, very moody. (Not flair)

So I decided that I needed to gather my life in. I wondered what would happen if I directed all my energy in one direction and not ten. Here's what I did:

I thought about where my home is. I thought about where my natural pathways are: where I live, where I walk, where I drive. I decided to focus energy there. I narrowed the scope of my life to a radius of a few miles (literally). Instead of spinning out of control, I gathered in. I cared for my neighbors as I walked to school. I helped launch a neighborhood fitness group. I didn't leave my neighborhood. I even attended a neighborhood church rather than driving to the other side of town. If some offer came along that made me leave these natural pathways, I said "no." I stayed in.

In my professional life, I gathered in by only teaching one course and directing energy towards making it great and teaching it multiple times. I directed my freelance writing projects to relate to my course work. I declined directing programs that didn't relate to this one course. I reduced my professional life to one natural pathway, and I developed it with flair.

Gathering in increased my energy and my capacity to be fully present and refreshed each day. Gathering in made me narrow my scope to my neighbors, my one course, and my family. I say "no" to everything else. It's simplified my life.

It's helped me live with flair. A scattered life, diffused and diminished of power, isn't a fun life to live. It's a tired life, a moody life, a life that feels spent before noon. A gathered life feels simple and energized. There's time to reflect, learn a dance, cook a gourmet meal, and keep a blog. There's time to drink coffee with a neighbor, hunt for a turtle in your backyard, or make homemade pizza with a child.

Living with flair means I gather in.

13. Hovering Over the Mess

I read a great prayer today in which the author talks about inviting the Holy Spirit to hover over the mess and chaos of the day and to begin exerting the creative, organizing, miraculous power of God.

In Genesis 1, I read how the earth was "formless and empty, darkness was over the surface of the deep, and the Spirit of God was hovering over the waters." And then, and *then*! creative power begins.

If I visualize the Spirit of God hovering over this whole messy day and infusing it with order, beauty, meaning, and purpose, I'm suddenly filled with great consolation. Where the Spirit of God is, formless, empty, and dark things change. New things erupt in otherwise desolate, chaotic places.

Just thinking of it gets me excited today.

14. 50 Ways to Stay Out of Trouble

It's a big weekend in my town. It's a big party weekend. This means I avoid campus and expect a really low attendance in my early classes on Monday. It's always the same story: students act out this script of what it means to be a college student.

Last year, a man came to my office and asked me if I had any ideas for how he could stay out of trouble. He'd been arrested, he'd had several underage drinking citations, and his GPA had plummeted from a 4.0 to a 1.7. Feeling like he'd squandered the last four years of his life, he asked me what I did for fun that didn't involve getting drunk. He wondered what a life looks like that doesn't involve partying. As I talked about my own college years, he started to make a list for himself. He was writing a new script.

So, as a shout-out to my students who want a different script for their evening, I'm providing 50 ways to stay out of trouble. I once heard a speaker say that the definition of pleasure is: "having fun with no negative consequences." Living with flair has something to do with experiencing pleasure in ways that don't harm you or anybody else. Hence, my tried and true 50 ways to stay out of trouble.

1. Learn the moves to *Beat It* (or any dance)
2. Cook a gourmet meal with your friend. (Remember: good things happen with cutting boards)
3. Play improvisational games. (Watch "Whose Line is it Anyway" or just play charades)

4. Organize your desk. (This will feel really good)

5. Do a movie marathon of 1980's John Hughes movies. Or James Bond. Or Spielberg.

6. Visit every coffee shop downtown and evaluate each one. (I did this one Fall semester)

7. Plant something. (I'm doing this now)

8. Call your parents. (I should do this)

9. Call somebody from your childhood.

10. Read a bestselling novel. Then go talk to people about it. Book clubs are cool.

11. Go thrift store shopping.

12. Find neighborhood garage sales and buy unusual things.

13. Go to a local park and swing very high so you can jump out of the swing.

14. Go for a long walk. See if you can walk for an entire hour.

15. Search for new music on iTunes. Fall in love with a new band.

16. Get into a fascinating conversation with a stranger.

17. Go to church.

18. Plan some dreams for the next decade. Write out your personal mission statement.

19. Help somebody do something.

20. Watch people. Tell a story about their lives.

21. Learn a new sport.

22. Start a "flair" blog and tell me about it.

23. Get a great night's sleep.

24. Go to a fancy grocery store and buy the most expensive chocolate.

25. Go to a pet store and hold all the new kittens and puppies.

26. Find a creek and sit by it.

27. Build your own kite and then fly it somewhere. You can Google instructions.

28. Start a collection of some really obscure thing.

29. Learn to draw something.

30. Make a flip book comic.

31. Go in search of the world's most comfortable slippers.

32. Learn a different language. (I want to learn Chinese this summer)

33. Go to a toy store and play with the toys.

34. Hang out at a bookstore and read for an hour.

35. Volunteer to help at a shelter or a community center.

36. Join a club.

37. Drive down a country road. (Rt. 550 changed my life)

38. Learn Double Dutch jump rope.

39. Do something that gets your heart rate up for 40 minutes and see how good you feel.

40. Practice being alone for an entire evening.

41. Donate stuff you don't need.

42. Read a chapter in a textbook because you want to learn something, not because it's on the test.

43. Reread a book from your childhood. (I reread *To Kill A Mockingbird*)

44. Hiking. Camping.

45. Make a scrap book.
46. Invent a game to play.
47. Create an ad campaign to motivate people to do something.
48. Teach somebody how to do something.
49. Watch an entire season of a show on DVD in one day. *24? Lost? The Office?*
50. Make water your beverage selection for the whole weekend. Hydration can change your life.

So there. Here's to living with flair.

15. Well, We Can Pray, Can't We, Mom?

Yesterday, my husband and I separate on the trail so he can retrieve our car. I take my daughters and follow the sign that says "Park Office." Easy. He'll walk the two miles to get our car and meet his tired ladies at the air conditioned Park Office.

However, the Park Office isn't at the end of our path. It's far, far away. The end of the path is a strange parking lot. No Park Office. We're lost.

I'm starting to get nervous. There's no way my husband will figure out what random parking lot we've reached in this huge state park.

I'm sitting there, worried. I'm trying not to panic. We have no cell phone service and no way to find each other.

What to do? Well, I decide we could just start walking and hope for the best. This is a terrible idea when you're lost. Suddenly, my youngest throws her hands in the air and says, "Well, we can pray, can't we, Mom?"

So we do.

Jesus, help us. Send help because we are lost.

Right then—right then!—a dear, sweet park ranger drives right up to us. He looks like a skinny Santa Claus, and asks us if we need help.

Right then! Right then! We pile into his car, and he drives around until he finds my husband for us. Apparently, the Park Office was miles away. The parking lot was where folks got their cars to drive back to the Park Office. Who knew?

All I know is we were lost, and God answered. I see the way that our getting lost helped build my daughter's faith. The purpose of that fear was to build faith, to get us to pray, and to allow us to experience God's provision.

Well, we can pray, can't we?

16. Even This By Faith: An Answer to Loneliness and Disconnection

I'm happily driving in my minivan (because "all seats provide equal viewing of the universe")[2], and I remember how pleased Jesus is by our faith. I remember Hebrews 11:6 that "without faith, it's impossible to please God because anyone who comes to Him must believe He exists and rewards those who earnestly seek Him."

I think about all the areas of my life that require great faith in God's precious promises—regardless of my circumstances or my feelings; regardless of what I perceive; regardless of the material reality about me, there's a spiritual reality that I want to access. I want to pierce right through into the truth of it and not live anymore in doubt, fear, or discouragement.

So anyway, I'm thinking about my struggle to find deeper connection with folks and those times when I or my children experience loneliness. "God, is this true? Is this really the truth of my reality, or is this a big lie, these feelings and these circumstances?"

Immediately, I remember 1 Corinthians 12 and the powerful, beautiful, and real picture of *what is true*: I'm part of a body. I'm deeply knit in. I'm deeply belonging to everyone else, and they belong to me. The great lie is that we're alone, disconnected, alienated, friendless, awkward, and too hopeless for community. I note how Satan is always, always driving people into solitary places. That's how he works best, like a beast isolating his next victim. By faith, I claim the truth of who I am. I am not alone now or ever. I'm not disconnected now or ever. I'm not abandoned now or ever.

I'm dropping my daughter off at Vacation Bible School, and so many wonderful friends and family greet me with great love. Suddenly, I see it like I've never seen it before. The spiritual reality of my connection is a truth I know *by faith*. My feelings and experience may contradict this on bad days, but the truth remains: I am part of a great community.

Once I choose to believe it, the fiery dart of loneliness and isolation folds and crumbles against my strong and very real shield of faith.

17. Becoming a People Gatherer

Lately, my community has been reflecting on how we came together. We've been in the news twice because others folks take notice of this strange phenomenon.

In the last few years, we learned the art of *gathering*. To gather means *to cause* to come together.

We figure out a reason to come together, and each neighbor brings his or her own flair. In the midst of Ladies Lunches, the Play Date for Dads, Saturday Pancakes, Monday Night Fitness (which grew from 4 people to 50!), community service projects, walking to school, potluck dinners, birthday celebrations, living room singer-songwriter concerts, or whatever else might happen in a week, we consciously decide to do it together.

We resist the temptation towards isolation. And we gather, even if the invitation puts us into unusual situations with folks we aren't used to. Whatever we are doing, we ask ourselves, "Which family can I invite along?"

Living with flair means finding a reason to bring the neighbors together. You have to pick up your phone or go door-to-door. Whatever it takes, you fight isolation and gather people into community. And once everybody has a place to belong, we all flourish and discover this is how it was meant to be.

18. A Rope and a Smile

Every morning, without fail, these two little boys find me on the walk to school, and they ask me for a "cat story." They know I have three cats. Don't worry: I heard that you don't become a crazy cat woman until you have five cats. I'm well below this threshold. And don't worry: this won't become a blog about my cats.

So the boys wanted a cat story. Here goes:

My little black and white cat likes us to run around the house, dragging a yellow rope she found somewhere. Recently, she's learned to find the rope, grasp it in her mouth, and carry it to wherever we are sitting (this is a big deal for a little cat). If I'm busy, she finds anyone who'll help. She brings the rope, drops it by a foot, and then meows and meows for somebody, anybody, to drag this rope for her to chase.

She's relentless.

You'd think this would annoy me; it delights me instead.

I recognized something about this little kitty. Cats are supremely independent, supremely aloof. And yet, what does this cat do? Learning to carry a rope to me, dropping it like that, needing me so much, is cat flair. She temporarily suspends her superior, I-don't-need-you-cattitude. She knows she can't make the rope jiggle and race across the living room. This cat knows her limitations. This somehow doesn't bother her. That's the flair.

Why is it so hard to admit when I have a need that only another person can meet? I'm the type of girl who would find the rope, even drag it someplace in hopes of playing, and figure out a way to make it move myself. What's with this attitude of independence? When was the last time I admitted to somebody that I needed them, really needed them?

Living with flair means acknowledging my limitations and approaching others for help. We think it annoys people, but more often than not, it delights.

Running around my house with an old yellow rope and a cat on my heels makes me smile. It's a gift to me, not her.

19. Finding Some Flair in Pain

I have a bad knee. One of these days I'm going to have to get a new one. My right knee has a personality of its own. Ever since a surgery I had in college, my knee has attitude.

Today it's in a bad mood. So it hurts. It really hurts. I can't sleep when it gets that way, and I wake up grumpy. And then I think about the fact that it's hurting all day. Then I'm mad at my knee. And then I go crazy trying to think about what to do with the pain.

So here's what I did for my out-of-the-ordinary flair moment:

I thought about all my knee has done for me in my life: the carpet burns it has endured as I crawled as a baby, the bike crashes it has absorbed, the stitches from that summer I fell at the pool, the times it had me kneeling in prayer, the beautiful landscapes it has taken me to, the nervous taps from my fingers it received all those long school days, the skirts it peeked out from when I was finally allowed to wear a miniskirt (hello 80's), the garter it held up on my wedding day, the babies it bounced, the dirty hands wiped on it from children, the floors it helped scrub, the way it lets me dance (I'm getting better at "Beat It"), the walks it takes to school, the way I slap it in the coffee shop when seated with friends who make me laugh, the Frisbee it lets me catch, impossibly, by the jump and the mid-air turn last night (that's why I'm in pain). . .

Oh, the knee!

I'm not mad about my knee. Living with flair means being thankful for that darn bum knee. So, yes, it's really painful today, but do you want to hear about how my knee once pedaled me along the Potomac River at dusk? That day, I remembered loving my life because of the fish surfacing, because of the golden sun that lit every leaf with some magic radiance, and because of the hope I felt back then that my life could become extraordinary. I was 10 years old.

It's not a solution to pain. But thanking my knee prevented another, more despairing pain: bitterness. Living with flair means I choose the beautiful and not the bitter.

20. Flair in the Face

I've never met anyone who loves his or her own face.

This morning, as I put on lipstick (hey, you can take the woman out of the South, but you can't take the South out of a woman), I had a flashback flair moment.

When I was eighteen years old, a woman I didn't know stopped me as I was bending down to talk to a group of children at a summer camp where I worked.

She pulled me aside as the children ran on and said, "You have such a loving face." Loving? *Loving?* Not *beautiful?* It was a strange and wonderful compliment. She continued to tell me that she saw how my face was loving the children.

As I put the lipstick down this morning, I thought about how that single statement changed how I think about my face. I started to love my face and what it could do. I still love make-up. I still curl my hair and pluck my eyebrows. I still conceal the dark circles under my eyes. It's fun to primp sometimes.

But I don't obsess about whether or not I'm beautiful.

Living with flair means loving my face because of whom it can show love to. And it means accepting (and giving) strange and wonderful compliments that have the power to change a life. That stranger used 5 words to strip away my fixation on beauty. It's over a decade old, that compliment. But it's my flair for today.

21. **What a Pancake Can Do**

I just threw a pancake across the kitchen, and my husband caught it on his plate. The sticky syrup helped snag it. He laughed and said, "Now that's flair."

We have a Saturday morning pancake ritual. Many families in our neighborhood do. There's something about all of the neighbors, nestled in their cozy kitchens, eating pancakes in their respective houses that triggers the flair sensor.

The pancake ritual connects me to my family and my neighbors. I'm thankful that I can expand my sense of family to include an entire neighborhood. Rituals are like that: they connect people. We have a great neighborhood, but we didn't always feel so connected.

This year, we put some rituals in place. We have a walking to school ritual, an evening bike riding and jump rope ritual, and a monthly potluck ritual. These patterns bind us together and create a wonderful community.

My sociologist friend (the same one who learned the "Beat It" moves in my kitchen with me) talks about the importance of ritual in relationships and in larger communities. Rituals are the mark of connectedness; they are sacred spaces that unite people. So when I'm drinking coffee with my husband at the same time every morning (7:00 AM—the kids are running around getting backpacks packed and teeth brushed), I feel close to him, secure, and connected. Our family rituals like dinner time questions, reading before bedtime, church on Sunday morning, or any host of regular, predictable events make us feel settled. In fact, if we try to change a family ritual, the kids will say, "But Mom, it's tradition."

So my flair for today is flipping pancakes with my family. I used to think that flair needed to be unique and unpredictable each day. But this morning, I realized the flair in the regular routine. The fact that it's regular (same time, same ritual) makes it flair.

22. **What If I Were Loyal?**

I had a sublime experience last night that carried into my morning so powerfully as to eclipse any other possible flair for the day.

I entertained a woman who owned a service dog. This black lab sat all night at our feet, waiting to take action in case my new friend had a seizure. The dog can predict up to two minutes in advance if the woman will have a seizure, and then he alerts her by tapping his nose on her thigh. Then the dog leads her to a safe location, helps her to the ground, secures a perimeter, and then stretches out on the ground beneath her head until the seizure ends. It gets better. The dog can also go get help by opening doors, retrieving cell phones, and even finding a dominant presence (usually an alpha male) in a room who can call 911.

I looked at that dog lying peacefully at our feet. No way.

Guess how he knows? Smell alone. The dog senses slight variations in the way my friend smells. Before a seizure, a chemical emits from glands on her neck that the dog perceives.

What? I looked again at the dog. I had to know more.

Apparently, the dog is just like other dogs: he plays, he runs, he eats, he poops. But at all times, he's tuned in to my friend. He senses any variation and takes immediate action.

I felt overcome by awe. I also felt something that surprised me.

As the woman talked about the dog sleeping close beside her, waiting with eagerness for her to emerge from a shower, or just noticing the slightest change in her smell, I considered how thankful I've been for people who "tune in" to variations in my moods, my health, or my well-being. I remember difficult times in my life when friends sensed a variation in me, led me to a safe place, tried to make me comfortable, and called for help if I needed it. Am I that loyal to my family, my neighbors, my coworkers and students that I can sense a variation, offer help, secure a perimeter, and provide comfort? What does that look like for me to "tune in" to people in my life?

When I'm not myself, I've had a friend say, "You don't seem right. Can I help?" Am I close enough—tuned in enough—to people in my life that I can observe these things? I want to be.

Living with flair means tuning in to others, providing help and comfort, and getting help for them if I need to. Living with flair means I notice subtle changes in others that might indicate something deeper. I want to be the one who secures a safe spot. Maybe one of my friends needs to rest on me until an episode passes. It's flair to be that loyal. It's not just for the dogs.

23. The Flair Disaster

Today in church, during the most reflective part, a little girl in a soft pink Easter dress spilled her grape communion juice. It trickled down her dress and pooled on the floor beneath her sandals. I was sitting two rows behind her.

Quickly, her grandpa and grandma (who happened to be the pastor and his wife!) found a cloth and began to wipe her dress and the floor. Her father joined in, trying to minimize the damage. And then, her mother—hawk-like and decisive—turned from her seat at the end of the aisle and made her way to where her daughter sat.

I felt myself bristle. Would this mother scold? Would she grab her daughter and drag her out of the church, shaming her for distracting the other worshipers? Was the Easter dress expensive, and would the little girl be punished for staining it?

The mother leaned down to her daughter. I couldn't see the daughter's face, but she had her head down, shaking with tears.

The mother took the child's face in her hands, firmly, tilting the chin up.

Then, looking clearly into that little girl's eyes, she kissed her cheek and smiled.

It's Easter.

Something about the way that mother held the girl's face, something about tilting a chin up, something about that soft kiss overwhelmed me. It was a picture of God's grace: choosing to love and not shame, lifting a face, covering a stain with a kiss. It was Easter flair.

Maybe I was so struck because I studied the emotion of shame in graduate school. When we feel tormenting inferiority because of a shortcoming, the body's response is to look down. We hide. We cannot endure the gaze of an audience.

But this mother tilted the child's face up. By refusing to allow the shame response, this mother locked eyes with her daughter and gazed with love and unconditional acceptance.

Later, I saw that little girl laughing and running around at an Easter egg hunt. The bright stain on her dress made no difference to her. But it could have.

Living with flair means I take a face in my hands (even if it's my own), tilt up the chin, and choose to love regardless of the deep stain. Who isn't walking around with grape juice on their clothes? Who isn't that child? Who doesn't need a love like that?

24. Commemorating with Milk

We couldn't make the Memorial Day blueberry pancakes this morning because we ran out of milk. I was the one dressed already, so I volunteered to drive to the store.

It was a little after 8:00 AM.

It was just a trip for milk.

I left my children in their pajamas and my husband hovering over his ingredients. I'd have to be quick.

I'm turning the corner out of our neighborhood, and all of a sudden, like something bounding out of a dark woods into my car, I'm aware that I'm really, really happy. The realization struck with such force that it astonished me. For someone who battled the black haze of depression for nearly a decade, I am still amazed and celebrate the sheer joy that accompanies feeling good.

I was so thankful this morning to be alive. I was so thankful for what the holiday weekend represented—commemorating soldiers who died to secure freedom. We'd commemorate them in ways they would want us to: we'd eat pies, swim in the public pool, gather for a potluck dinner. What a gift this life is—this simple life that bursts with beauty in all these hidden places if I just look . . .

Living with flair means I commemorate, with ceremony and observation, how thankful I am for battles won, large or small. And I remember the fallen by being fully alive—fetching milk early Monday for blueberry pancakes eaten in peace, with a family, around a simple kitchen table.

25. The Burn

I shouldn't like to watch things burn so much. Think about it: I'm taking pleasure in the disintegration of something, the dissolution of some object into nothing but gray ash that floats up into the atmosphere or settles hopelessly beneath my feet. Last night I sat by a beautiful campfire in my neighbor's back yard. The children, otherwise distracted, came around the fire just to watch things burn.

I could have sat there for hours. Transfixed, I had to wonder: why do I love to watch things burn? Why do most people?

Living with flair means asking the sort of question to get beneath my experience. So I stared at the fire. My children stared, hypnotized. I even recalled my entire history with campfires and what things I used to throw in. Magazines burned with prettier colors. Marshmallows exploded and elongated into these snake-like black creatures.

My children, too, enjoyed watching marshmallows burn more than eating them.

Why?

I finally thought of this: We really don't expect things to fall apart. We're used to permanence. I see things around me as intact, stable, and predictable. A stick is a stick. Newspaper is newspaper. Marshmallows are marshmallows.

But put them in fire, and all of a sudden, the true constitution appears. These stable objects transform into mere ash, residue, that looks all alike no matter what unique appearance it had to begin with. It's just a chemical reaction, completely understandable, and yet it produces such wonder, such peace even, as I watch the burn.

Outside of the boundaries of the campfire, though, that fire has such destructive power that it could take down my whole city.

It terrifies me, that power. And yet, sitting around a campfire, I get to observe that power from a position of safety. 18th century philosophers would say this is a sublime experience; it's a simultaneous fear and attraction. And when I encounter a power stronger than myself, even in a little backyard campfire, I'm humbled and put in my place. I see into the reality of my world—the black ash underneath it all.

Fire makes me think of the fragility of things (my own fragile self). Living with flair means appreciating a campfire for more than just the s'mores it makes. It means understanding the fear and power that accompanies all truly beautiful things.

26. Infusion

A popular blog I read this morning suggested that one pathway to happiness is to "imitate" a spiritual master—someone like Jesus. I cringed. The not-flair bells rang. I frowned and felt the same way I do when somebody tells me to just "try harder" and I'll find holiness. It's just not true. Telling a person to imitate a spiritual master to find real life and joy is like telling a cardboard box to act more like a computer in order to come alive.

Imitation doesn't change the inherent problem I have. I need an infusion of grace, not an imitation of one.

Imitating a master is also like telling two people to stare at each other and imitate a relationship. I don't want to imitate love. I want to be in love. Imitation isn't the trick.

A relationship with God is a romance. It's an infusion of power, of love, of joy, of deeply knowing. It's not imitating a master or doing what Jesus would do. That kind of life doesn't work. It never has.

That's why the gospel is good news. I want to know Jesus and have him give me the power to live the life I'm supposed to.

Christianity isn't a religion of imitation—of acting more like Jesus. It's exchanging our weaknesses for his strength, for inviting his presence into our lives, and for depending on his love and peace on a daily basis.

It's not imitation. It's infusion.

I'm off to the pool. My children have been in their bathing suits since 8:30 AM. The towels and sunscreen are all in a row. The snacks are ready. The goggles are tightened. We could sit on the couch and imitate swimming, or we could dive into that delicious water. I think I know what we'll choose. Living with flair means I'm experiencing a life of joy, not imitating one.

27. Resilience

Driving home from preschool today, two bubbles floated across the street like they had somewhere to get to. I couldn't see any sign of someone blowing bubbles, or even any other bubbles, anywhere. They must be mighty resilient, I thought. One was bigger than the other, and it looked like a mama bubble and a baby bubble. I imagined the wind, the buildings, the people, or even the animals they might have encountered before crossing my path. And yet they remained intact, beautifully sparkling in the sun while floating just above my car. Resilient.

I said the word aloud, and my daughter repeated it.

"It's a great word," I told her. I had actually looked the word up that very morning. My friend and I were talking about parenting, and she mentioned wanting to raise resilient children. She advised me not to constantly rescue my children, to not be afraid to let them suffer, and to realize that adversity creates strong children.

All week, I've been trying to rescue my older daughter from the bossy, mean girls who roll their eyes on the playground and insult her. I'm the mom who calls the teacher and wants to be there, mediating, controlling the situation, and ensuring total peace and happiness for my child.

Last night, I gave up the fight. I'm lying on the bed with my daughter. I'm listening to her talk and talk and talk about the mean girls, about the bullies, about the gossip and jealousy. For once, I don't try to solve it; I don't go email the teacher again. I've been doing that all year. For the rest of my daughter's life, there will be mean girls. I can't save her, no matter how hard I try.

"Look," I said. "You are just great. I love everything about you. You will figure out a way to handle those girls. I believe in you. God is with you. You can figure this out."

"I know," she said, smiling with that one loose tooth hanging by a thread. "I totally will."

The dictionary tells me that a resilient person possesses the ability to recover readily from adversity. In science, resilience refers to the energy a thing can store up as it deforms or is put under stress that it releases as it reforms. In organizations, resiliency is the ability to positively adapt to the consequences of a catastrophic failure.

I'm praying that she's storing up energy from this, that she'll learn that ready recovery skill, and that whatever catastrophic failures come, she can positively adapt. Tonight, I'm telling her I'm so proud of the resiliency she's already shown in these enormous eight years.

Resilient girls can handle anything. Put that on her résumé! Put that in the cover letter! *I survived recess today. What did you do?*

This way of living with flair is the only way I'll survive parenting. Living with flair means I value raising resilient children. It means I embrace adversity myself for what it's storing up in me.

28. My Huge Gardening Mistake

Last night I bragged all about my blueberries, my strawberries, and even my blackberries. My dear friends, older, wiser, and experts in gardening asked if this was their first year in the ground. When I said, "yes," they cried:

"You need to remove that fruit! Pinch off the blossoms, too. Do not let those plants produce! Not this summer, and not next summer either."

All week, we'd been so happy about those blueberries and those ripening strawberries. I had imagined my blueberry pies, my strawberry smoothies, my blackberry jam. There was no way I was going to destroy that young fruit and those beautiful blossoms. Who were these people to suggest I would have to be patient for two more summers? (I realize that most of my friends know this about berry plants. I somehow missed the information.)

"You have to. You just have to do it. Make your husband do it," my understanding friend said. "But it has to happen."

This counter-intuitive and destructive move would make my plants thrive. If I take away the fruit, the plant directs the energy and nutrients to the most important part of the plant: the root system. A new berry plant needs a few years to make an indestructible foundation of roots. Then, we can enjoy the fruit. It would take three summers.

"I know it's hard. It killed me to do it to my own fruit plants," another said.

So this morning, with my daughters (and me!) safely away from the garden, my husband prepared our plants for abundance by deliberately diminishing them. All night I'd been thinking of what my friend said as I sat there with my mouth hanging open, refusing to believe the truth about my plants. I had to figure out what spiritual process this represents, what truth about the universe this destructive act mirrors. The flair project depended upon my ability to find the right in the wrongness.

She said, with such love and wisdom: "You've lived here three years, right? Weren't the first two hard? And now, in your third year, everything's going so well." I thought about the principle of three years. Maybe it was true. Maybe God knows that I need seasons of total emptiness, no fruit, not even blossoms, in order to get my roots deep and strong. I thought about marriage, of raising those babies to toddlers, of moving to new places and starting new jobs. I thought about years waiting for manuscripts to be published, friendships to form, community to thrive. It never all came together that first year, and maybe not even the second. But the third year? Fruit did come.

Maybe God feels like I do—the sadness, the loss—pruning away the obvious signs of productivity. In those years when nothing seems to happen, where nothing seems to bloom in my life, I'm putting down these awesome roots.

Just wait. It might not be this year, or even next year. In her book *Anonymous,* Alicia Britt Chole describes the spiritual process of our hidden years. She writes, "Abundance may make us feel more productive, but perhaps emptiness has greater power to strengthen our souls."[3]

Living with flair means I'm strengthening my soul when there's no fruit in sight.

29. One Good Prayer

This morning, I had a few minutes before the walk to school, so I took out my prayer journal. What did I need? What did the neighbors need? Many things came to mind, but one thought kept recurring. I knew I might pray for prosperity, for health, for safety, for success, or for any host of material things. God says we can ask for anything. But I knew to pray this:

"Jesus, help us see you today."

Jonathan Swift wrote that "vision is the art of seeing what is invisible to others."[4] When I look at this day, right now, I know that God is at work. And he sees what I don't see. Through suffering, through disappointment, through fear, through loneliness, God sees what I don't see. I want vision to see, with God's help, what is otherwise invisible. That's flair.

I want to see what God sees. I want to pierce through that layer of my circumstances to perceive that invisible script that God writes. These marks of God's intentions, of God's goodness, of God's love, are here. I pray that God sharpens my vision so I can see them.

My sleuthing for daily flair is really a prayer to see the invisible thing—that underlying beauty and goodness in any situation, no matter how bleak. It's a prayer to identify, in every circumstance, the marks of a spiritual process. When I see that process, I'm suddenly released from fear. I can find hope and love here, even in pain or confusion.

Living with flair means seeing the invisible thing. It means offering up a prayer to find God in whatever situation I'm in because, surely, He is here.

30. Bad Day Slogan

As far as bad days go for a five year old, this one ranks high. While at her yearly check-up, she discovered she might need glasses, was told her spine might be slightly crooked, and, to make matters worse, endured two shots in both thighs. My job was to "restrain" her arms and legs as the nurses jabbed the needles in.

Not flair. No, this was not flair at all today.

We left the doctor's office right at lunch time. Dairy Queen was on the way home, so we pulled in. The whole time, I'm trying to comfort her, but nothing's working.

As we order food inside, I begin telling our server all about my daughter's horrible day. Hopefully, some ice cream will help matters. A few minutes later, this same server came to our table. Seeing my daughter still tear-stained and sniffling, I said, "We are just having a really bad day."

"Well," she said as she handed us our food, "there's a lot of day still left."

My daughter looked at her and smiled. The thought of "a lot of day still left," worked. The radical concept that the day wasn't doomed just because of a bad morning transformed this little girl's world. There was still time—seconds, minutes, hours even—to redeem the day. There was still time for flair.

I wanted to kiss the server. I told her that her comment would change the course of our whole day. Once again, language well-timed and well-spoken can create a new reality. The comment created anticipation. Something good would come. And by the time we'd finished lunch, ice-cream, and some laughs in our booth, it already had.

Living with flair means remembering "there's a lot of day still left." Even if we're down to seconds, there's still time for flair.

31. The Blessing We Need

A girl with a stuffed unicorn stood by the restrooms at church this morning. I've been seeing unicorns everywhere, and each time, I have a little flair moment. Here's why.

I learned recently that a gathering of unicorns is called a *blessing*. I just love that. Animal groups have some strange names. Alligators are a congregation; barracudas are batteries (did you know that?); sea birds are called wrecks; bullfinches are a bellowing; zebras are a crossing; rhinos are a crash, and owls are a parliament.

But a group of unicorns is a blessing.

The gathering of beautiful creatures, more divine than earthly, isn't just the stuff of lore and legend. As I left the bathroom, I walked into the worship gathering of our church. It suddenly occurred to me that I was in the presence of the divine—the holy—in the people.

It suddenly stuck me how much I loved the people. I knew all those people, and all those people knew me. I could probably raise my hand and ask anybody for anything and the answer would be, "no problem."

One man had broken his ankle and, on crutches, rose to the applause of the rest of us as we cheered in hope of his full recovery.

And those people—those creatures more divine than earthly—were my blessing. They were my group and my joy both.

People go crazy in isolation. People die in isolation; they can lose their vitality and their strength. But in groups, they thrive, they enhance one another, and they accomplish more together than they could alone. They bring forth the glory of God.

In the Scriptures, Satan drives people to solitary places. In fact, his best work is accomplished when we are alone. For example, Jesus encounters a demon-possessed man who "drives the man into solitary places" (Luke 8: 29). And we learn in the book of Peter that the enemy of our souls "prowls around like a roaring lion waiting to devour" (1 Peter 5:8). He must search for the loner. When I watch nature shows, I'm always struck by the skill of the lion. He preys on the lone gazelle, the one that gets away from his group. The isolated, the ones separate from their group, are the ones in the most danger.

If only we could see that left-out person as part of ourselves. If only we could boldly move forward, extend a hand, and invite a stranger into our blessing. Our story has many more characters to include.

If only we could see the divine calling to participate in each others' lives.

We are interdependent at our best, much like tiny streams that, when we link up, become mighty rivers that nourish entire landscapes.

I need to join my blessing. Whatever it takes, I need to. Living with flair means seeing my community as more divine than earthly and part of my own self. Within my blessing, I gather in the stray gazelles when I'm strong. And when I'm weak, I look to the others to circle around me and bring me to safety.

32. The Best Definition of Courage

My daughter and I were talking about taking her training wheels off and learning to ride a bike. She became very quiet and said, "You know, Mom, little hills mean little boo-boos. And big hills mean big boo-boos."

I said, "So I guess you want to avoid the big hills on your bike."

She paused and said, "Oh, no. It just means we need a bigger first aid kit."

There you have it: Courage means I ride full speed ahead, anticipate the wounds, and prepare with a great first aid kit. For my daughter it means Hello Kitty band aids. For the rest of us, it might mean we fill our kits with authentic friendships, strong ties to a community, a vibrant relationship to God, and the kind of space to heal. It's not the height of the hill that matters. It's not the danger, the risk, or the potential for failure. Wounds are likely. So I build the best first aid kit I can. That's some 5 year old flair.

33. Bring on the Whimsy

This morning, I saw my neighbor's dog, Murphy, walking in a bright yellow doggie raincoat. He stood up on his back paws and greeted me, looking more human than canine. Then, I saw a little girl carrying an umbrella shaped like a dragon over her head . Huge pointing scales, triangular and menacing, slithered down her back. I felt like I had temporarily entered some whimsical world where dogs act civilized in bright yellow rain gear and little girls enjoy the protection of dragons atop their heads. I looked up just in case an owl should swoop down to deliver my mail.

Why do whimsical things delight us so much? Why do we recite *The Jabberwocky* or go see *Alice in Wonderland* and *Avatar*? Why are we so entranced by the world of Hogwarts or Narnia or Neverland?

The little dog turned human or the girl with her dragon ripped open the rational world for me this morning. All at once, I thought of a fantasy world, an alternate reality existing parallel to my own. In this world, the rules are all different. It's the Mad Hatter's tea party on this side of things, and I barely know how to get my footing. It's dangerous, weird, and most of all, wonderful.

Whimsy refers to something playfully odd, something unpredictable, childish, and given more to imagination than reason or experience. Whimsy indicates a suspension of the rational and predictable. It opens a doorway into another realm, another way of thinking.

In this way, whimsy helps my spiritual growth. It's a whisper of the supernatural.

Whimsy and fantasy—the odd, the seemingly impossible—give spiritual truth a plausibility structure. I want to encourage the type of living where we can believe in what we cannot fully fathom. Whimsy, which makes me stop and reconsider, tears apart the structure of my otherwise orderly and rational day. And in that sliver of space—that wrinkle in time—a life of faith blooms.

So bring on the dogs in raincoats, the dragon umbrellas, the fantastical, and the absurd. We are made for more than we can imagine, and to stop and consider it—the flair of it—ushers in the spiritual.

Whimsy lets in the crack of light that pushes me onward to truth. Living with flair means I consider the crack of light. It opens my eyes to another reality—the kind of reality where God tries to get my attention through the out-of-the ordinary thing. Living with flair means to be attentive enough to see and respond.

34. A Tool to Measure Success

Somebody asked me recently what my professional goals are.

I used to be incredibly ambitious. Now, not so much. Part of the reason is that, as I age, I realize the things I was ambitious for—money, prestige, fame—don't retain the same shimmer after too long. The problem with ambition is that it keeps my focus on some future manifestation.

I will know I am successful when. . .

I ask myself, and my students, to find a career that they love so much they'd do it for free. Today I will add: love it so much you'd do it for free and *for absolutely no recognition*. You love it so much you could do it anonymously. You'll measure success, in this case, by a completely different standard.

Imagine!

It's hard to talk about these things when we need to earn a good living. We need to pay the bills, provide for our children, and stock the refrigerator. We often don't have the luxury of thinking about the larger questions about our work when we have to pay the electric bill today. But sometimes it's good to ask ourselves what motivates us to try so hard all the time. Beyond the paycheck, what are we really doing?

With money and prestige out of the picture, what would motivate someone to succeed in a particular line of work? And how in the world would they define success? As I think about living with flair, and in particular, working with flair, I wonder what to be ambitious for. Is it to serve others well, to advance knowledge in my particular field, to love every coworker, to build community in that workplace, to think about a mission to create beauty, order, or healing somewhere? Is it to fight for injustice or to awaken spirituality? Is it to provide for my family? It is to work with excellence, to the best of my ability? Or is it because I must do it because of a calling—because I'm made to do it—regardless of how my gifts are received or if they do anything?

These things are good and right.

Another friend asked me what the goal of my blogging adventures are. A book? For the first time in a long time, I was able to say that the goal was just to write, every day, and record special moments that made the day great. The project is its own reward. I'm ambitious for living intentionally enough to find joy in the common thing.

When I measure success by a different tool, I'm suddenly free to do what I'm supposed to do—what I'm made to do—and not imprisoned by any other standard.

Living with flair means being ambitious for the right things—for the sorts of things that can't be measured by dollar signs or followers.

35. When It Looks Like Chaos and Abandonment

My sassiest daughter was playing school with her big sister this morning before church. Apparently, they'd set up a whole imaginary classroom with imaginary students. All of sudden, the little one starts stomping around with her hands on her hips.

"I can't do imaginary anymore!" she yelled.

I laughed out loud. Watching her with her hands on her hips, saying in exasperation, "I can't do imaginary anymore," gave me the same feeling as when I hear her singing that Sugarland song about not settling. There I am, driving down the road, minding my own thoughts, and this little girl will belt out every line about living a full life.

It's the kind of sass I like in a girl. She doesn't want so-so or imaginary, and neither do I.

We want to fully inhabit the lives God gives us. We are learning that ordinary is extraordinary when you figure out what you can learn from it.

We aren't settling if we can help it.

We aren't letting one moment go by without finding out what it means.

We are getting better at it. This morning, in the cool breeze of 9:00 AM, something caught my eye as we pulled out of the driveway.

Blue and wispy like the tip of some fairy's wing, leaves danced across the base of the oak tree by my house. I stared harder, confused about the blue leaves tumbling around on the lawn. My husband stopped the van, and I got out. There, like tiny crumbled scraps of blue construction paper, balls of feathers unfolded to show little beaks. Obviously abandoned, obviously fallen from a high nest, these bluebirds strained their heads and wings hopelessly. They seemed cold, sure to die, and starving. I looked up through the branches of the oak tree. High up, higher than the rooftop, the tangle of sticks and leaves sat.

The whole family gathered solemnly around the oak tree. Believing we were seeing dying birds, the girls shouted: "We need to call the pet store! We need to call animal rescue! Help!" We all ran inside, frantic as we tried to find the phone book. My husband, calm and sure, went to the internet to find out what to do.

And we prayed.

A moment later, my husband spread the good news: These weren't dying birds. They were fledgling birds. There's a big difference.

Fledgling is a great word. It describes a young bird (or person) who is new to the scene. This person has just left the nest and is almost ready to fly. They still need help, but as they flop around, looking hopeless, they are actually building strength to fly. To the inexperienced observer, a fledgling looks like a dying bird. The feathers look all rumpled and broken, and the body is limp. What I saw, when I looked at those bluebirds, was chaos and disaster and, worse, abandonment.

But it was actually a highly controlled, intentional situation.

Later, I sat in church, so thankful for the truth about my fledgling times. What I see as chaos, disaster, and abandonment (by God or others) is actually a highly controlled, intentional situation. God knows I need some time to strengthen my character and my resolve. He knows I need to flop around a bit first.

And I was thankful that my daughter who can't do imaginary didn't have to this morning. She could sit and look right out at the real world in her front yard. And this girl who won't settle for so-so learned that rescuing birds isn't about removing them from their situation or creating better circumstances. Sometimes it means keeping them right there in it because it's where they are supposed to be.

Living with flair means that I might reinterpret chaos, confusion, or even disaster as part of a highly controlled, intentional situation. God, like the mother bird, knows exactly what's going on. Later today, I saw that mother bird seeking out each fledgling with a worm in her beak. She found all six of them, no matter where they had tumbled, and nourished them fully. They'll fly by evening.

36. Seeing a Newborn Foal

Last night, I heard a rumor that newborn foals were in the campus barn. Campus barn? Where was that?

"Honey! Baby horses at some barn! Let's go." He got in the minivan without even thinking this might be a strange activity so close to bedtime. But if we are going to live with flair, we want to embrace some adventure.

We drove to campus and found the right road. "This doesn't look right," I kept saying (I'd never been before, but it just didn't feel like it could be a magical place with newborn horses. It was too urban, too busy). My husband encouraged me to "just keep going" and that we'd find something eventually. I took a sharp right and then a left down an unmarked dirt road.

"Just keep going," he said.

I did. In silence, we drove. We should have turned around and gone straight home. It was bedtime, and besides, the sky was threatening some thunderstorm. We'd never find the place anyway.

Then, like we'd entered Narnia through the wardrobe, an enormous expanse of rich green meadow opened before us. To the left, a single white barn. The surrounding campus evaporated; there were no other buildings in sight.

We had entered a hidden pocket of paradise right in the middle of a town.

The setting sun made the meadow golden and deeply green with light and long shadows. The brewing storm made the air heavy and electric. The barn was quiet. Was this the right barn? We left the minivan, not even bothering to close the doors.

In the cool of the barn, we walked by each stall, one by one. All empty, except for two stalls near the end. We peered in, straining our necks. We held the girls up so they could see. There were real live horses in there.

Two chocolate brown mares and caramel one-month-old foal snuggled into one another in separate stalls.

I'm a city girl. I grew up outside of DC, and I've never seen a real foal before (except on TV or in picture books). Amazed at the tiny legs, so unsteady, I held my breath. He was. . . tiny. I couldn't believe that just a moment before, I was driving through suburbia, and now this. What could be more beautiful on this evening?

A few minutes later, we left the barn from the opposite entrance. As I turned the corner, I froze. Six enormous mares, their coats shining with light, hovered over six separate foals—right in front of me. Each foal mirrored the mother's movements exactly as she roamed the meadow. That fragile creature was not only guarded by the mother, but by all the mothers.

Here, in this place, all is well as a mare protects a newborn foal.

We discovered a young woman who rents a room by the barn to care for these horses night and day. Her face shines and her heart seems at peace. Nations battle, people suffer, but here, in this barn, a girl cares for horses and instructs visitors when they can come back to see a new foal due in just a week. The pregnant mare, Skipped Emotion, stood proud and tall in her stall.

We'll be back in a week to see the newcomer. We'll be back to congratulate the mother, whose presence brings forth everything but skipped emotion. In fact, for once, we are fully in our emotions—awe, wonder, joy. We are coming back for more.

Living with flair means marveling at foals. It means leaving your home, even though it's bedtime, to find a secret barn cloaked by campus all around. It means you "just keep going" until you find the right road. You'll find it if you just travel in far enough.

37. The Best Verb to Keep in Your Notebook

Great living is a lot like great cooking. You want to take the ingredients of the day and create 5 star masterpieces. You want to arrange what's given to you (like on *Iron Chef*), and make something so fantastic that you close your eyes and sigh (like the judges) when you think about it.

I'm not a great cook. Fortunately, I have a chef friend.

Today she explained what "braising" meant. Braising something means you apply low heat, lots of time, and moisture in order to soften something hard and unsavory into something delicious. She was braising cabbage, I think.

I stood there and wrote in my little notebook the definition of braise (you have to keep a notebook if you are searching for flair). I like this new verb. I'm going to tell students they need to braise their ideas, break them apart with some intellectual heat, some time, and some emotional juice in order to present that concept the best way.

I use cooking verbs like percolate, stew, and sauté, but I haven't used braise ever in my whole life. It's a great verb for cooking, writing, and now, living.

Everything that happens to me in any given day passes through some intellectual heat, some time, and some emotional juice in order to arrive at flair. I braise the day to get to the good stuff. It keeps the hard parts in me soft.

It's the art of reflection, and it teaches me how to have insight. It's not as if we wake up and find flair arriving on our pillows in a package we recognize. It takes some work: some heat, time, and moisture. It takes energy and emotion to actively find the larger importance.

Insight means to look within the thing, to go deeper. It's mining for a new understanding about my day using the common, daily ingredients I'm given. People with insight train themselves to see, not just with the senses, but with the mind. In other words, as I live, I think about what something symbolizes or represents. I put a flair lens over my eyes and pray I see it when it comes.

Braising my experiences creates steady hope and steady joy for me. It feels so good to have this lens, especially after knowing the dark days of depression and hopelessness for nearly a decade of my life. I want to braise the day and make it all soft and delicious. It makes me live well and intentionally. Living with flair means writing down the word "braise" in a little notebook and thinking about living (not just cooking).

38. What to Offer a Mean Person

Something spiritual happened in the drive-thru as I was paying the cashier today. Everybody inside the place was scowling and sulking around. They seemed so angry and so inconvenienced by my presence at the little sliding window. These people need some flair, I thought.

I decided to ask God for help. Those people needed a blessing.

To bless is a way of inviting the power and presence of God in. It's a means of imagining the best for someone and infusing some situation with hope and joy.

"God, could you bless these people?" I muttered. But then I rolled my eyes at myself. Was that the best I could do? That blessing had no pizzazz. If I'm going to pray for good things for people, I want to do it with flair.

I tried again: "God, could you give these workers unimaginable strength and joy today? Could you somehow remind them how wonderful and beautiful they are? Would you bring good things into their lives? Would you fill them with the kind of hope and security that will sustain them forever?"

Then, as I was leaving the drive-thru, a frowning older man nearly drove into my car. It looked like he hadn't laughed in decades. I took a deep breath, still wondering how I could be more creative in blessing people. I wanted to get specific.

"God, I hope this old man can laugh so hard that tears come out of his eyes today. I want him to slap his thigh and hang onto his friends for balance because he's laughing so hard."

I pulled out of the parking lot, and a frantic and stressed-out UPS man darted in front of me. I prayed he would enjoy a profoundly delicious lunch. It was all I could think of at the time! Then I drove past some stern looking utility workers who seemed annoyed that I was driving past their work zone. I prayed that they would have wonderful evenings with their families—the kind where everyone feels cozy and loved.

Offering blessings today saved me from a bad mood and road rage. It reminded me that, in some mysterious way, I can invite the good and the beautiful into a stranger's life. God commands that we bless and not curse, so I want to do it with flair. What if I did this more often? What if everybody did? Living with flair means I'm not just enjoying this power and presence, but I'm also giving it. Next time I get in my car, I'm going to eagerly anticipate meeting grumpy people who need a stranger to bless them. And I hope that, when I'm a grouch, somebody is blessing me.

39. When Temptation Comes, Tell Yourself This Story

Today I celebrated not giving in to an obvious temptation. Perhaps this victory will carry over into larger, more insidious ones.

I've been thinking about temptation all day. Daniel Defoe, one of the first known novelists, wrote that "we are instruments of our own destruction."[5] We hurry towards things that are not good for us. We run away from things that are. Why can this be?

This concept rings true primarily because we are experts in self-deception. We are very good story-tellers.

I wonder what story I'm believing that makes the perceived benefit of that thought or action outweigh the harm it causes. It's amazing to me, for example, that a bowl of chocolate ice cream can overpower me. I can be ruled by appetite. Here I am, a full-grown woman, strong and sure, and yet, I'm brought down by sugar and chocolate. No matter what resolution I make, it wins. Sugar wins. Sugar! Isn't that just. . . ridiculous?

And it's not just food. It's overindulgence in many things.

But not today. I had this moment—this flair moment—when I figured out why the temptation wins in my life. Temptation wins when I change the story of what harm that thing I want brings. I tell myself only half the story (the good part). And it makes sense. I teach rhetoric. I was a debater. I know how to persuade, and I'm really good at convincing myself.

Today I told the whole story. I told the story of what happens when I do what I shouldn't do. I stopped and worked out the extended narrative—the director's cut. I let myself imagine myself doing that thing (in this case, eating the entire carton of ice-cream). But then what? If I tell the whole story of what happens next—after giving in—I remember the false promise. I unmask it, reveal the lie, and tell the truth about it. There's no life in the chocolate ice cream. It's just empty calories that provide exactly 3 minutes of chocolate pleasure followed by 3 days of getting back on track with my diet. It's not worth it. It's not that good.

Telling the whole story of what happens when I give in to temptation helps diminish its power. It's one way out. Living with flair means I see the full story regarding my choices. It means I become aware of my capacity for self-deception and tell the truth instead. That thing I want to do is just not that good.

40. 3 Questions that Set Me Straight

This time last year, I was mad about everything. I was jealous of other mothers and their resplendent brunches, their new jewelry, and their country club life. Why couldn't I just have more money?

I was jealous that Rob Reiner was filming the movie *Flipped* in my old backyard (the one I left to move here). I should have been there, serving coffee to Hollywood celebrities and awaiting my invitation to star in the movie.

I was jealous of other women (friends from college) who had political and academic power. That was supposed to be me there on Capitol Hill or at that podium. It was weird how jealous I was. It was the kind of jealous that ate my insides and made me stomp my feet in the kitchen as I told my husband how wrong everything was. I was supposed to be a different person by now. Why was I here, in this town, with this life?

The rhetoric of my life was "if only."

So exactly one year ago today, I sat in church, jealous and ridiculous. I had just finished writing something about how if you ask yourself a good question, the right question, you could get yourself out of any bad mood. I knew I need to ask spiritual questions. That seemed right (after all, I was in church). So I wrote:

1. Is knowing God better than anything? (as J.I. Packer asks: "For what higher, more exalted, and more compelling goal can there be than to know God?"[6])

2. Will I live the life God asks me to? (Here, in this town, with no retail, no glitz?)

3. Will I pursue wealth or godliness? (Seriously? I need a whole new summer wardrobe with sparkly flip flops.)

These questions mattered so much to me because in a split second, like lightning forking through the roof and straight into my heart, they reoriented me. They set me straight. They reminded me that my happiness comes from surrender to the spiritual truth that governs my life.

The first recorded question that Jesus asks in the Gospel of John is, "What do you want?" I love this question. I love the disciples' answer even more. They essentially ask him where he is staying. They want to be where Jesus is. They would leave everything to be in his presence. So Jesus says (strangely), "Come and see."

When God says, "What do you want," the answer from my heart is: "To be in your presence."

God, always the pursuer, always setting up a way to delight us, just says, "Come and see."

That morning, a year ago today, I imagined God asking my jealous heart: "What do you want?" And I wrote in my journal: *To be in your presence. But is it really enough? It is really worth it to pursue spiritual instead of material wealth?*

And God said: "Come and see."

It's been a year. What a year of enjoying the life God has given me. Nothing more, nothing less. When I open my eyes to see the wonder and mystery of God, the jealousy dissolves. Living with flair today means I continue to "come and see" what God wants to prove to me about the sufficiency of Himself.

41. A Gift for Every Mother You Know

Today was chilly, windy (hair in my face no matter which way I pushed it around), and gloomy. We drove out into the country to a far-off nursery to buy some berry bushes for my latest gardening adventure. And when I say country, I mean *country*. The roads were unmarked, narrow, and tumbling over the landscape like an afterthought. A creek skipped by on the right, and cows fed in fields on the left. They were so close to my window I thought I might reach out and pat a nose.

Eventually, we arrived at a huge nursery. We left the car, met the wind and cold, and, hunching down and running, we slipped into the first greenhouse.

Immediately, warmth. My daughters sighed with pleasure and stretched their arms. Everything here seemed abundant: the moist air, the fragrance of blooming things, the tangle of vines and hanging plants overhead. I looked at all the gorgeous flowers and thought of the ripping winds outside. They'd have never made it without this greenhouse.

Standing there, seeing that little Eden of beauty set against the gloom and fierce wind, I thought of—not flowers—but people. More specifically, I thought of mothers.

I think of the moms I see that remind me of myself back then. I see the vacant stare, the lifeless smile, the numb conversation of a mom who is just trying to get a warm shower and go to the bathroom without somebody crying. Beneath the exhaustion, the stained t-shirt, and the post-pregnancy figure, there's a woman in there—vibrant, sassy, powerful. There's something in her that wants to bloom.

If only she had a greenhouse—a little paradise to keep her safe and warm so she could grow too. If only we could create the conditions that help her put down strong roots, stretch high out, and bloom, bloom, bloom.

What does a mom need? She needs to be protected and nourished so she can fully develop into the woman she's supposed to be. She needs friends who ask her about her ideas and her dreams; she needs a community who will spur her on and enable her to take risks in any direction she chooses. A mom needs people who don't limit her scope, who don't assume anything about her, and who recognize that she is a growing thing—like a tender vine in a greenhouse. Our children aren't the only people that need to grow in our homes. Babies aren't the only people that need swaddling.

If a mom doesn't grow and ripen, she shrivels. Moms need communities that value her spiritual, physical, social, emotional, and (if she wishes) her professional growth.

As I stood in the greenhouse today, I thought of how much I want moms everywhere to live with flair. A great Mother's Day gift (that we might give all year to every mom we know) is the mindset that the mother you see wants to grow too. The roads are unmarked for her; she's out in a far country. Motherhood can be her time to shrivel or bloom. Get her to the greenhouse!

42. Why You Should Make a Fool of Yourself

Some students who regularly frequent local bars recently told me that the reason why college students drink so much is because it's the only time they don't feel self-conscious. Alcohol makes them feel free to be themselves. Without it, they worry so much about making a fool of themselves.

Today I reasoned that making a fool of yourself might not be such a bad thing. In fact, it might just be flair.

I remember being terribly self-conscious in high school and college (who isn't?). I remember agonizing over whether people liked me and whether I was impressive. Years of trying to manage other people's perceptions of me exhausted me.

But in one terrible semester of graduate school, I stopped trying to impress people.

That year, I nearly failed out of school. A certain professor mocked me publicly, claimed I wasn't fit for graduate school, and implied that there had been a mistake in the application process that allowed me into a Ph.D. program. The tormenting shame I felt for that (and for nearly every mistake I was making personally that year), drove me into hiding and despair.

And it was the best thing that could have ever happened to me.

Before that year, I was self-conscious to the point of never being my true self. But when my worst fears were imagined and everybody saw me as a failure, a beautiful thing happened.

It wasn't that bad. It actually felt like freedom.

I was free to be exactly who I wanted to be. I stopped expending energy on wondering what people thought (I already knew—it wasn't good), and instead I asked myself what I could do to serve the academic community there. I figured out how much I loved teaching, I wrote an entire dissertation on the emotion of shame (how convenient!), and I didn't have to try to earn anyone's approval (I already lost it). And of course, as these things always go, I had more friends, more accolades, and more respect from professors than ever. That one grumpy professor even apologized to me. People like people who aren't self-conscious. They like people who can make a fool of themselves.

I haven't struggled with self-esteem since then. What drives self-esteem issues is a profound fear of being exposed as a loser, a fraud, a fool. Well, maybe we need to be exposed.

I wonder if college students wouldn't drink so much if they gathered their friends together, admitted their weaknesses, regularly did ridiculous things that made them supremely self-conscious, and tested the theory that we'd all love them more because of it.

Why not practice letting people see you at your worst? When it happens to you (like it happened to me), you recover, you find that people love you even more, and you stop trying to impress everybody.

Living with flair means testing the theory that we'll love you when (not if) you make a complete fool of yourself.

43. Imagine the Kite

Last night I watched my children fly kites. A kite is what I feel like when I'm undergoing a transition. I dip and I dive, I crash land, I jitter and jounce. But if I remember I am tethered and held by a Strong Hand, I can relax and know that eventually, I'll find the right air current and soar.

Living with flair means I'm assured of my mission, and I relax on the journey up.

44. Why You Should Sneak into the Kitchen During a Wedding Reception

During a wedding reception today, my youngest was fascinated by the food servers. They'd disappear behind swinging doors and return with iced tea at exactly the same time you needed more. After the cake cutting, several servers took the cake away on a little silver cart.

"Mommy, where are they taking it? When am I getting my piece of cake?"

As we waited, she became more and more agitated about the cake, her piece of it, and what in the world was happening behind those swinging doors to the kitchen. As a way to pass the time, I helped her try to imagine the secret world of reception hall kitchens.

"Can't we just go back there?" she asked.

I asked one server if we could watch the cake being cut for the guests, and he reluctantly agreed. We tip-toed back, deep into the heart of the kitchen, lifting our dresses to keep them out of the way.

Seven sweaty servers, like nervous surgeons, stood around this delicate and elaborate cake. My daughter peeked around my back to view this inverted perspective of wedding receptions. Back here, in the heat and pressure of food service, the reception experience was being made for the rest of us by real people. Tired people. People who looked up at us, embarrassed, like we'd just caught them all skinny dipping.

They apologized for not working faster.

When we returned to our table, my daughter waited with her hands in her lap. She didn't say a word. The cake came in due time, and instead of just enjoying it, she appreciated it.

Sometimes I need to remember to take myself and others back behind an experience—to see how it's being made for us. There's an infrastructure to our lives that other people make on their backs. It's not just food service. It's any service that we take for granted that makes our days happen. Someone is picking up the garbage, sorting the recycling, delivering my mail, or keeping the street lights working. Maybe I wouldn't demand so much if I could just journey back and see what's going on from a different perspective.

Living with flair means to sit with my hands in my lap and not demand my piece of cake.

45. When You Don't Get Recognition

All day, I think about the verses in Colossians 3 that implore, "Set your minds on things above, not on earthly things. For you died, and your life is now hidden with Christ in God. When Christ, who is your life, appears, then you also will appear with him in glory."

What does it mean to have a hidden life?

I wake up to a snowfall. The forest that just yesterday made a glorious, boastful display of buds and bird nests and bullfrogs now stays silent, keeping secrets.

It's deathly quiet on the way to school. Snow buries the crocus and daffodil shoots. Oh, that I could bear the weight of a hidden life with such grace! Oh, that I could see the beauty in this tomb of snow when I was expecting Spring's grand performance!

What if we are hidden away at the moment when we're supposed to bloom?

The temptation to be seen, to be public and praised, to be recognized and valued loses its power when I think about what it means to be hidden.

Later, I stand in my kitchen. I'm crying about hidden things: the years behind us and the years ahead of us of invisible labor. We do beautiful things today that nobody awards or congratulates.

But God sees. Being a hidden treasure is a way to live with flair. And the scriptures teach that God "who sees what is done in secret, will reward you."

46. Finding the Worst Parking Spot Ever

There's some convention in town, and the campus swarms with people in every direction. I turn into my usual parking lot to find that there's no parking on any of the lower levels. I'm driving around and around the parking lot, whiplashed and frustrated.

Finally, I'm spit out into the light of the uppermost deck of the lot (nobody wants these spots because everybody knows about the pigeons that assault your car with excremental gifts).

I pull into a spot far, far away, and as I walk through pigeon droppings, I look out over the valley (I'm that high up).

It's gorgeous. The sky is clear blue, and the wind whips across my face. I take a deep breath and look out across the mountains in the distance. I actually stop right there in the pigeon droppings and gaze out. I'm humbled and diminished by how small I am compared to this huge valley.

I'm thankful for this particular inconvenience and this particular mess. It's beautiful up here, and I wouldn't have seen it had I found a spot lower down.

Living with flair means I realize my missed opportunity might spit me out onto a higher level—the one that has the thing I'm supposed to see.

47. The Greatest Thing I Learned After Blogging Every Day for One Year

I woke up to an ice storm complete with power outages and school delays. In spring! What's happening!? This cannot possibly be the kind of day to celebrate a Year of Blogging with Flair.

But one thing I've learned after blogging every day for a year is that I can choose to find the flair in an ice storm.

What's it going to look like to embellish with wonder and deeply infuse the ordinary with some spiritual reality? Can I do this again today in the midst of the humdrum and the common routines?

I've taken on the spiritual discipline of finding God's truth reflected in the ordinary object: acorns, a cat's injured eye, a snowflake, a wandering albatross. I find that bit of truth that shows me, by analogy, a kingdom reality.

The ordinary day shimmers with God's radiance. The mundane does indeed become marvelous, and we simply have to worship.

Even when the ice storm destroys the freshly bloomed daffodils. All the fresh buds bend down. There's beauty in the ice. There's beauty in the bowed head of that daffodil. The daffodil, after all, is a narcissus plant whose name derives from the Greek myth about Narcissus. As you may know, Narcissus becomes obsessed with his own reflection at the water's edge, falls into the water, and drowns.

Is it God's loving hand that sends the thing into our lives that invites us to bow down in worship? The thing that reminds us that He is God and we are not? The thing that forces us (for once) to take our eyes off of ourselves and instead gaze upon the beauty of the Lord?

Send the ice storm if it means I bow down.

48. Give Your Life Away

My arms are sore from turning Double Dutch jump ropes.

From 6:30 PM-7:30 PM, 30 (yes, thirty!) parents and children came out to the parking lot for Monday Night Neighborhood Fitness. Imagine a swarm of children riding bikes and scooters or playing football and Frisbee. Imagine a car blaring music from an iPod so a group of children can dance. Imagine moms and dads walking together and connecting in their own neighborhood.

Imagine a little boy tugging on my sleeve to announce he rode ten times around the lot which I clocked for him as one mile. Imagine another little girl finally learning to jump rope.

I need more kites! I need more cones for obstacle courses! I want hula hoops and another set of ropes!

Why am I so happy when I'm turning jump ropes? It makes no sense that something like this would so deeply change my life.

Over the weekend, I hear Christian psychologist Larry Crabb talking about the goal of Christian therapy. As someone who battled depression all those years and reads everything I can about finding happiness, I drop everything to listen.

Crabb tells me that, typically, we think about counseling and our own happiness as answering the question, "How much can I get out of my life?" But therapy in the truest, Biblical sense asks, "How much can I *give* of my life?" In practice, I have found my own happiness bloom fully when I'm involved in tasks that serve others and let me forget myself.[7]

I want to give my life away. Turning jump ropes isn't glamorous, and it doesn't generate any revenue. But something about this task has secured more happiness for me than anything else I've done this year.

49. Do You Know What Quiescent Means?

It means "tranquil repose."

I find the word this morning when trying to determine if it's true that my daughter's silky dogwood has grown this winter.

Can trees and shrubs grow in winter? We stand on the back porch in our rain boots. Huddled together in the pouring rain, under a huge blue and white umbrella, we examine the silky dogwood. The snow has melted (finally), and my daughter races outside to check the growth of that tiny little wisp of a sapling she planted two years ago.

We haven't even had breakfast yet. Even my coffee can wait; I've learned this year to follow a child where she wants to lead you.

We peer over the deck. It grew! It grew into a whole bush. I can't believe it. I thought everything went dormant in winter. I imagine trees and shrubs in suspended animation.

Apparently, even in the winter, trees can grow. Dormant isn't the same thing as quiescent. In winter, roots experience "winter quiescence." They are resting but ready. As soon as roots encounter nutrients, water, and even a slight elevation in temperatures, they spring into action.

The dogwood was resting but ready all season. It took advantage of every warm day, every bit of moisture, and every nutrient. In tranquil repose, it waited and experienced growth as the days allowed.

I like to think of living in tranquil repose. I'm *resting but ready* as soon as my environment offers nutrients for spiritual and emotional growth. And I have to remember that the sapling wasn't dormant—growth happened—it only looked like suspended animation on some days.

Living with flair means we embrace quiescent days. We are resting but ready, and we are growing.

50. Screaming "Base!"

Today I chase my daughter around the living room to tickle her. At one point, she defiantly stops in her tracks, places one hand on the couch and screams, "Base!"

"I'm safe! I'm safe on base! You can't touch me!" she insists, nodding her head and putting one hand up as a stop sign.

I wait patiently for her to move from "base" only to find that as soon as she's nearly in my grip, she just touches the wall and screams, "Base!" again.

For little ones, the concept of a "moving base" saves them every time. They just have to touch something—anything—claim it as their safe haven, and stop the attacker (in this case, the Tickle Monster).

She's onto something.

I imagine enemy attacks against us in various spiritual forms. I reach out my hand, wherever I am, cling to God and scream "Base!" You can't touch us here. We are safe.

Living with flair means I realize I'm on base.

51. Rearrange the Day!

This morning, I scrape egg off of a blue and white plate.

I overhear a pastor, Tim Keller, speaking about work in a sermon video. I wipe my hands on the dish towel and strain to hear.

Keller says, "Work is rearranging the raw material of a particular domain for the flourishing of everyone."[8]

I think about what "raw materials" make up this day.

So far, my raw materials are dirty dishes. Later, I rearrange letters to make words and then rearrange words to make sentences. Now, I position red peppers in a pan to roast for dinner. At 6:30, I'll open the front door and welcome the children for Neighborhood Fitness Group.

I also have the raw emotions of fear about my sick friend and sadness over tragedies all over the world. I take the feelings and do the work of prayer.

Suddenly, I look at my work in new ways. Cleaning the kitchen, teaching grammar, making dinner, praying, and then hosting the Neighborhood Fitness Group tonight all represent ways I rearrange raw material into new positions for flourishing.

And if what I'm doing doesn't contribute to our flourishing, then it's not the kind of work I want. I think of Proverbs 14: "The wise woman builds her house, but with her own hands the foolish one tears hers down." I want to be the kind of person who rearranges whatever she's been given today to allow everyone (including myself) to flourish.

Living with flair is a kind of rearranging: We rearrange our circumstances, turn them towards the light, and find the good, the beautiful, and the hopeful.

52. "Do Everything, Even the Insignificant Things, in a Significant Way."

Early this morning, before the chatter and patter of little girls and the swish and push of backpacks and coats, I read this quote:

"Do everything, even the insignificant things, in a significant way."[9] I'm reading the ancient little devotional by E. Stanley Jones again, and his words hit me stronger than the aroma of the Dunkin' Donuts coffee I have brewing behind my back as I write.

As I ask God to show me how to do this—how to make each moment truly significant—I'm interrupted by the purrs and meows of hungry kitties. I stoop down to feed them, and as they swirl about my feet like I'm within some tornado of fur, I pause and thank God for these furry friends. I thank Him for One-Eyed Jack and all I've learned. I thank him for the companionship these faithful cats provide as a refuge for little girls.

It becomes a simple moment of worship right there by the cat food bowls.

I turn back to my question, and I already know the answer.

I infuse each moment with a thankful heart and invite the glory of God in. I want to amplify each moment like that. I want to fold laundry and worship. I want to empty this dishwasher and encounter God's glory.

I want those moments to be as powerful and symbolic as when I put my American flag out each day. I stand on the porch as the sun rises, and I tell the girls how thankful we are to be citizens of a great nation. I remember my friend Charity's brother who died in Iraq. I ask God to protect our soldiers and to help my family honor their sacrifice. I make a ridiculous bugle call sound with my mouth as if I'm raising a flag (I really do this, and it's completely ridiculous, but it's how I sanctify the moment).

I'm moving forward today into a thousand insignificant tasks that now have monumental meaning. I'm sanctifying mundane moments.

Living with flair means I do everything in a significant way.

53. A New Approach to Serving Others

Today, I hear my husband explain a new way to care for folks in our community. He says that we do things "with" people and not "for" them. As a scholar obsessed with the nuances of language, I find myself baffled by how a simple change in a preposition revolutionizes how we act.

Prepositions reveal relationship. Am I doing things "with" my community or just "for" my community? For years, my husband and I followed the model of doing things "for" other people. But two years ago, we wanted to belong to our community and not stand outside of it.

We had recently heard a Navajo Indian speaking about various groups that would visit his reservation. They'd bring help or aid and quickly leave. Yet what the Navajo truly wanted, more than anything else, was to be known, understood, and valued. They wanted the organizations to be "with them" and not just come do things "for them."

In our community, I have learned (finally) to be with people. The walk-to-school campaigns, the Monday Night Fitness Groups, and the Saturday Pancakes are all about being with my community. We mutually encourage, mutually support, mutually serve.

In my parenting, I have learned (finally) to do things with my children and not just for them. I'm learning to say, "I would like to do this with you and not just for you." That philosophy seems to honor their dignity and mine as well.

It's the same with teaching. It's the same with blogging. There's a "withness" about this work that transforms it. We are with each other.

My husband reminds me that the incarnation is God "with us." Immanuel—God with us—represents a prepositional phrase that's changed my life.

Living with flair means I learn the meaning of "with."

54. Tied in Place

When you're growing climbing roses on your trellis, you tie the vines in place so they don't go where they're not supposed to go.

You also invite a particular type of growth:

My husband ties the main runner vines to encourage them into *horizontal* growth. With horizontal growth, the main vine sends out many stems to move upward and creates beautiful flowers all over the trellis.

With just *vertical* growth, the runner won't stem off, and you'll only have blooms at the very top of your trellis. It's a growth that happens too quickly and without any branching.

I glance at my trellis today and feel thankful for those years I felt tied in place somewhere. I wanted all this growth and excitement and movement, but instead, I stayed put and moved deeper into my community.

I sent out stems that bloomed.

If I feel stuck somewhere spiritually, emotionally, or physically, perhaps I'm being tied in place for some horizontal growth. This kind of pruning makes for something *exquisite*, but it takes time and what must feel like an imprisoned kind of binding. It's not this at all, but rather the necessary training for the roses to bloom abundantly.

55. What Has to Die in Me?

This afternoon, I notice my Winterberry bush budding in the backyard.

Those blooms hold particular significance this Easter season because I've beheld their cycle this whole year. I see death and resurrection, and I suddenly remember the importance of death.

For months, this bush seemed more acquainted with death than life. The brittle and barren branches!

This bush endured the assault of ice storms. Those branches seemed hopeless, trapped, and unchanging.

Things were being put to death in her.

Now, these new buds burst forth.

I remember my Winterberry bush when I think about God's work in my life. I go through seasons when things have to die in me. The soul in winter feels like death, but with every burial, there's a resurrection. What will Jesus bring forth in us? We await that bloom even when we cannot perceive the secret work happening deep within our souls.

56. A Turning Point Statement

During the summer of 1994, a friend told me she thought I had the spiritual gift of encouragement. She posted a little note by my bed. It said, "You are an encourager." I remember exactly what it looked like—the handwriting, the color—and how it felt to have someone name something like that about me. My friend saw what I couldn't see.

That single comment shaped the next 15 years of my life. I wasn't just an average girl; I was a hope giver, a courage finder, and an inspiration provider. I wasn't just a nobody. God wanted to use me to point others towards a beautiful future.

It took someone naming it to help me see it.

I had a student who told me that of all my weeks and weeks of teaching, the most memorable thing from my class was a single comment I wrote on one of his many essays.

In the margin of his paper, I wrote: "You sound like a great teacher right here." He was overwhelmed that I named that in him, and he later wrote about his dreams for graduate school to become a teacher. As my husband and I discussed these turning point comments, he told me he remembered the exact words of a Scout leader who pointed out some unique gifts he saw in my husband. Those were turning point words.

Today, as I guide students through their memoir drafts, I realize that I'm not naming what I see enough. I wonder what I need to name in my children, in my friends, and in my students. *I see this in you.* Maybe God will use it to shape a life. Maybe those words will be a turning point for someone today.

57. The Text Message I'm Waiting For

The text will arrive sometime today. I don't know when.

All it will ask is, "What do you see?"

Today marks the beginning of the "What Do You See?" campaign on campus. Students in the graduate student campus ministry receive a random text message from my husband every day for two weeks. When I receive the text question, I'm challenged to do three things:

1. Look up and see who is around me.

2. Pause and pray for a few moments, asking God to open my eyes and to show me how He sees those who are around me.

3. Think about what God shows me and contemplate how that is different from how I typically see that person/those people.

I'm also challenged to record what happens—who I see and what I do about it—when I get that text.

The last time I agreed to this challenge, I received the texts at the most inconvenient times. Every person in my path seemed angry and unapproachable. But I'd look down at my phone and see the question, "What do you see?" and pray for God to show me what He sees instead.

I found courage to stop my minivan and ask my neighbor how she was doing. I turned to complete strangers in elevators and perceived them in light of eternity. I looked up and saw the office assistant as precious to God.

In John's gospel account, I learn that Jesus tells the disciples to "open their eyes" and see the fields are ripe for harvest. Jesus tells the disciples to "open their eyes" right after His encounter with the Samaritan woman (who everybody saw as an outcast). Jesus saw her differently.

I pray my eyes are opened today to see people as God sees them. I don't know where I'll be when that text comes, but I pray I have the courage to love the way God does. Eventually, I won't need a text message to remind me to see folks in my path differently, but for these two weeks, I'm training my heart to love.

58. Hearing the Falconer

I love the satisfaction that comes from enjoying the meaning of small things, small moments, that shimmer with the glory of God. How did this happen? When did the whole world become an allegory that taught me something about God and myself? It's a rich and glorious gift to read the world through the lens of mystery, wonder, and divinity. How could a day be bad or boring when the smallest detail teaches me?

I remember this quote that helps me shape the way I want to experience my life. Sue Monk Kidd writes, "I realized it for the first time in my life: there is nothing but mystery in the world, how it hides behind the fabric of our poor, browbeat days, shining brightly, and we don't even know it."[10]

When I look for meaning and symbol in my world, I enjoy the mystery of things: acorns, a cat's purr, a sprouting seed, a snowflake, a candle. . .

When I learn about myself and God through these simple, ordinary objects, I help develop a certain unity and purpose to each moment. Everything feels at peace and right; everything feels orderly and reasoned. I peer into the fabric and find that Christ "is in all things and in him all things hold together" (Colossians 1:17).

I wonder if modern despair and cynicism have something to do with meaning-making that fell apart. I wonder if we might recapture a way to see the world again. I wonder if we might train our minds to see beauty, allegory, and design right down to the smallest fleck in this day.

Then, the whole world would call out to us, like a falconer to the falcon. We could hear God's voice and see His fingerprints everywhere.

I tune my ear. I sharpen my eyes. I prime my fingertips. I lick my lips. I flare my nostrils.

I'm ready, Lord.

59. When You Stop Resisting God

Last week, I was asked to write a piece on depression and Lent for *The High Calling*. At my lowest point, I imagined God asking this question:

"Will you live the life I ask you to live?"

Yesterday, I'm walking to the vernal pond and recalling that depression. I remember how many years I resisted the reality of my life. It didn't look like it was supposed to.

But God knows what I don't know; He sees what I don't see.

But I wasn't ready to surrender. Nothing felt right. Nothing felt abundant.

Humbled again, I'm silenced as I walk in the woods.

We find our secret pond, and on the surface, I see the blue sky reflected.

My daughters peer deeply, waiting patiently. All of a sudden, we see the new frog and salamander eggs. They might even be turtle eggs.

Then, the water's surface trembles: little salamanders, spotted bright red and orange, dart beneath the leaves.

I look out, and I see an entire pond filled with eggs, and tiny creatures move about everywhere. Those white cottony puffs are great big globs of frog eggs. Next week, we'll see unimaginable numbers of tadpoles.

As I think about my life (the one I resisted all those years), I hear another whisper of the Spirit. Underneath that trembling surface, that dark and murky mess of mud and fallen things, something was being birthed.

Something was happening.

I look deep into that pond, and I see how fertile, how bountiful, how rich and teeming this exact spot is.

This very spot where I find myself (no matter how wrong) will produce life in abundance as I cooperate with God. And when nothing seems to be happening, I just have to look beneath the surface.

60. Loving by Faith

This morning, I remember the simplest of truths: I love others by faith. There's a supernatural, unconditional, pure and deep love that God wants to produce in me for others (and myself). But I cannot conjure it from my own flesh. I cannot think or feel my way into loving folks that, for whatever reason, are difficult for me to love.

And God commands I love others—especially enemies, especially the unlovable—with that pure and deep love.

Impossible! Yes. In my own strength, it is impossible.

I pull a little booklet off of the dusty bookshelves. It's *How You Can Love by Faith*, by Bill Bright. I flip through the pages, hungry for the truth there. He writes:

"God has an unending supply of His divine, supernatural, agape love for you. It is for you to claim, to grow on, to spread to others, and thus to reach hundreds and thousands with the love that counts, the love that will bring them to Jesus Christ. In order to experience and share this love, you must claim it by faith; that is, trust His promise that He will give you all that you need to do His will on the basis of His command and promise."[11]

Suddenly, I'm parenting my girls with the pure, deep love of God flowing through me. I'm overwhelmed with divine love for my husband, my neighbors, my students, myself.

When God gives a command in scripture, He gives the power to fulfill it. Living with flair means I enter, by faith, into that divine flow of agape love. I love the unlovable. I love the ones hardest to love. I love in a way that counts.

61. A Great Big Show-Off

This morning in the garden, I turn the corner towards my little peony plant. Every time these buds fully bloom, I always think to myself, "Now that's just showing off!" A peony is just an over-the-top kind of flower. What flair!

I lean in to observe what seems just like all the popular bunching up patterns I see all over skirts and shirts this season. God indeed clothes nature in a kind of splendor we can only copy. I look up that word, "splendor," because I begin to recall how frequently it appears in Scripture. It means magnificent, gorgeous, and brilliantly distinct. I find references all over the Bible that we worship the Lord in the splendor of His holiness and majesty. I also learn that God says we are His "splendor" and that He displays His "splendor" in us.

He shows off in us. I even read that the splendor the Lord gives makes our beauty perfect.

I finally recall when Jesus says in Matthew 6: "And why do you worry about clothes? See how the flowers of the field grow. They do not labor or spin. Yet I tell you that not even Solomon in all his splendor was dressed like one of these. If that is how God clothes the grass of the field, which is here today and tomorrow is thrown into the fire, will he not much more clothe you—you of little faith?"

God is all splendor. He displays that splendor in us. When I look at peonies showing off, I remember a magnificent, gorgeous, and brilliantly distinct God who, in turn, clothes us with all we need to display that kind of splendor. I want to open my eyes and see that splendor in every face I meet today.

62. Do You Know a Mama Like This?

Do you remember the Italian Mama? She taught me how to have a soundtrack to my life a year ago as I learned about sauce. Then I studied meatballs and how to clothe both them and my own children. In November, she instructed me in the fine art of relaxing and throwing those meatballs. In December (during that awful cold) she brought enough baked ziti, turkey noodle soup, bread, and chocolate to feed a village.

Today, just when I needed it most, she hosted an Italian Mama's Lunch. Since I'm partly Italian (and studying how to be an Italian Mama), I skipped down the street like a little girl going to her first party. I couldn't wait! I arrived to this:

Roasted peppers, tomatoes, basil, four types of cheeses, meats, olives, artichokes, fresh bread, cannoli desserts, and freshly ground espresso comprised this lunch. As we dined, I learned that Italian Mamas are always authentic, passionate, honest, generous, and so vibrant that they literally have to hug you, use hand gestures for every word, and talk about everything.

Italian Mamas live with a particular kind of flair. They can hold the whole neighborhood in their embrace. Whatever suffering—whatever hunger—they can soothe it. I know this: Everyone needs an Italian Mama for a neighbor. And even though I'm still learning how to be one, I know that I can also be that Italian Mama for someone else. I want to live that passionately and generously. I want to hug you and talk about everything.

63. Why You Belong Right Here

I'm walking with my neighbor in the woods.

All of a sudden, she cries out, "The Lady Slippers have bloomed!" She's pointing to the earth, and at first, I do not see anything.

Then, I see them.

I don't even really know what I'm seeing or why it matters.

My friend tells me something wondrous. Lady Slipper Orchids are extraordinary.

It's illegal to uproot them. It's actually against the law to harm these wild orchids. I learn two amazing facts that explain why.

First, the US Forest Service reports that Lady Slippers depend upon a very special fungus in the forest that allows the seed to grow. The fungus cares for the seed—passing on nutrients—until it grows older. And when the plant matures, it then sends nutrients back to the fungus through its roots. That symbiosis will be destroyed if we harvest the orchids.[12]

Second, I learn that the intricate system of orchid roots means that if you take even one plant away, you harm the entire network of orchid plants.

Every single one matters. And the location isn't an accident.

As I think about the impossibly complex design that allows these orchids to thrive, I consider my own community. Every single person nourishes each other, and we're here for a reason. There's nothing accidental about it. The conditions for our growth exist only here.

Doesn't God tell us that He "searches out the exact places where we live" (Acts 17) and that we are "all part of one body"? (Romans 12)

You are here for a marvelous reason. We need you! And even when these growing conditions seem like, well, fungus, this is what we require to thrive.

Living with flair means really seeing ourselves as a community and knowing why it matters. We are part of each other.

Finally, it took another person to reveal this beauty to me. I would have never noticed these Lady Slipper Orchids without her. Living with flair means that when our neighbors don't see it, we show them.

64. What Would You Wish For?

Just a few days after mowing, our backyard transforms into a wonderland of wishes.

My youngest calls me outside and hands me a dandelion and tells me to make a wish. She closes her eyes, takes a deep breath, and whispers that little girl wish that sends the seeds flying.

"Now you do it! Make your wish!"

I stand there, holding my breath, and just as I begin to exhale, I realize I don't know what to wish for.

Sometime this past year, my desperate longing for something more became satisfied. I had all I needed because God was sending the flair right into any circumstance. It didn't matter where I was because He was there.

Even in the weeds of suffering, illness, and disappointment, there was always some flair.

So what's left to wish for? I'm holding the weed in my hand and asking God what His wish for my life is.

I remember that God's name and His renown are the desire of my heart. What does it mean to wish that your life radiates with the power and presence of God? What does it mean to wish for a life that brings the most honor and glory to God—that His name would be made great through your life?

These are serious wishes. These wishes include sacrifice and dying to self. These wishes invoke a sort of hope and intention that invites God to work in my life no matter what the cost. It's a surrender that sends my life flying out into the unknown.

Is this a wish I'm ready to make? I exhale everything out across the landscape. I don't know where these seeds will land, but land they will. This is my life that I'm scattering out. It never belonged to me anyway.

65. Released from the Snare

All day, I've been thinking about a verse from Psalm 25:15.

"My eyes are ever on the Lord,
  for only he will release my feet from the snare."

A snare means a trap. It's a deceptively enticing situation or mindset that captures us. These past few days, I've repeated this verse over and over again. I've applied it to unwise relationships I've formed (professional or personal), foolish commitments I've made, and ungodly mindsets I've adopted. When I feel ensnared by something, I'm learning to ask God to set me free.

And He does.

Living with flair means I keep my eyes "ever on the Lord." He knows exactly how to "release my feet from the snare"—whatever it may be today.

66. A Strange Lesson from My Mother's Day Candle

My mother was the first to teach me that candles have "memory." When you light a jar or pillar candle the first time, you must let it burn for a few hours until the wax pools all the way to the edges.

You see, the candle remembers how far the wax pooled that first time, and it will only burn to that boundary every time you light it. A small wax pool means your candle will tunnel as it burns. It will waste the majority of the wax. It can't break free of that early pattern. It remembers.

This morning my family comes into my bedroom with presents for Mother's Day. Two scented jar candles, wrapped in tissue, roll out on the bedspread. My oldest daughter has breakfast on a tray for me, and as I look at this little family around me and light my candles, I think about candle memory.

Will I ever break free from old patterns? Am I doomed to candle memory in my own soul?

Sometimes life feels so limited by our destructive patterns—set deep in stone—that we cannot change. But I don't want a narrow life! I don't want to tunnel down—bringing my children with me—because of old patterns set by the world, the flesh, and the devil (as Scripture teaches). All morning in church, I think of the hopelessness of that candle memory and of a life that cannot ever break free from a set pattern or false belief.

I need to recover from the patterns of thought—lies I believe—about where my hope and security originate.

In church, I look and see rows and rows of folks in recovery from drugs and alcohol. A few minutes before, I shake hands with a woman who tells me (in the same breath) her name and her reality: I'm in recovery. She's been clean two weeks.

What can break the old pattern? Who can erase the narrow boundaries and set us free? That new friend knows her name and her reality. She's in recovery. Day by day, she embraces a new reality, a new pattern. It's Jesus in her—the only One who can set us free from the prison of ourselves.

That's what I think about when I light this Mother's Day candle. Candle memory may seem final, but there's a Light that knows no boundaries and can expose any false pattern. I invite Jesus in—all the way to the far edges—and let my heart melt and pool deep and wide.

67. Mothers are Beanstalks

This afternoon, the children run outside and design a bean garden for themselves. They want a beanstalk.

I discover that we need a structure in that bean garden around which the bean plants can twine.

I love that verb, first of all. To twine means to interlock tightly, twisting up and coiling about.

Beans are twining plants, and this means they cannot support their own weight. For vertical growth, they circle around a support in order to grow. They exert continuous pressure against this support so they can rise tall and strong.

They will not survive without interlocking tightly, twisting up and coiling about a supporting structure.

I needed that truth today as I think about motherhood and this life of faith. I cannot do this on my own. I lean hard against the Lord as that internal structure around which I cling. I interlock. Every tendril of thought and action encircles one singular support.

If I'm exhausted, shriveled on the vine, and incapable of doing this alone, I remember I wasn't meant to. I'm supposed to twine.

68. Making Us Suitable

Do you remember my huge gardening mistake?

This morning, I look out the window and remember how difficult it was for me to remove all the blossoms and young fruit from my blueberries, blackberries, and strawberries that first season. I didn't understand it! I didn't want to wait! But I learned this:

This counter-intuitive and destructive move would make my plants thrive. If I take away the fruit, the plant directs the energy and nutrients to the most important part of the plant: the root system. A new berry plant needs a few years to make an indestructible foundation of roots.

I walk out to the garden and notice the morning dew on the strawberries.

The berry patch has tripled—maybe quadrupled—in size. My deliberate attempts to diminish these plants by removing the fruit worked.

Even the raspberries come back larger and more abundant. This bush was one shoot last summer.

I'll never forget this. What looks like a fruitless season—cut short, wasteful, damaged, stolen—is preparation for abundance. We are being made ready and suitable in advance. My roots are being nourished and strengthened to support what's coming next. It may take a year or two (even three), but it's God's preparation for the fruit to come.

69. Without You, We're Doomed

I learned something astonishing about my new blueberry bush. She can't produce fruit alone. She not only needs pollinators to fertilize her, but she also can't be fertilized with her own pollen. In the case of these blueberries, for example, you need *different varieties* to cross-pollinate in order to have fruit.

So confusing! So dependent and conditional and troubling! Can't she just produce *alone*? I call my husband: "Sweetheart, did we plant two different varieties of blueberry bushes? Did we? Because you know that. . . "

"Yes," he interrupts. "Yes, I know that you need different kinds in order to cross-pollinate. We're good." He hangs up and returns to work. I'm so thankful that he knows what he's doing.

Because I don't.

I'll never make it without you. The older I get, the more I realize how much I need others and they need me. We are as interdependent as pollinators, one kind of blueberry, and an entirely different kind of blueberry. If even one component doesn't show up, we're doomed.

70. Your Chilling Requirement

This spring morning, we all notice the gorgeous peach tree blossoms set against an ominous morning sky.

We know what's coming. At the end of the summer, we can pick peaches on this walk. This one little tree produces so many peaches that the owner actually begs us to pick his peaches each year.

So we do.

Many folks plant peach trees in Pennsylvania because peach trees, like other fruit trees, have a chilling requirement. Some peaches require over 1000 hours of below 40 degree days in order to go into the dormancy that allows a new season of peaches. Without those 1000 hours of rest, the peach tree simply won't bear fruit. Here, a peach tree gets those crucial chilling hours.

So if it's bearing great fruit, it means that tree had the right amount of rest.

I have my own chilling requirement. For days, months, sometimes years, I go dormant to prepare for the next year's fruit. We have to see rest that way. It's preparation. It's a requirement.

71. What You Lose in the Getting

I'm standing in front of my beautiful white Weeping Cherry, and I tell my neighbor, "I wish the blooms were pink."

Pink is so glamorous, so very Spring. Pink has always symbolized energy, love, zeal, and beauty. Instead, I have a white Weeping Cherry. Boring. Usual. Pure, but bland.

"If only it were pink like some of the others!" I shake my head and go inside. That very night, a storm passes through the valley, and I wake up to a *pink* Weeping Cherry.

Has some magician come in the night? Really, the rain and wind turn the blossoms down. The weight of it transforms this tree from the inside out. The once white blossoms hang low, closed for the season. Closed, they are pink.

Pink signifies the end. It means the tree submits to the storm. These blooms will fall by tomorrow.

I consider what it means to want something. I wanted pink, but I see now so very clearly the great cost of it.

You lose something in the getting.

God shows me this with every unfulfilled dream. He sees what I'd lose in the getting. He sees what would fall.

If I don't have pink, it's because of what I'd lose in the getting. Thank you, Lord, for the bright white blossom.

72. Just This

On the walk to school, we notice the tiniest Weeping Cherry. Amid the oldest and the tallest, the brightest and the best, this little tree—so humble and no bigger than a chair—makes her contribution.

In the shadow of the tall oaks on either side of her, she seems so very small.

Stand tall, Little Tree! The whole world might not see you, and you don't stand nearly as tall as the rest, but for this one walk to school, this one street, and this one patch of grass, you bring joy.

I want to be the kind of woman who brings pleasure and joy, even if I'm not the best or the most important. Maybe my assignment from God is to bloom small for just one street.

73. In God Alone

This morning, I remember a great truth—the Greatest Truth—that sets everything right.

In Psalm 62 King David writes, "My soul finds rest in God alone; my salvation comes from Him. He alone is my rock and salvation; He is my fortress, and I will never be shaken."

When it comes right down to it, all my coping mechanisms and all the wonderful things in my life (family, community, beauty, writing) do not provide true rest for the soul. Even when everything's in place and I'm doing all the right things for mental health, God reminds me that the rest I need comes from Him alone. He alone is my rock and my salvation. Not family. Not even amazing community. Not even beauty that points to His glory. These things reflect and remind. But they aren't Him.

My soul finds rest in God alone.

I pour coffee, sit in the morning sun, and read the ancient words. I cry out to the One who alone gives rest.

74. The Best Worst Thing

My husband and in-laws are driving with me to run errands, and my husband tells the story of the worst internship he ever had as a veterinarian's assistant. It involved losing a dog, being attacked by a cat, and other tales too graphic for my blog.

"It was the best worst thing," he claims. That experience helped direct him to his true calling—far away from the vet—and towards another field.

The best worst thing! I just love the expression.

We decide to ask one another for our "best worst thing" stories.

"The military. The worst experience of my life and the best thing that ever happened to me," my father-in-law says.

I offer my battle with postpartum depression as my best worst thing. I learned things I could only know through that darkness.

I also laugh about nearly failing a biology course in college and realizing the medical field would have to do without me. I think further back to particular heartbreaks that led me to a deep and abiding relationship with Jesus.

They were the best worst things.

And just last week, I ask my sweet daughter why she was turning into such a confident young woman with so much joy and wisdom inside. She says, "Being bullied and made fun of in the second grade. That makes you so strong."

It's her best worst thing so far.

I love that our worst things become our best things. I think that's the whole point of living with flair, don't you?

75. The Making of a Great Person

I'm at a very special birthday party last night for my dear friend (the one who says the sign of a happy childhood is dirty children, the one who taught me to tell my children how much I want to be with them, the one who sent me double-dutch jump ropes to advance the Neighborhood Fitness Group, and the one with five beautiful and creative children who inspire me).

This friend has invited women to journey to a restaurant to celebrate her 50th birthday, and her two oldest daughters also attend. Women come from all over the East Coast, and I've driven all the way from Central Pennsylvania. I would have driven from California if I had to.

We all begin to share how much we love this woman and how simply great she is.

As my friend introduces each guest around the tables, she tells everyone why that woman matters so much to her. She finally concludes by offering her motivation for this wonderful party: "I wanted to show my oldest daughters what makes a person. It's our friendships."

She shares about the women who've journeyed with her through her life, and I find myself in tears at the beauty of it. Here I sit with 20 women who all don't know one another but who all know my friend. At this party, we're not talking about the birthday girl's accomplishments, her advanced degrees from Harvard and Princeton, her publishing, her work with the school district, or her time in China.

We talk instead about friendship.

Guests pass photo collections around highlighting *us*. The conversation around the tables is about *us*.

Even during her 50th birthday celebration—when she's supposed to be the star of the show—she's talking about others.

That's living with flair.

76. An Impossible Path

I'm driving on Route 76 in Somerset County, and as I approach the Allegheny Mountain Tunnel, I have the strangest feeling that such things cannot be. A tunnel through the mountain? How? The mountain rises up to block the path, and yet I'm sucked into the tiny black hole in its side. I'm driving in that silent tunnel, and I'm thinking of impossible pathways.

The Red Sea. The Jordan. I think of Psalm 77: "Your path led through the sea, your way through the mighty waters, though your footprints were not seen."

I think of all the strange and unfamiliar and just impossible paths God sets us on. When I ask, How will I get through this? I remember this from Isaiah 42: "I will lead the blind by ways they have not known, along unfamiliar paths I will guide them; I will turn the darkness into light before them and make the rough places smooth. These are the things I will do; I will not forsake them."

When I'm on what looks like an unfamiliar (strange, impossible path) these days, I know that every obstacle has an equally powerful tunnel that God cuts in the unmovable rock.

That's how I get through.

77. Returning with Treasure

Today on the walk to school, my friend suggests that we are all on a Hero's Journey, and sometimes we stop at Step 2: The Refusal of our Calling. His wife pulls up the steps of the Hero's Journey on her phone and recites the narrative pattern for us. This pattern, noted most famously by the American scholar, Joseph Campbell, follows various steps which we find in so many stories but also in our own psychological development.

The steps include a Call to Adventure, a Refusal of the Call, Meeting with a Mentor, Crossing the Threshold into our calling (where all the rules and values seem strange), the Period of Testing, Joining with Friends on the mission, the Main Ordeal, the Reward, the Road Back, Death and Rebirth, and finally, Returning with Treasure and Power.[13]

The hero, after these steps, emerges transformed and renewed.
We ask ourselves where we are on our own journey as Ordinary Heroes. Some of wonder what our calling is. Others know but refuse it. Others are in their period of testing while still others are on the road back.

Thinking of the journey in this way, we remember that it's natural and patterned to go through refusals, trials, ordeals, and deaths. But we remember that most important step of joining with friends on the mission. And we remember that one day, we'll return with treasure.

On the way home from the morning walk, I realize that I'm returning with treasure indeed.

78. On This Day: A Promise to Yourself

On this day, I will, as Oswald Chambers writes, let God "fling me out."

Let God fling you, my friend reminds me all week. She's talking about letting God send me out into those unknown and unsafe purposes, those amazing and unimagined plans.

Before school, I push my daughter on the swing, flinging her as far as she'll go. She can't stop giggling. She's terrified and delighted in equal measure. This is what it feels like to let God fling me. Am I ready for this whirlwind?

Chambers concludes: "The only way God sows His saints is by His whirlwind. . . Let God fling you out, and do not go until He does. If you select your own spot, you will prove an empty pod. If God sows you, you will bring forth fruit."[14]

I walk on with all the neighbors to school, and I see a blossom stretch out to me, strangely distinct—flung out—dangling. How beautiful to see what this tree brings forth in this spot, right here, today.

79. Forget Not His Benefits

This morning, after I find myself elbow deep in a strawberry patch, I spend some time reading Psalm 103. No matter how many times I read this Psalm, I'm struck by the simplicity, truth, and joy of it. Other than Psalm 16, I can claim Psalm 103 as a favorite.

Just the first five verses set my mind right: "Praise the Lord, O my soul, and forget not all his benefits. . ." And what follows is that beautiful list of verbs: He forgives, heals, redeems, crowns with love and compassion, and satisfies.

He satisfies! The verse reads that God "satisfies your desires with good things so that your youth is renewed like the eagle's."

He satisfies indeed. I begin to consider how this happens. I realize a pure truth that I've learned after all this time: He satisfies in the precise way that fits our needs. He satisfies in creative, often unusual, unexpected, and unimagined ways.

He invents these ways, and they almost never match my ideas of what will satisfy me. Almost never.

I want glamorous living, but He gives me a strawberry patch to love.
I want an international bestseller, and He gives me a daily blog to keep.
I want fame, and He gives me friendship.
I want to collect extravagant works of art, and He gives me a camera to make my own art.
I want global influence, and He gives me two little girls to raise quietly in a small community.

It's like He knows the desire beneath the desire. He knows what I really want.

So today I make a list of all the good things He's given me that fulfill the desires beneath the desires.

And off I rise like an eagle.

80. Fresh From the Nest

On the walk home from dropping the children off at school, the neighbors and I see a baby robin leave the nest.

He stands there ready to start really living.

He tries his wings out, and the neighbors lean in and begin cheering for him.

"You can do it! Fly little bird! Fly!"

What a great day this one has ahead of him! Flying! Juicy worms! Oh, what it must feel like to be fresh from the nest, exploring a new world!

I want to live this day as if I'm fresh from the nest. Whatever I need to leave behind—whatever dependencies, spaces, and old, comfortable ideas of what life should be like—I do it, stretch out these wings, and go.

81. Well Worth the Waiting

Do you remember exactly two years ago my huge gardening mistake? I put my strawberry plants in the ground, and I bragged about all the glorious berries I'd have that summer. Remember how the older, wiser folks told me that I had to pinch off every blossom and not, under any circumstances, let that plant produce?

I had to do it. I had to deliberately destroy even the possibility of fruit.

I wrote this:

This counter-intuitive and destructive move would make my plants thrive. If I take away the fruit, the plant directs the energy and nutrients to the most important part of the plant: the root system. A new berry plant needs a few years to make an indestructible foundation of roots. Then, we can enjoy the fruit.

Today, *two years later*, my youngest daughter rushes in from school, and the first thing she grabs is a bowl for harvesting berries. We have so many that we can't eat them all. We will begin storing them this weekend. And they're huge.

Don't ever let me complain about waiting again. Don't ever let me tell you that unproductive seasons with no fruit in sight are wasted in God's economy. Remind me that my roots are going deep, and I'm nourishing my system. That's the way it has to be if we want any kind of harvest.

82. Finally Accepting God's Boundary Lines for Your Life

All week, I've considered how beautiful it is to finally surrender to the limits of your own life. You stop resisting. You stop wishing for a different life. You stop living in an imaginary future.

Instead, you look at all the perfect boundary lines in your life. You thank God for the places He never let you go and for the people He never let you marry. You rejoice with every single rejection because time always shows you a Divine Hand of protection and guidance. You giggle with joy over every thing you wanted that God withheld because you know by now that He sees what you don't see.

You actually even come to the point of celebrating emotional, physical, intellectual, financial, and relational limits. Why? Why could you?

It's because you know God, and you know what He's up to.

You begin to realize that limits breed innovation and creativity. They usher in freedom and joy as you relax into the borders God places. They are good! They are perfect!

Most of all, limits protect and nurture you.

You read Psalm 16 again and thank Him that "the boundary lines for [you] have fallen in pleasant places; surely [you] have a delightful inheritance!" You finally understand that God has "hemmed [you] in, behind and before" (Psalm 139) because He knows exactly what He's doing for our good and His glory.

Living with flair means we thank God for all our limits. We accept them and let Him work.

83. Even in the Not Yet

This morning, my youngest takes me to the garden to see the very first blush of red on the huge strawberry in the patch.

Almost. Soon. In due time. I nearly turn away because it's not ripe yet.

But wait.

I spent so many years hurrying through the stages of motherhood. I spent so many years hurrying through the stages of my own life. I wanted the next thing. I wanted to chase the next great dream.

I realize that in all my hoping for the next thing, I often forget to live the life that's right here.

I pray that we love each and every stage—wherever, however, and whenever. Even in the unripe. Even in the not yet.

84. When God Asks You to Give What You Do Not Have

This morning in church, we read from 1 Kings 17 the story of the Widow at Zarephath. Elijah comes to her and asks of her what she does not have.

Elijah insists that she give him what she does not have (in this case a loaf of bread). And when the Widow acts in faith, God graciously and miraculously supplies flour that is not used up and oil that does not run dry.

Does God ask of me what I do not have in order that He may supply it? In order that He might usher me into that wondrous place of miracles?

It suddenly occurs to me that the life of faith begins when God asks something of me that requires absolute dependence upon Him. I do not have what it takes here. I do not have the resources or the talent. I do not have what you're asking of me, Lord!

He asks of me what I do not have in order that He may graciously, miraculously supply it.

85. Open Wide Your Mouth

I arrive at another Italian Mama's Lunch (this time, eggplant parmigiana, pesto, roasted peppers, mozzarelle, anchovies—and that's just the beginning), and I'm told to "bring a container" to take home the pizzelles.

Apparently, I severely underestimate what's in store.

"Oh, that's way too small," the hostess says, laughing as she eyes my small plastic Tupperware. "You'll need something much bigger."

When you're with the Italian Mamas, you have to remember abundance and over-the-top feasting. You have to remember that you'll get more than you can possibly contain.

I think about Psalm 81 again (just like I did with those baby Northern Cardinals), and I consider that sometimes, I just don't open my mouth wide enough to receive the abundant, over-the-top joy and blessing God has for me today.

I'm closed off. My container is way too small.

I feast on my stack of fresh homemade pizzelles, and I know the truth: God longs to be gracious to us (Isaiah 30), and He wants us to revel in His great goodness (Nehemiah 9).

When you're feasting with the Italian Mamas, you learn how to revel. You learn how to receive.

You just have to bring a big enough container.

86. **Stay Quiet, Look for Clues**

A writer's life has seasons, too. After output, you gather yourself back in, plant new seeds, and let things percolate deep inside until they're ready to emerge. You stay quiet. You think. You watch the snow fall and listen to music. You reread old poetry books.

You discover dusty old college papers about language—when poetry was a matter of life and death—and realize you can't recall what it felt like to experience things so deeply.

Back then, I used to walk around and quote Walt Whitman, and I wonder why twenty years later I don't.

Maybe I should.

I find these words of old Walt in college notes. He proclaims, "I fully believe in a clue and purpose in Nature, entire and several; and that invisible spiritual results, just as real and definite as the visible, eventuate all concrete life and all materialism."[15] His writing reminds me of my *Live with Flair* mission; I'm looking for clues, and I simply cannot stop.

I find myself loving poetry again, especially when Whitman explains, "The greatest poet hardly knows pettiness or triviality. If he breathes into any thing that was before thought small, it dilates with the grandeur and life of the universe."[16] Yes, let this very common day dilate with grandeur. Let us not know pettiness or triviality.

God's grandeur is here.

87. **"That will be enough for us."**

This morning before church, I read a paragraph in that little book, *We Would See Jesus* (Roy and Revel Hession) about all the ways we use Jesus as a means to an end. We might hope for great ministry, happiness and peace, freedom, ease, blessing, revival, or any other wonderful thing but just Jesus himself.[17]

The writers remark that Philip in the book of John begs Jesus to "show [them] the Father, and that will be enough for [them]." Then, Jesus claims that "He who has seen Me has seen the Father."

And, that, according to Philip is enough.

An encounter with God was enough.

Then in church, the pastor remarks that "nothing is better than an encounter with God." He jokes about how excited we get about retweets, likes on Facebook, or blog followers (hey, why not add on book contracts?). These things that we seek, when placed against encountering God, seem downright silly. Or what about other things like marriage partners or children or houses or careers or health? Great things, yes, but not the Greatest Thing.

Show us the Father, and that will be enough.

88. "He has reached the place where he is not thinking about himself anymore."[18]

The Freedom of Self-Forgetfulness: The Path to True Christian Joy, by Tim Keller, is a small little book that reorients the soul. I've been personally struggling with the writing life—the public writing life—because it feeds into a dark side of me. All the self-promotion! All the self-focus! How can I escape it? When I'm admired, it feels wrong. But I also find myself sad and jealous when I hear about the publishing successes of others. It feels like a terrible sickness in my soul either way.

This book provided a great answer. Keller talks about coming to the point where you stop thinking about yourself (successes or failures). You do things out of love because you're so secure and accepted in Christ. You aren't trying to prove you're special.

Keller writes, "Wouldn't you like to be the skater who wins the silver, and yet is thrilled about those three triple jumps that the gold medal winner did? To love it the way you love a sunrise? Just to love the fact that it was done? For it not to matter whether it was their success or your success. Not to care if they did it or you did it. You are as happy that they did it as if you had done it yourself—because you are just so happy to see it."[19]

He further explains that when folks live in the freedom of the gospel, they no longer attach accomplishment or failure to their identity. How wonderful!

Finally, I love what Keller says (in summary of C.S. Lewis), that when you meet truly humble people, you don't come away from them thinking about how humble they are. You leave their presence thinking "how much they seemed to be totally interested in [you]."[20]

My prayer is that I don't think great things of myself. Also that I don't think less of myself. I just don't want to think of myself much at all.

89. The Best Parenting Advice: Ask This Question

Two years ago, I asked a wise, older mother for her best parenting advice. I marveled at the way her grown children loved to talk with her and spend time with her. I marveled at how not one of them went through silent, rebellious years. I marveled at how open the children were about their own lives.

Her best advice? She told me to sit on the end of my daughter's bed every week and ask her if there's anything I've done to hurt her.

That's it. That's the simple question.

"Ask her if there's anything you need to apologize for and see what happens. Do this regularly."

The mother said that children close down when they're hurt.

They stop talking.

They don't want to be touched. They don't like to look at you.

The relationship suffers, and the hurt feelings just pile up until there's a huge wall between family members.

The wise mother says, "Parents often don't realize that they've hurt their children. To prevent a communication breakdown, simply ask if you've hurt them and seek their forgiveness."

In my mind, I'm thinking this: "Surely no. Me? Hurting my own daughter's heart? No. We're fine! All is well here."

But I promised to try it.

The first time I asked one daughter that question, she paused, looked up at me, and said, "Well, yes, actually. Remember this, this, this, and that? Remember when you said this and that and how you embarrassed me here and here?"

The list was long.

I apologized for each and every thing. I've been asking my daughters if I've hurt them in any way every few weeks, and each time, there's something I've done that I didn't perceive. When I apologize and make it right, suddenly, we're talking, hugging, and gazing right into each other's eyes. We want to be together again.

Asking my daughters this question might be the best parenting advice I've received in a long time.

90. Remember the Gamma Girls: A Must Read for Moms of Pre-Teen Daughters

I'm sitting at the kitchen table, doling out after-school snacks and casually talking to some preteen girls about their lives. I hear about the playground drama, the hurt feelings, and the popular girls who control the whole scene. (This is 5th grade, by the way.)

"You have to be gamma girls," I tell them, remembering my friend Kellie's advice about popularity and teen drama.

"What's a gamma girl?" one girl asks, chomping on trail mix.

"Well, one sociologist wrote about how the popular girls you see on the playground in their tight circle are the 'alpha girls.' The girls jumping all around them and trying to get their attention all day long—those are the 'beta girls'."

The girls nod.

"Then you have the gamma girls. These girls are smart, confident, creative, funny, and just plain awesome. They're out building forts in the woods, talking about literature and music, and enjoying their lives. These girls love their parents and God and don't care one bit about being popular."

It's like I've shared some deep secret, some key to unlock the universe for them.

The girls don't say a word, waiting for me to tell them more.

I pull up the "Meet the Gamma Girls" article from 2002, and I read some excerpts.[21] I remind the young girls that certain teen girls don't do drugs, get drunk, obsess over boys, or do poorly in school. They choose to be gamma girls. They have close friends, tons of ambition, and great relationships with their parents. And they are not popular.

That was it. End of conversation. The girls left and went to rescue that baby squirrel.

Four days later, a mom finds me and gives me a big hug. She tells me how her daughter was on the playground trying so hard to get the attention of the popular girls. The daughter said: "They kept abandoning me and walking away."

163

I imagine the pointing and whispering. I imagine the gossip. I imagine the girl standing on the outside, wishing with all her heart to be popular.

"My daughter told me that she stood there, and all of a sudden she said to herself, 'I'm not doing this anymore. I don't have to be alpha or beta. I can be a gamma girl'."

The mom tells me that then, her daughter looked around the playground to observe who was actually having fun. She ran to where some creative kids were building forts and talking about their spelling tests. She was warmly welcomed and spent the afternoon enjoying herself with girls who couldn't care less what the popular girls were doing.

Besides, who has time for drama when you want to write a new song on your guitar, hang out with your family, make cupcakes with your friends, and play with your little sister?

There's another way to be.

91. "God will fulfill His purpose for me." Psalm 138:8

I've been taking great comfort in a simple truth from scripture. In Psalm 138, David claims, "God will fulfill His purpose for me."

It's true. I don't have to worry. As I think about all the times in the Bible that "purpose" occurs, I remember that nobody can thwart God's purposes.

Nobody. And nothing.

The Lord's purposes prevail.

They do.

In another translation, I read that "God will accomplish all that concerns me."

When I think about all that comes against the child of God—rejection, discouragement, disappointment, suffering, death, depression, and every terrible thing—I remind myself that God fulfills His purposes for us.

92. To the Cynic

I'm studying cynicism. It's the philosophy of the day amongst many college students, and I wonder how to combat it. Cynicism is trendy. It's so very sophisticated to be detached, sarcastic, pessimistic, suspicious, negative, and bitter.

It seems so intellectual. The cynic recognizes the fake because it's all fake to her. It's all hopeless and pointless. The best the cynic can do is to detach and complain. She pretends she's outside of the system so she can criticize with supreme arrogance.

When the cynic meets me—in all my flair—she finds I'm naive, Pollyanna, and filled with false hope. She can't believe I actually believe the Bible or in any type of God for that matter. She rolls her eyes at my optimism and my sincere hope. She's angered by my unshakeable belief in beauty, wonder, and joyful living.

She hates me. I remind her of something she wants to forget.

It's called hope.

The author Michael Crawley wrote this: "A cynic is a coward .... Cynicism always takes the easy way out. It is a form of laziness that provides someone with an excuse for not making any attempt to change the world. . . Cynicism is a way to hide. . . Cynics are afraid . . . So, instead, they pass judgment on anyone who is trying to make a difference. They ridicule the efforts of individuals and organizations that are working hard under incredibly difficult circumstances . . . Being cynical is often thought of as being composed and detached. It is considered to be a sign of sophistication. Cynics are mistakenly given credit for possessing a deep awareness regarding the limits of what humans can accomplish which is somehow lacking in those who spend their time in passionate efforts to change the world .... Being filled with cynicism is indeed a cowardly and sad way to go through life."[22]

I want brave. I want to change the world. I press on into the hope even more. Maybe the cynic will give hope a chance today. Besides, today already has too much wonder and joy to fill a million blog posts. Don't get me started.

93. Warning: What Not to Do With Your Restless Heart

Every few years, I grow restless.

I begin to believe that a more exciting life exists in another town or in another career. My soul feels sick inside, and my imagination tells me I'm living the wrong life. My instincts tell me to beg my husband to take our family and flee. Everything in me believes something must change.

This week, I hear the gentle admonition: *Do not flee. Do not change.*

I'm learning instead to settle deeper into my own soul. The restless heart isn't a cry for new and different; it's a longing for truth. It's a longing to go even further into the restlessness till you strike pure gold.

I'm not there yet. I write things in my journal about whether I'd stake my life on the truth that Jesus brings the life that is truly life; that you lose your life and find it; that you come to God and never thirst again; and that the restlessness is there to drive you to a different kind of vibrant living.

Yes. Yes, these things are true.

Do not flee. Go deeper in.

I'm wandering the garden, and I see the stakes around my blueberry bush. I observe the impenetrable netting that keeps the birds away. The beautiful bush is trapped on all sides except one: beneath her. So she sends down roots so unimaginably strong. And within the cage, she produces the kind of fruit only possible here.

After all, these boundaries are protection. They exist to ensure her fruitfulness.

When I feel restless, I send down roots instead. I go deeper into the very soil I think holds me back, and I rejoice in the pleasant boundaries around my life.

94. Something to Enchant the Rest of Your Life

Today I recall E.O. Wilson's confession in his memoir, *Naturalist*, that his searching the sea for mysterious creatures was really about something else. He says, "I also hoped for more than sharks, what exactly I could not say: something to enchant the rest of my life."[23]

Aren't we all searching like that? Aren't we all secretly hoping to come upon the sort of mystery and beauty that will fascinate and enchant our whole lives?

As I think about my love of art, music, poetry, and theater, I know I love it because it fascinates. It enchants. But it cannot be the end. I remember the way C.S. Lewis came to know Jesus. He was searching for a form of enchantment he called Joy, but he realizes that everything he observed or experienced was a reminder of God—the Real Joy.[24]

I think about the most incredible sights and the most sublime experiences I might have on this earth; even the very best is a shadow or an imprint of something far grander. Every wonderful thing gestures back to God.

When I encounter beauty, I remember it's a imprint. It's a reminder.

Everything we experience—the best of it, the absolute most enchanting thing—is simply a signpost pointing to God.

I believe I have found something to enchant the rest of my life.

95. 10 Things You Learn About Healing When You Raise a Wounded, One-Eyed Cat

A few nights ago, Jack starts pushing his nose against us and rubbing our legs with his face as we approach him. As a classic cat declaration of ownership, this behavior is Jack claiming we belong to him.

It's authoritative. It's bold. It's a way of leaving a territorial mark upon us.

He never did this when we first took him in.

If you remember his journey, healing came slowly and curiously. With one eye, a broken tail, an infected mouth, and no interest in being his true cat self, he seemed half-alive.

And then—then!—he learned to purr again. He figured out how to meow and finally spoke to us one day in the kitchen. Then, he began caring for another cat. One day, he stood up to our dominant cat. A month later, instead of moping, I found him basking. Sometimes, his wounded eye would leak, and I felt like we were back to square one. He then learned to do things normal cats do that he had forgotten. Then, he bonded with our cat, Snowflake, began napping only with her, and seemed he had found his true love.

And now, he's rising up and declaring what belongs to him.

As I think about healing processes, I've learned some things from Jack:

1. Wounded cats (and people) slowly find their voices.
2. They'll cry out when they're ready.
3. Part of healing is caring for others.
4. You have to stand up for yourself and your needs.

5. Begin to worship again. Let yourself experience beauty.
6. You'll have setbacks.
7. You'll remember what it feels like to be healthy.
8. You'll find friends.
9. You'll let yourself love and be loved again.
10. And finally, you'll be strong enough to claim who you are and where you belong with a particular type of authority.

I love my little wounded cat.

96. Praying Away the Thing You Should Welcome

I had just been lamenting the fact that ladybugs will most certainly bother me again as spring turns to summer. It drives me crazy when they sneak in the windows and end up in my house. One year, the whole wall seemed covered with them.

Another year, I spent each week vacuuming more dead ladybugs than you can imagine.

Oh, the ladybugs drive me crazy! Oh, Lord, just send them away!

Later, I'm out in my yard near my most precious Winterberry Bush, and I notice a sticky substance on each leaf. Then, I see them.

Black aphids everywhere! They're eating my bush!

But then, I see what's eating the aphids: ladybugs.

Come, ladybugs! You're welcome here! We love you! I know you are the predator of the very thing I need removed!

I wonder how many things I pray away that I should welcome instead.

97. A Spiritual Lesson from My Compost Bin

I stick my hand into my compost pile to pull back a space to dump some more fruit peelings, coffee grounds, eggshells, and vegetables.

It's so hot in there under the leaves and grass that I actually pull my hand back in shock.

(Aerobic bacteria that's breaking down my bucket of offerings releases so much heat as it works. Decomposition isn't easy. It's hot work. It's a smoldering mound that you can't use for a long time.)

"It's working! It's really working!" I tell my chemist husband who agrees it shocked him the first time he felt the heat of composting. The heat is a sign of conversion: what we put into the pile transforms into nutrient-rich soil that allows our garden to bear glorious fruit.

In the process of breaking things down inside my own heart—of purifying, refining, and becoming a useful vessel for divine activity, I remember that in that dark space of change, it's real work. There's a heat involved in that refiner's fire—that compositing bin—that lets me know I'm changing.

It's working.

It might take a long time, but I can feel the heat in my own heart.

98. It's Sort of Awkward

My youngest daughter shares the incredible news: The classroom eggs have hatched!

"Wow! What was it like?" I ask. I've never actually seen anything hatch before— at least I can't remember that I have. I imagine it's very fast. A few taps, and then the duck just comes out.

That's how I want it to be. I imagine a little tap, chirping, and a beautiful fuzzy duckling popping out.

"It's takes an hour," she reports.

"A whole hour?"

"Yes!"

We watch the tail end of the hatching video her teacher records and posts.

It's not pretty. It's sort of awkward, time-consuming, and unattractive. It's floppy and strange.

I suppose we imagine our own hatchings into God's new plans for us to be very fast. I think of suddenly arriving into some new part of my life with ease, beauty, and speed.

No. I think it's more awkward, time-consuming, and not always attractive. But once you dry your feathers, get your bearings, and shove off that shell, you finally do come into your own. It's just not struggle-free. It's just not quick.

99. Life Changing Advice for the Exhausted and Irritable: Stay at 60%

This morning, my friend tells me her secret for sanity in the midst of pursuing a Ph.D., raising young children, maintaining a great marriage, and hosting neighborhood events.

"I live at 60%."

"What do you mean?" I turn to her, curious, and confused.

"Some women live their lives at 90% capacity. They are already nearly at their energy expenditure limit each day. So when a new stressor adds into the mix, they explode. They go ballistic. They're atomic bombs that go off in their own homes."

"That was me last night," I confessed. The tiniest comment from a child set me off into tears.

"But if you live at 60% of your energy capacity, you're ensuring you have buffer for emergencies and any changes. You're able to deal with life as it happens. You have reserves."

She walks on, smooth and carefree, while I'm chasing after her to learn more.

"How do you live at 60%? What's the secret?"

"Well, I was chronically ill for six years, so I know how to ask myself what I have to offer energy-wise each day. Then, I do even less to protect myself from what might come. I say 'no' a lot. And I know what I need to reenergize."

She lives less than what she's actually capable of each day. Instead of do more, it's do less.

I live at 99%, nearly maxed out, wild, multi-tasking, over-producing, checking-off-my-to-do-list kind of living.
I want to live at 60%. I need to live at 60%. I think I need to slow my own children down as well.

I don't want to snap at my family because I have no reserves. I don't want to raise my voice because I'm maxed out. I don't want to fret when the car needs repair, if dinner burns, or if a supervisor gives me a new assignment.

Today, I slow down. I don't jam everything in. And sure enough, at 2:00 PM, a neighbor calls with an emergency. I was ready. I had energy to spare.

The Robin knows this. I check the nest today, and she has stopped laying eggs. The nest, with four gorgeous eggs, is at capacity. Natural processes tend to stick within their boundaries. Animals rarely do too much on purpose.

Living with flair means living at 60%.

100. Not If But When: The Fine Art of Expectancy

Years ago, folks would ask me if I was going to write a blog that day.

Now, they ask not if but when. When will the moment arrive? What will the flair be?

Not if but when.

There's really no question now. It's going to happen. No more if. No more doubting. We move from doubting to waiting.

And then from waiting to watching.

And then from watching to seeing.

And then from seeing to proclaiming.

I don't live in if anymore.

Summer

I will praise the Lord, for He has dealt bountifully with me.

Psalm 13:6

1. Fire Ants

I'm walking in an area where fire ants bite us as we travel from the front porch to where our cars are parked. A fire ant bite can be extremely painful and, for those of us with allergies to bites and stings, potentially deadly.

A family member calls out: "Just keep movin'! They won't get ya if you just keep movin'! It's when you stop that those fire ants get into your shoes!"

It becomes a family joke whenever we leave the car. "Just keep movin'!" we repeat, laughing but also running to the porch as fast as we can.

Something about that phrase made the flair bells ring. To avoid those ants, it's absolutely critical that I don't stay in one place. I have to move. I can't be stagnant or else trouble comes.

If you look up the word "stagnant" you'll find it means this: *Lacking freshness, motion, flow, progress, or change; stale.*

I want a life that moves. I want motion, flow, progress, and change. I want fresh. As I age, I realize I have to create motion. I have to choose progress and flow. Maybe it means I read a new book or find a new friend. Or it means I learn a new skill. Or I learn a new dance.

Left to themselves, things do stagnate. Without thinking, I could stay right here, doing nothing. And in that place of *stale*, unwanted things invade and take over—like fire ants. Friendships, marriage, parent-child relationships, spiritual growth, my relationship to myself, my relationship to the natural world, my teaching, my writing—it can all stagnate unless I develop a plan for fresh flow.

Living with flair means creating fresh flow. It means running like crazy so the fire ants don't get into my shoes. Whatever it takes, I want to avoid that sting of stale.

2. Feeling Homesick at Home

Sometimes I feel homesick. It's not for any particular home or family.

It's the weirdest feeling. I'll be sitting there, doing the dishes or folding laundry, and I'll feel that something is horribly wrong. I'm in the wrong place, and everything feels sad, and I just need to take my husband and children and *get home.*

I feel like the wild daisy in A.R. Ammons's poem, "Loss." He describes a wild daisy "half-wild with loss" who turns "any way the wind does" and lifts up her petals to float off her stem and *go*.[1]

It's an image of terrible longing.

What must it feel like to be rooted nowhere, to belong nowhere, and move like that with the chaos of the wind? Some of us live that way simply because we don't know where to put down roots. We can't find a sure place to land. On those days, we are wanderers, and even if we have the strongest physical sense of home and place, we still feel lost at sea.

There's a homesickness in our soul, even on our best days.

So I'm doing the dishes, longing for *home*, and I recall Frederick Buechner's book by the same title. Buechner's writing soothes my soul because he says we are *all* longing for a spiritual home. The sense of belonging and rightness comes when we put down deep spiritual, not just physical, roots.

Maybe there's hope for me.

Buechner's book, *The Longing for Home*, reminds me how narrow my ideas of home are.[2]

My home is not my house.

That homesick feeling is a cry for heaven, my real home. I remember the great statement by the psalmist in Psalm 90. He writes, "Lord, you have been our dwelling place."

The Lord is our dwelling place! We are "in Him." It's mysterious, sublime, and wonderfully comforting. No matter where I am, I am at home in God. I'm dwelling in Him.

He is my refuge. He is my fortress. He is my home. Home is inside of me.

This is how I manage my homesick feelings:

I can find my home in this very day, with God, and belong somewhere while I long for *Home*.

Living with flair means I find that internal home, even while wandering here below.

3. Swimming Beneath the Geese

I'm swimming in a lake with my daughters, and another family nearby starts feeding the geese. Within seconds, a gaggle surrounds us. They come from every direction, leaving the shore and their organized formations across the lake. Our heads bob along in the water right against their soft, wild feathers. I'm so close that I can look into those deep black eyes and touch the fuzzy heads of the goslings.

It doesn't seem right how close we are. It seems other-worldly. We aren't separate from the wild; we're swimming along with it.

The family with the goose food offers me a handful. If I'm *still* enough, someone tells me, the geese will eat from my hand.

And so I am. And so they do.

I'm told we can swim *under* the geese and even touch their webbed feet. Because the geese are used to floating logs and debris, they don't mind when you *hold* their feet. My daughter tightens her goggles and dives under the surface to swim beneath the geese.

She reaches out, and she holds them.

My five year old has pink goggles that sit on the pier. My husband tosses them out to me, and I dive deep under the gaggle, turn myself over, and look up towards the heavens. It's all feathers, little webbed feet, and the jeweled water swirling above my head as the sun shines down.

I stored that experience away, like I hope my daughters did, in that place in my imagination reserved for the magical, the heavenly, and the purely happy. Maybe one day, when life bears down on my children with that weight of sadness that comes to us all eventually, in its own way, they would recall this morning swim beneath the geese. They could live again in that moment when something rare and beautiful happened. And they'd catch it—all feathered, webbed, and jeweled—in their hands.

It could be their flair for that day.

4. Of Courage and Second Chances

I had a huge revelation while shampooing my hair this morning:

I keep praying for God to save my daughter from mean girls, teasing, and any and every bit of suffering. I've spent eleven years protecting her, caring for her, and using all my energy to keep her happy. And now, it's middle school. It's a whole new ball game. As we transition to summer, I realize how tired my prayer has become.

So I begin the same old prayer, and then I stop mid-rinse.

No. This isn't quite right.

The better prayer is that God would be with her—that she'd experience His power and presence right in the middle of all the drama. There's no end to drama; my supposedly mature and wiser self experiences the exact same kind of exclusion, cliques, and general mean-spirited behavior from adults.

The secret isn't about creating a life that shields us from any drama. The secret is abiding with God *in the midst of it.*

In that presence is fullness of joy. In that presence is peace. In that presence we overcome.

Suddenly, peace fills my own heart. My daughter just might have a great day today, or she just might experience teasing (towards her or others), but either way, God is with her.

Besides, she is learning to stand up to mean people. And when she doesn't—because of fear or feeling "weird" that she champions kindness—she prays for second chances to be that one girl who has the courage to say, "Hey, let's stop gossiping and invite the one sitting alone to come eat lunch with us."

5. A Stranger Tells Me His Secret

Many of my flair moments in the past 90 days occurred during conversations with strangers: the tired woman at the grocery store, the neighborhood boy, the hard-working Amish man, the precious waitress who gave my daughter a bad day mantra, the mean people at the drive-thru, that wonderful unknown woman who gave me the compliment that changed my life, the curious woman and her service dog, the man at Starbucks, the man chasing trash in the parking lot, or the little boy explaining why he loves the rain because it makes the worms come out.

Remembering these conversations—and the flair they brought forth—reminds me to challenge myself to engage more with people who cross my path.

There's flair there, I just know it.

I am leaving a restaurant, and a man whose job it is to hold open the door greets me with a big smile. He proudly holds open the door with such gusto I have to stop.

"Thank you!" I say happily. And then again: "Thank you *so much*."

He smiles bigger (if that were even possible). This employee is happier than he should be in this heat with this on-your-feet job. I have to find out why.

I say, "When you hold the door like that, it makes us all feel like celebrities."

He frowns and shakes his head. He says, "You should feel like that *all* the time, not just when somebody is holding a door."

"All the time? How is that possible?" I say, my arms crossed. The rest of my party is already in the parking lot, and I'm hanging around to talk to a strangely happy man.

"Above ground," he says softly.

"Huh?"

"Above ground," he repeats.

I lean in and whisper, "What in the world does that mean?" People stream past us, a whole crowd of them, and I'm ducking my head back and forth to try and maintain eye contact.

He waves his hands like he's shooing me away. I stand my ground.

"I'd have to explain it and it takes too long," he said.

"Well," I say, raising my eyebrows. This was flair, and I wasn't about to leave it.

"OK," he says, the crowd thinning so he can give me some time.

"You just say to yourself that you're *above ground*. You aren't stuck where you are, on this ground. It's not about where your feet are or where you are hanging out. You can be above it—above it all. You are *above ground*. Do you get it? It's not about where you are or what you are doing. That's why you can be the celebrity every day."

He's already on to other parties. He's like a rock star that bothered to take a moment to talk to the little people. He's big stuff, the real deal, and he's *happy*.

And I'm writing down his words, learning from a stranger, because he was there, *above ground*, holding the door for me.

6. What Gets You Out of Balance?

A couple of days ago, everybody complained about the water in the pool. After a rainstorm, the pH levels of our public pool were "off." Our eyes stung, the water felt weird, and some people complained that their bathing suits were changing color. It was strange. The pool staff adjusted the pH, but it still took time to stabilize.

I learned how sensitive a swimming pool can be. Did you know the pool levels need to be monitored daily, sometimes several times a day? Did you know how easily the pH levels change? I had no idea. I had no idea the *delicate balance* of chemicals involved in daily pool maintenance. It's a lot of work! And results don't come immediately. Sometimes it takes 24 hours for a pool's normal pH to be restored after an imbalance.

I liked learning that about my pool. My pool's imbalances remind me of my own. It's not so strange to monitor my well-being daily, sometimes several times a day, and recalibrate based on what's out of balance. I'm like a lifeguard holding that chemical kit and pH tester. I'm armed with tools to get myself back in balance.

If I'm not feeling good, if the family is stressed out, or if we aren't experiencing peace and joy, we stop and ask: "What's out of balance?"
Then we recalibrate. Sometimes, we recalibrate twice a day. We make any and all adjustments to find balance again.

Just as rainwater and outside chemicals and debris radically alter the pool's functioning, I've learned after all these years 10 things that get me "out of balance." I wonder if you could add something to my list.

I don't feel so happy! I wonder:

1. Have I had too much junk food, sugar, or processed food?

2. Have I had enough sleep?

3. Have I had time to pray and connect with God?

4. Have I exercised in the last 48 hours?

5. Have I deeply connected with my husband and each child recently?

6. Have I had enough social time with friends? Have I had too much?

7. Have I had a creative outlet in the last few days?

8. Have I conversed with too many toxic people (manipulative, guilt-trippers, complainers, gossipers) in my day?

9. Have I assumed too many responsibilities and not delegated enough? (Especially when it comes to keeping an organized and clean home—I don't have to do *all* the housework, ever)

10. Have I let my mind wander and create irrational future scenarios of doom (finances, health, etc.)?

What sort of things get you out of balance? What brings your mood down most of all? I'd love to hear what else we could ask ourselves to check our "balance levels." Living with flair means learning to monitor myself, ask what's out of balance, and then, recalibrate.

7. In Only Five Minutes

I look up at the clock and realize I haven't posted my blog, and my personal deadline is 5:00 PM. There's no real punishment for not blogging every day; nobody penalizes me, and most people just don't care one way or another.

But I care! I love having that moment of reflection just to ask what great thing happened—what moment of flair—that's worth sharing. After all these days of finding that thing, I'm amazed I just simply forgot to think about it today.

Can you believe it?

But I still have five minutes left of this blogging day.

In five minutes, I *remember*.

I remember to reflect. With four minutes left now, I think of the deep purple in the blackberry cobbler we ate, the sweet forgiveness we all had to ask of each other, the cool blue neighborhood pool, and the great storm cloud that hovered over it. I'll never have this day again. You'll never have this day again. What made it shimmer for you?

I have two minutes now, and I think about how tomorrow and every day after that, I'm pushing as far into my experience as I can to find that *one beautiful thing.*

One minute left.

Living with flair means we remember not to forget. I can't skate on the surface of my life any more. I want to dive deeply into it, even if I only have five minutes to do so.

8. The Fame That Lasts Till Lunch

My daughter tried out for the end of the year talent show yesterday.

I'm amazed that she would do this. *Amazed.*

Last year, she didn't receive even one vote from her class for her dance routine. (It was freestylin' to "Accidentally in Love"—the worm, the spins on your bottom—I'll spare you the details because she would want me to.)

And this year has been heartbreak. The mean girls! The fickle crowd! When she told me she planned to audition in front of her class, I wanted to scream: "Are you crazy, foolish child? Will you cast yourself to the lions? Let's preserve what little reputation you have left! You will be devoured and humiliated! Stay safe in my arms! You've endured enough!" I knew she'd be competing against a kid with magic tricks and a girl with years of elite gymnastics training.

She had no chance.

But she really wanted to audition.

So there I am, preparing mentally all day for her sure failure. I'm visualizing my parking space, closest to the school, so I can pick her up in my arms and carry her to the car so nobody can see her tears. I'm imagining a special comforting dessert that will await her homecoming. What helps a child recover from. . . losing?

She walks out of the school building, and I can hardly face her.

She calmly approaches me with a little folded piece of paper.

She doesn't say anything but just points to the note.

I unfold it and she's written in yellow marker: "I won the vote. Yay!"

Oh, me of little faith.

As we drive home, she tells me about the other acts and how nobody was that good. But when she performed her piano act (after dragging the class to the auditorium just so they could hear her 1 minute of music), everybody started cheering. *They voted for her. The hands went up in the air!*
What world is this where things go well for her? Did God hear my prayer, her music teacher's prayer, and all my frantic text message prayer requests to please pray for my daughter today?

I think so.

"How did it feel? Did you feel just great?" I asked her, beaming but definitely trying to hide my proud parent, over-the-top enthusiasm.

"It was awesome." She paused and looked out the window.

"But my fame ended by lunch time. People forget you."

She changed the subject and told me to look back to see her amazing ceramic turtle she made in art class. We were on to new adventures, new topics—art, her summer reading plan, and what computer games she wanted to play.

Whatever it was that allowed her to walk down that hallway to the auditorium, her little chin up, it's another thing I'm putting on *my version* of her résumé. Right next to "Survived Recess," I'm putting, "Auditioned in Front of Hostile 2nd Grade Crowd to Win Spot in School Talent Show Despite Totally Bombing Last Year's Dance Routine."

And I might add: "Learned that Fame Ends By Lunchtime so Don't Bother Wanting it So Badly"

That girl has flair. I would have never had the guts to do what she did.

And God answered an even better prayer than my superficial "grant her success." He showed my daughter that winning the love of the crowd doesn't last. And it shouldn't.

There are *much better* adventures awaiting.

9. Flair in the Terrible Storm

I practiced one of the oldest ways of storm forecasting today:

I watched the leaves.

As families hurried into church under a darkening sky this morning, my children clung to either side of me as I welcomed newcomers.

I looked out at that smolder of sky and clouds. Everything in sight seemed dark and braced for the worst.

Everything, that is, *except the leaves*. My daughter pointed outside and said, "Mama, the leaves are dancing." I smiled at the verb choice.

It was beautiful to watch. Dry leaves on the ground swirled up in this ballet of movement. And in the distance, every tree turned its leaves up, anticipating the storm. My friend who reads botany told me that the undersides of leaves contain stomata, or little pores, that help soak in moisture. When they turn up like that, they position themselves to receive nourishment from the sky.

"Can they turn themselves up?" I wondered aloud. I imagined little leaf arms that flexed tiny muscles to turn those leaves over. That would be so cool! So flair!

It turns out that the leaves don't do any of this themselves. The coming storm creates changes in pressure that actually move up from the ground and turn the leaves upside down. The atmosphere conspires, it seems, to force these leaves to receive from the heavens.

I looked again at those leaves, enabled like that with no effort on their part, to receive. As I turned to enter the sanctuary, I considered what it takes to stir those fallen leaves to dance and those branch leaves *to receive*. I know God brings the storm, the pressure system, to invite my undersides to be exposed, to turn me to the right position. From that place in the storm, I'm in the best place to receive what heaven pours down. Only from there can I dance in that particular storm's wind.

10. Reinvent the Course

I've been thinking about what it means to instruct, to offer suggestions, and to speak in the imperative mood. My love of verbs means I know they sometimes take the form of commands—*imperative* forms—that we use to express suggestions or advice. This morning, I used the imperative on myself. Here's what I said: *Reinvent the Course*

It's like I'm running, and potholes and roadblocks stop me in my tracks. I think to myself that it's all over. My dreams, my goals, my projects all fall apart with the slightest bit of discouragement. Sewn together in particular ways, my life dreams must take shape *exactly* as I form them.

But pull one thread, and the whole thing unravels.
At that moment with a heap of disaster uncoiled around my ankles, I'm learning to reinvent the course I was on and recalibrate till I'm aligned with what always turns out to be better and a much purer form of what I really wanted all along. For example, nothing in my life has ever come about in the right place, at the right time, and in the right form. But it always ends up being. . . *just right.*

I met my husband in the wrong place (he was supposed to be in the South), at the wrong time (finishing a Ph.D.—who has time?), and in the wrong form (where was his little poet pony tail and John Lennon spectacles?). But he was just right. *Exactly right.*

And children? Born in Michigan when my whole family was in Virginia, during my dissertation writing, and a girl instead of boy. But she's just right. *Exactly right.*

Or moving here in a mad rush to a house I never imagined in any dream. Or to a teaching career that came in the wrong place, at the wrong time, and in the wrong form. It was supposed to be a tenure track job at some Ivy League school. But teaching was the goal and God put it in the right place, at the right time, in the right form.

Finally, my publishing dreams. No book contract, no bestseller. And yet, I learned to reinvent the course. Blogging? And look! A half a million views from 77 different countries or territories. I didn't even know how to make a blog 125 days ago. I wanted to write, and maybe this new course would let me. It seems just right. *Exactly right.*

I think of life as a maze with only one path to my dreams. But it's not a maze. It's a beautiful landscape with trails we haven't even imagined. I'm just so thankful we have a Faithful Guide.

Living with flair means I'm discouraged when I have to reinvent the course.

11. A Solution to Insecurity

Today, I remembered something unique about God's economy. In Christianity, the more you give, the more you receive. The times when you feel last, you are actually first. The times you act as a servant, you become the leader.

I wonder about this upside down approach to living.

Some mornings, I feel the weight of various insecurities—mostly *relational* or *financial*. I worry about all sorts of relationships: family, friends, co-workers. And then I worry about financial things: what I need, what my children will need, what our future might require of our resources.

What a debilitating way to conduct myself during the day! Insecurity becomes a prison. Insecurity keeps my focus on *myself*—what I need, what I'm getting, and what I'm not getting. I feel insecure because of what I think I'm missing. What's the solution to insecurity?

Insecurity arises out of a heart that's concerned with what it's not getting. When I turn the kaleidoscope and focus on *what I can give, who I can love,* and *what I can provide* for others, I see the day in a whole new way. I stop worrying so much about myself because I'm living abundantly according to *spiritual* and not material principles.

I'm trying to teach my children that as long as they worry about who likes them and what they can accumulate, they will continue to live under the illusion of security. Their souls won't rest. But when they choose to love and give generously to others, miraculously, they find the kind of relational and financial security they seek. It's the model that Jesus teaches, however confusing and however counter-intuitive.

I pray we can have the wisdom to live like that.

12. What the Heart Needs Most

As I walk around the church parking lot today in the summer heat, I reflect on all the things I've been telling my husband I need and want in my life. These conversations are ridiculous. I'm such a brat! It gets so bad that sometimes I lament the fact that there's no good fine dining in this town or great live music. I get in these "if only" kinds of conversations: If only we lived in a big city. If only we owned this house. If only this happened, if only that happened. . .

I'm so focused on what I need all the time. As you know, I'm always asking my heart what it's missing because I'm a walking existential crisis. I've already confessed this problem to you, so bear with me.

I decide to ask God to show me *what the heart needs most of all.* I was inspired to ask such a question because I was reading Hannah Whitall Smith again this morning, and I love how she asks God to reveal to her the "secret" of a happy life. She wanted happiness! She was tired of miserable Christians who walked around in perpetual angst (oh, she would have been so annoyed with me). She wrote a whole book on God's answer to her question about happiness called *The Christian Secret of a Happy Life*.[3]

But back to my question to God. I'm tired of perpetual angst (even if it is part of the poetic sensibility, the divine madness of the artist, and the dreary lot of the writer). I'm tired of struggling so much for peace in my heart. I'm tired of not even knowing the answer to a question two different friends asked me this week. They looked at me with such love in their eyes and said, "Heather, what do you really want?"

What do I really want, God?

As I'm rounding the corner, I imagine God answering me. I think of this truth:

I think of how David begs God in Psalm 51:12, "Restore to me the joy of your salvation." He doesn't ask for more friends, more wealth, more wisdom, a different city, live music, fine dining, or more fruitfulness. *He asks God to restore the joy of salvation to him.* What the heart needs most is the joy of our salvation!

I think about this as I walk, and the fog clears inside of me. Everything I most desperately want, I already have: the righteousness of Christ, the immediate and unmediated access to God, and the knowing and being known by a Savior. Yes, forgiveness of sin that separates me from God—this is what I most desperately need. And because I have it already, I ask God to restore the truth of it to me, the pure and raw joy of it.

When I lose my focus and wonder what I'm missing, I'm going to think about this summer morning walk and how I remembered the joy of my salvation. It was a great little walk with God.

13. Why We Need Impossible Goals

I remembered lines from Lewis Carroll's characters this morning about "impossible things."

Alice laughed. "There's no use trying," she said, "one can't believe impossible things."

"I daresay you haven't had much practice," said the Queen. "When I was your age, I always did it for half-an-hour a day. Why sometimes I believed as many as six impossible things before breakfast!"[4]

A few hours ago, someone tried to encourage me by telling me I should set a goal I think I can't achieve. What?! That doesn't make any sense! A goal I think I *can't* achieve? Isn't that a recipe for failure, hopelessness, and shame?

I thought about it more. Something about setting an *impossible* goal, one I think I can't accomplish, sets me up for an extraordinary challenge. It's not a great goal if I know I can reach it. But if there's doubt in my mind—if there's the potential for devastating failure—then that's an honest goal.

That kind of goal-setting beckons a life of adventure, faith, and *flair*. It lets God in.

I remembered today that God specializes in impossible things.

I called one of my best writing friends during my late morning rest between dusting and vacuuming. She said that she was going "to pray for three impossible things today." We talked about the impossible dreams we have for our children and for our own lives.

Why not dream big? Why not set impossible goals and just see what we're capable of and what God does in that moment of extraordinary belief? I want to believe six impossible things before breakfast. That seems a lot like living with flair.

What seems impossible might just not be.

14. A Science Experiment About My Mood

Last night we picked wild Queen Anne's Lace for a science experiment. I wanted to show the girls how capillary action works.

The stem of the Queen Anne's Lace in a cup of dyed water will, within a few hours, suck the water up into the flower and turn it the same color as the dyed water.

We put our Queen Anne's Lace in water dyed dark purple, neon blue, and pink. This morning, sure enough, the flowers were the same color as the water.

Amazing! The color was striking, and it occurred to me how trusting the Queen Anne's Lace is, how *indiscriminate*. Whatever liquid environment you place the stems in, they draw it in deep within themselves and assume that color.
I imagine my living room as one big vase of water and my family as Queen Anne's Lace. I'm thinking about what they draw in from me, from my attitude, my hope, my flair.

It's just too easy for the stem to draw in whatever it's near—no matter what shade. Hopefully, that color is bright and joyful.

15. What Only Slow Makes Happen

We're growing many unusual things in our garden, things like artichokes and radishes and eggplant. Every morning, barefoot and chilly, we all go to the garden to check the progress of things. The basil is growing well, and so are the tomatoes. We find little blossoms on the peppers and the cucumbers. The carrot seeds have finally sprouted across from the beans.

It's a funny concept, but we go out there to *love* our little garden and encourage it.

We've harvested enough strawberries to freeze two bags for winter pies. Blueberries ripen alongside the flowering blackberries and raspberries.

It's a *slow* kind of thing that's full of love and gentle care. Even the composted dirt is a slow kind of thing.

Slow, slow, slow.

I love the patience of it and the way I feel when I'm out in the garden. The Slow Food Movement agrees, and I'm having a good time learning all about it. I want slowness to seep into other areas of my life because if you know me, I'm the exact opposite of slow! There's no slow in me at all! Well, maybe there's some.

I've been a proponent of Slow Parenting (I didn't know that was a real thing) for all these years, and I learn today that in addition to Slow Food and Parenting, you can have Slow Church, Slow Art, and all sorts of other Slow Things.[5] It's all about slowing down one's pace to *savor*. It's about relationships and community and not over-scheduling. It's about natural processes and having the time and space to let God work.

You can't rush God, and you don't want to.

It's about loving well because you have the time and space to let things unfold. Most of the beautiful things happening in my life come from *slow* things. The walk-to-school community, for example, has wasted thousands upon thousands of hours when we might have just dropped off children from our minivans. Instead, we've savored our friendships and our neighborhood because we took some time for a slow walk to gather up all the children. On that slow walk, we talk and talk. We laugh and observe.

We grow in ways that only *slow* can make happen.

16. The Spiritual Principle from My Hair

Our hair is dry and completely damaged by all the chlorine we swim in.

I've tried special shampoos and various conditioners, but nothing seems to repair that absolutely stiff-as-straw, greenish hair adorning my daughters' heads.

I decided to do some research. I found out that if you wet your hair in the shower first, you help prevent some of the chlorine damage. Apparently, if you let pure water saturate your hair, the strands swell, and this prevents them from soaking up the chlorinated water. The hair just isn't thirsty for it.

I kept thinking of the devotional literature I read in the morning. I've been trying to saturate my mind with good things every morning. I think about my heart swelling up with true, right, noble, and lovely things.

Soaked like this, I'm not thirsty in a way that will damage me. I'm not thirsty in the way that lets whatever is nearest, most available, and most naturally compelling *in*. Chlorine, for example, strips the hair of protective oils and dries everything out. The hair thirstily takes in what actually dries it up. That kind of quenching creates more thirst and *damages*.

My hair is teaching me a spiritual principle that I want to remember: Saturate and swell with the Good. Then I'm not thirstily soaking up what damages.

Living with flair means I saturate and swell and soak up the good.

17. "Missing this, we miss everything."

I find myself reading the old classic, *We Would See Jesus*. In the introduction, the authors make the claim that if you miss the concept of grace in coming to Jesus, you've missed everything.

In fact, they argue that, "the moment we have to do something to make ourselves more acceptable to God, or the moment we have to have a certain feeling or attribute of character in order to be blessed by God, then grace is no longer grace."[6]

We have nothing to offer. Everything is bestowed freely because of Jesus. If we miss this, we miss everything.

18. Writing Atop a Double-Decker Bus with Wi-Fi

I'm doing something I've never done before: I'm riding atop a double-decker bus on the way to Manhattan.

I'm with complete strangers. But here's what I know:

The woman beside me was homecoming queen, and I know the whole story about the boy she met when she was 14 who visited, only in the summers, his grandparents who were her neighbors. I know about their long distance relationship, the time they broke up after they already paid for airline tickets to visit Chicago, and how, even though they doubted the other would actually still go, they found each other in that city and fell in love again.

I also watched a storm brew through the windows above my head with the older man next to me. He has a hearing aid, and I'm not sure would speak if I engaged him, but when that storm barreled in, he glanced at me, looked back up at the dark clouds, again at me, and then back again. We both saw it happening, and this was important.

I had 15 minutes at a truck stop, and I was late because I was listening to a man describe his writing project. The bus driver came in to find me. He looked down at me, shook his head, and smiled.

For the woman who hates to travel, I'm learning to find buried treasure in the people around me.

I'm having the time of my life, and we are just in New Jersey.

19. How to Live in Luxury

Luxurious or lavish things do not need to be *expensive*.

I'm learning that luxury can be sought in the right mindset. There's something biblical about luxury properly applied. But, by definition, luxurious implies indulgent, excessively expensive, and unnecessary.

Even the word seems excessive. The way it sounds seems. . . *luxurious.*

The word connotes an entire world of very fine and very unobtainable things. But in my house, we use the word to mean anything rich in goodness and superior in quality. We can make luxurious fruit tarts and paint our toenails with luxurious colors. We can lay out in the grass, luxuriously, and watch the lightning bugs. We can swim in the public pool with luxurious backstrokes. We won't be on boats or eating fine chocolates today. We won't be vacationing on a far off island.

And that's fine.

There's something so uncertain about wealth and luxury. Today, as I was painting my daughter's fingernails with the cheapest bottle of bright pink, I remembered one of my favorite Bible verses from the book of Timothy:

"Command those who are rich in this present world not to be arrogant nor to put their hope in wealth, which is so uncertain, but to put their hope in God, who richly provides us with everything for our enjoyment."

Does God really richly provide everything for our enjoyment? Not for our needs, but for our *enjoyment*? How lavish! How luxurious! This means I only have to wait and see what luxurious experience God might send my way today.

Maybe it's the gorgeous deep purple blossoms on the eggplant I'm growing outside. I've never grown eggplant before, and I'm amazed by how beautiful it is. And the fruit hasn't even come yet. Eggplant is excessive and probably unnecessary (although I did learn how to make Eggplant Parmesan), but my goodness, I love those blossoms.

Thank you, God, for the luxury of purple eggplant blossoms. They have flair indeed.

20. To Get a Great Thing, You Have to Lose a Great Thing

Last night, I explained to my sister how my new 5:30 AM wake up routine meant that I have lost my night life. I was snuggling up in bed at 8:30 PM before even my children were sleeping. She quoted someone I can't remember (can you? Maybe Tom Brokaw?) who said:

"Sometimes to get a great thing, you have to lose a great thing."

All morning, I'm reminding myself that every yes is a no somewhere else. The great thing I want means a *loss* somewhere else.

And this is perfectly reasonable, good, and right.
Marriage, children, working part-time, waking up early—there are *losses* associated with these choices. But nobody talks about them enough.

Nobody tells you what it will feel like to get the great thing you want.

They don't talk about what you will lose in the getting of it. Maybe if we did, we could understand more fully the weight of our decisions and the flip side of every "yes."

What great loss do I need to consider, weigh, and let go of? I'm reminded of what it costs me to embrace God, marriage, children, my health, my work, my community with radical commitment.

When things cost me nothing, are they really *great things*?

Living with flair means that sometimes to get a great thing, I will lose a great thing.

And that's what makes it a *great thing*.

21. 4 Questions to Protect Yourself

Our family has been on a mission ever since Monday.

Monday afternoon at precisely 2:20 PM, I look out at my beautiful garden and smile at the huge squash, the cauliflower, the tomatoes, the cucumbers, the eggplant, the herbs.

Then, I see him.

He's literally looking up at me with a smirk on his face, holding a juicy cucumber between his paws.

I start screaming and waving my arms in front of the window. I run like a mad woman down the stairs and out into the yard. The groundhog merely saunters off and finds refuge under our back porch.

He's huge. He's eaten all my cauliflower, stripped the green beans, destroyed the squash, and decimated the cucumber.

We gather the family together and set up garden surveillance. My children watch from the window and begin making a list of questions like:

1. How does the thief enter?

2. When does he come?

3. What attracts him to the garden?

4. What will keep him out?

My dear, dear husband puts up a beautiful fence that very night. But the thief knows how to tear through the wooden fence. He can also dig underneath it. So my dear, dear husband returns from the store with chicken wire that buries deep into the ground and ascends up high around the garden.

Finally, we can sleep easy. What's left of the garden can grow in peace and produce a bountiful crop.

All day, I've been considering the vigilance of our family against this intruder. It was silly. But what isn't silly is *real* threats against the garden of my own heart and the hearts of my family members.

Scripture teaches us that there's an enemy of our souls, and my daughters' list of questions sparked a new awareness of ways I protect myself from "anything that contaminates body and spirit." That groundhog contaminated our garden, and we found a way to protect it. We learned to recognize the how, the when, and the why of harmful intruders.

When things intrude and contaminate my own heart, might I ask myself that list of questions and devise a plan to ensure safe growth and a bountiful crop in my life? What must go deep and ascend high about my life to ward off spiritual, physical, and emotional contaminates?

Living with flair means I protect and defend against contamination.

22. A Little Garden Magic

Early this morning my daughter picks a cucumber from our garden. It is shaped exactly like a "C." The wonder of this! A vegetable shaped like its first letter!

196

She holds it up and shows me, eyes wide. Would our eggplant come out like an "E" or the pepper in a big, plump "P"? It is fun to think of it until we realize that it's entirely normal for cucumbers to turn into long "C" shapes. The youngest knows this already, and my gardener husband confirms the truth.

There was no magic in the garden.

No zucchini coming in "Z" shapes or squash in long yellow "S's." No enchanted alphabet vegetables.

The disillusionment lasts only a millisecond. My daughter, still in pajamas, decides to pick the basil for pesto. Then she turns around and whispers: "I'm picking some parsley for us too. It's the *secret ingredient*."

Her eyes sparkle to think of the secret ingredient from the garden.

The wonder returns. Tonight we are having *enchanted* pasta with pesto.

Living with flair is finding a secret ingredient when you've reasoned the wonder away.

23. The Beauty in Sorrow

To know sorrow is to know loss.

Sorrow represents one of the most complex human emotions because it's a sadness tinged with beauty and joy. We are sorrowful because we miss what was once, or could have been, *wonderful*. We remember the joy but are simultaneously aware of its absence.

I think of Eve, leaving the Garden, unable to ever return.

I'm driving in my car, remembering lost things, people, lost experiences, places. I'm trying desperately to get out of the sorrow. Maybe I could exercise or distract myself somehow. Besides, the day was nearly over, and I hadn't had one moment of flair.

This sorrow was overtaking *any* chance of flair.

And then I wondered: What if the sorrow *is* the flair? Just because it's a negative emotion doesn't mean it's not extraordinary and full of the presence of God. There's a theology behind sorrow that tells me something about myself. I inherit sorrow as part of the Fall. I'm that figure looking back at the East Gate of Eden.

And isn't that curse accompanied by hope? Doesn't God promise a way to rejoice in sorrow? Isn't He called the Comforter in Sorrow? Aren't Christians described as "sorrowful yet always rejoicing?" (2 Corinthians 6:10) How can this be?

Is our coming joy dependent upon our present sorrow?

When I'm sorrowful, I let my heart break apart so God can enter and heal. Sorrow accompanies me—a true companion—that reminds me what I have lost but also what will one day be restored in God's way and in God's time. It's a beautiful reminder of an unusual form of flair.

24. A Taste of My Own Medicine

For all my talk of releasing *children* into nature, with nothing but pure imagination and the grass beneath their feet, I'm not one to take any time—as an *adult*—away from technology to just relax outside with no plan, no agenda. Is nature only good for the young? What would happen if I joined them?

How would I do it? Would I be barefoot? Would I look for frogs or collect random sticks?

Leaving the cell phone and the netbook behind, I placed myself under a tree in my front yard. The children played by instinct with the sort of freedom and abandon of fish finally released into water after nearly suffocating on land.

But for me, this environment of dirt, grass, pebble, and twig threatened to destroy my pedicure more than relax me.

But I stayed on, noticing the shade and breeze against my body. I settled into the earth, introducing myself by removing my shoes. I curled my toes around the grass and took a deep breath. A moment later, a single white garden spider crawled over my big toe, and two ants found my left arm: my welcoming committee.

I'd been incorporated. I was *in*.

At one point, I opened a book and leaned back to read in the grass. Afternoon shadows grew long, and the wind was cool. The girls laughed and chased an enormous toad.

Their voices faded into the background of songbirds, the rustle of leaves above my head, and the hush of my own slow breath. What peace was this in my heart? What soothing balm?

Tomorrow, I'm telling my children to send their mom outside. She can't come in until dinner.

25. When You're Disappointed and Bitter

With so many tomatoes, how could I not make homemade sauce? Warning: It's *violent.*

You take tomatoes and submerge them in boiling water for a few seconds. Then you drown them in ice water. Then you skin them. Then you remove their seeds. It feels like some torture process. I chop; I puree; I simmer everything down to a thick sauce.

You have to do it this way. No other process removes the bitterness; no other process releases the flavor.

My daughter's helping me peel and chop garlic. We've been disappointed, *bitter*, all morning because she didn't get the teacher she wanted for kindergarten. None of her friends are in her class. Head hung low, mouth in a frown, she's experienced this first violent assault on her expectations, her hopes, her dreams for her life. "Sometimes it's like that," the older one says. "But the best thing about kindergarten is making brand new friends. You'll see."

She *will* see. It *is* like that. No other process will teach her how to rise above her disappointment. No other process will release her from her rigid control of what must surely be the best life. Released like that, her life can be that sweet aroma—that beautiful flavor—of a person who knows how to find good in any pain.

No other process will do that for her.

26. Delighted In, Rejoiced Over

While trying to get the children back on their school bedtime schedule, I have them tucked in at 8:00 PM. They are hardly tired. I tell them I'll sit in the armchair in the corner of the room while they fall asleep

I feel like the Mother Bunny in that old favorite, *Goodnight Moon* (only I don't have knitting needles, and I'm not one to sit still).

I have a gazillion things to do.

Besides making lesson plans, I could tidy the kitchen, fold another load of laundry, mop the kitchen floor—the usual.

Instead, I stay put in that soft corner-of-the-room armchair.

And then the most unusual thing happens. I think it would be a good idea to *sing*. It almost (don't think I'm crazy) feels like God wants me to sing. I have never been able to sing. Couple nerves with probable tone-deafness, and you have a recipe for musical disaster.

But I start singing every old hymn I know. I'm singing over my daughters and imagining wonderful things for their lives. It feels like I'm rejoicing and that I'm taking enormous delight in them with those warbling notes.

The girls quiet down and fall fast asleep in 15 minutes. I stay put in that chair and sing for a half hour more. I feel closer to my family and somehow closer to a picture of how God feels about *me*.

Something calls out to my soul as I sing. I remember this verse from Zephaniah 3:17:

"The LORD your God is with you,
 he is mighty to save.
 He will take great delight in you,
 he will quiet you with his love,
 he will rejoice over you with singing."

I think of God sitting in the armchair in my own bedroom.

I fall asleep—delighted in, rejoiced over.

27. When You Have to Wait for Something

I've been watching a chrysalis in my garden for a week now, and today a gorgeous butterfly emerged. She's finally here!

She's a female Eastern Tiger Swallowtail.

She waits for the right time. If it's too cold, too windy, or too wet, she *knows*. She'll proceed another day, another month, when conditions are perfect.

Today's her day! So why in the world is she just *sitting* there?

I read that after she comes forth from the chrysalis (a great word: from the Latin *chyrsallid* and Greek *chrysos* meaning "gold") she pumps her wings full of blood, and then she's required to sit *very still* and let her wings dry. They have to harden in order to support her in flight.

This could take *three hours.*

How hard must this be for her to wait, very still, when she was made to fly, when she's been waiting for this her whole life?

As she waits, she's extremely vulnerable to many predators (birds, spiders, ants, wasps, snakes). She's delicious and vibrant and without any defense.

I think about her all morning. My youngest daughter and I creep around the garden barefoot, dew soaking even our legs. We approach her, and she doesn't move. She can't. She's not ready, not even a little bit.

How could I not think of those of us waiting for things—letting our wings harden—in that fragile and *dangerous* time (dangerous because of the lies that assault us) when something's just about to happen but we aren't quite ready? We have to stay still and obey the process. We can't rush. Our whole flight depends upon it.

28. Am I Fond of Them?

In Titus 2:4, we learn that older women are supposed to encourage the younger women to love their children. Isn't that weird? Why wouldn't they love their children?

I learn this morning that the admonition in this verse to *love your children* is about being fond of them, delighting in being with them, and enjoying them.

What does it mean to be "fond" of your children? I learn that it means to have a *great affection and liking for them. It means to have a passion for and an inclination towards them.*

Yes, it means to actually enjoy them. The etymology of fond means to be foolishly infatuated. It does! It really does!

Do you ever feel like this enjoyment gets lost somewhere in dishes and laundry, bills and scrubbing? Do you ever feel like you don't enjoy your own children because you have forgotten how?

I prayed that God would fill my heart with fondness for my children and that they would feel my fondness toward them. Why would I need to pray this? Well, my heart veers towards selfishness on the summer days when I'd rather drink coffee, write, and read a novel alone. Sometimes, I'd rather escape because I've spent so much time in meal preparation, cleaning, and housekeeping.

So I ask God to do this fondness thing in my heart.

Guess what? I found myself playing again. I found myself putting goggles on and exploring the depths with them. I found myself hiding and seeking and imagining I'd come upon foundling children who urgently needed strawberry pie and tickling.

And when I was alone reading my novel later, I threw it down and called out down the hall, "Where are you two? I want to be with you! What are we doing next?"

Oh, dear! I'm foolishly infatuated!

29. "Pull Yourself Together!"

This is a strange little statement: *Pull Yourself Together.*

It's been a hard day of learning about terrible deaths in the news, comforting close friends who grieve, and enduring a general weariness over evil and brokenness in the world.

Years ago, I might sit in my minivan, tilt my chin up, and say, "Pull yourself together, Heather! Find some flair!"

I realize how much of my life has been about doing this. It's been all about gathering in all my wild emotions, terrible wanderings, grieving thoughts, and bizarre behaviors into some kind of order.

Today, I realize a better quote is this: "Let Yourself Fall Completely Apart!"

That's when I stop trying so hard to make sense of anything. That's when I break open so God can do that mighty work.

Pulling myself together has something to do with being in control and *making sense* of what's happening. I want the narrative. I want to know the why behind it all.

I want to make sense of it all.

But what if I can't? What if I just can't find the narrative in senseless deaths? What if I just can't find any reason for anything anymore? My wise friend said this: "*Why* is not the most important question."

We talk about how God owns our life, and if He chooses to withhold any order or sense of narrative—a *why* behind a senseless thing—then I submit to not knowing. I submit to falling apart and moving forward with faith.

I'm not pulling myself together anymore. I don't have to. That's living with flair.

30. "If you lose your mind, you lose it into the hand of God." Elizabeth Goudge

A new friend recommends one of her favorite books to me. It's *The Scent of Water*, by Elizabeth Goudge. It's a wonderful book! One character who fears for her mental state as she battles depression receives wise counsel from a spiritual friend. When she expresses how terrifying it is to lose your mind, the man replies, "If you lose your mind, you lose it into the hand of God."[7]

As someone so afraid of returning to depression, I find such comfort here.

Even my mind can rest in the loving hand of God. I don't need to worry; my soul—different and distinct from my brain—doesn't deteriorate or fail. It doesn't waver or betray. My *mind*, however, might—and most likely will—betray me in the end. I will not fear.

If I lose my mind, I lose it into the hand of God.

31. The Easiest Way to Persevere

There's just too much to do. That's the problem today. Most people have a threshold. They can balance just so many plates in the air, and add just one more, and the whole operation comes crashing down. Some of us respond with a paralysis and a moodiness that we can't beat. We are overwhelmed and stressed out.

I'm lying in my bed, and I think of what needs to be done today. It's huge. It's mammoth. It's *impossible*. But then I remember one of the best coping mechanisms for that overwhelmed, stressed out, paralyzing, moody feeling of "I can't do this."

I think about *tiny chores*. It's a simple truth your own mother probably told you when you had to clean your room. When the chores seem too much, you just break them apart into *teeny, tiny chores*.

And they have to be *tiny chores*. Remember, we are overwhelmed and stressed out. We can't tackle cleaning the basement, but we can clean this *one inch* of desk. I need that small accomplishment as activation energy, as catalyst, as fuel. Then, a reaction starts. A glorious, vibrant one.

So I start in the smallest division of my mammoth task as possible. I do one *inch*, then the next inch, then the next and next and next. You fold this one shirt. You clean this one dish. You study this one page. You write this one sentence.

And soon you've written a dissertation.

I'm persevering through the day, and all of a sudden, the stress drains. The finished tiny chore gives me a power that moves out in concentric circles like a stone I've thrown on the surface of the water. I can do this next thing and then this one and that one. I'm inspired! I'm energized!

Perseverance is "steady persistence in spite of difficulty." I don't have to do everything right now. There's difficulty here, opposition there. But I can do *one inch* and see what happens. I can keep doing my inches, steadily. It's like starting to exercise. You just put on your shoes and say you'll go these few steps. Maybe you'll walk or run to the mailbox out front. That's good. That's the inch. Later, you could run to the stop sign. Next week, I won't even be able to catch you.

Do the inch. Living with flair means I think of this task in terms of *the inch*.

32. Surprise!

"If God knows everything, then He never gets to be surprised." This is my daughter expressing sadness over what she feels is one of life's greatest pleasures: the feeling of surprise!

She loves surprises. She loves unexpected little gifts and friends arriving unannounced. She loves it most when I say, "I have a wonderful surprise for you." Maybe it's a treat I've baked or a new book I've found for her that's hiding under her pillow. Maybe it's a movie I've rented or a special event I've planned.

Her love language is *surprises*. She loves them so much that I try to create a few each week.

"Doesn't God ever get that feeling?" she wonders. "He doesn't, does He?"

I think about this today as I smile with joy at the red ripe strawberry in the patch. I knew it was coming all along (just like it has the past four years), but each time, it's a delight. Each time, it's astonishing and wonderful. Some things are just so beautiful that it doesn't matter if you *know* they're coming. It's deeper and better than surprise; it's wonder and worship.

But I'm still thinking about this.

I'm thinking about how much a child loves surprises. Then I'm thinking about how much I absolutely love creating the perfect surprise for this child. I've grown up into the person who loves surprising instead of receiving surprises, so maybe that's part of God's character. There's more joy in making the surprise than in getting it.

This makes me wonder how God must be fashioning the perfect surprise for you right this moment. You have no idea it's coming, but it's coming. You have no idea what it will be, but it's going to be so amazing that you'll be simply astonished all day.

It's coming!

33. What's on Your Kitchen Floor?

Late last night, I get out the bucket and the mop.

I mop my kitchen floor.

It's nearly 10:00 PM. I fume that no matter how clean I try to keep that floor, it gets *filthy*. Cleaning day is Saturday. It's only *Monday* night, and here I am, mopping the filth. I can't bear to wake up to it.

The children sleep soundly.

I mop, and then I start seeing the whole thing differently. I'm not mopping. I'm *reading*. I read a narrative on that floor. I have filth because we run through mud and sand. We drag wet towels in from the pool. We spill cinnamon and sugar and butter that missed the toast. There's spaghetti sauce here, honey there. I mop ground-up glitter from the fairy doors we made that morning. Bits of twigs and parsley from the butterfly pavilion we constructed for the monarch caterpillar just now building a cocoon, scattered into the corners, come clean with my mop.

Peanut butter, eggs from the omelet my daughter made herself, pencil shavings from her new pencil for her journal, coffee drips from my own cup, a cat treat crammed into the tile. You can read a kitchen floor like some book of days. We have *lived* for the past 48 hours.

One day, my kitchen floor won't need a mop at all. It will shine clean. This won't be a good day.

I leave the bucket and mop out when I finish. I will need it again tonight and every single night for the next 18 years. By the time the floor shines clean, I have tears in my eyes. Thank you God for this filth. My kitchen floor has the kind of flair I love. It's a book I could read every night before bed. Let it be a *good* one.

34. Just Because There's Space Doesn't Mean You Have to Fill It

For the first time in 9 years, I'm going to have *space*. Space and time. Both my daughters will attend elementary school from 8:30-3:00 PM.

Already, I'm filling up those future days. I work part time and help coordinate ministry events with my husband. I write novels and design college writing courses on the side. Saturday morning I clean the house. If you read this blog, you know that I keep *busy*. I'm driven by some unseen force to produce, to achieve, to be recognized. That's my dark side.

And it's showing up again as this new school year approaches. I'm already thinking about new projects and new campaigns. I'm wondering what group I can organize, what new courses to teach, and what new novel I'll conceive.

My husband, the wise Eagle Scout that led me to the still water on our anniversary hike, said this:

"Just because there's space doesn't mean you have to fill it."

I stare at him, mouth agape. Whatever can that mean? I don't even know what that would look like.

This morning in church, I talk to God about my drive to fill space with as many things as I can. What am I *doing*? Whose affection am I trying to win? What prize am I racing toward? I ask God to show me how to be led and not driven. I ask

God to show me what it would look like to have so much space in a day that I could rest, listen, and respond to my life rather than reacting in a rush of furious energy.

So I'm not filling space this fall. I've turned down 3 offers for more work this week. I even said "no" to a teaching offer and a writing project. Cheers! High-fives! I'm going to feed my soul and practice not filling space.

I need space to be *led* by God and not driven. I'm still not sure what it looks like to slow down and sit in empty space. But whatever it is, it's a new thing. It will be my less frantic form of flair.

35. They Will Keep

I remember an exchange in the recent movie *Jane Eyre* (also in the book) between St. John Rivers and Jane. It's so simple, but it showcases a great character who isn't consumed with ambition or personal gain.

St. John Rivers worries that Jane's simple work and life is somehow beneath her or wasteful. He asks: "What will you do with all your fine accomplishments? What, with the largest portion of your mind—sentiments—tastes?"

Jane Eyre replies: "Save them till they are wanted. They will keep."[8]

While I'm remembering this quote, two different friends point out the incredible story of the American Agava plant that has waited 80 years to bloom. This very week, the plant has bloomed at Michigan's Matthaei Botanical Gardens. I learn something about this plant whose fine accomplishment has been kept for 80 years. Nobody knows why it waited so long. Nobody can explain the particular timing of it. It's a mystery.

All I can think about is the truth that our gifts and offerings to the world will keep until the right time—when they're needed. Until then, we live in the mystery of it and the comfort that we can save all our offerings until they're wanted.

They will keep.

36. Stop Comparing and Make Your Own Fun

Sometimes we get into a terrible thought pattern where we truly believe everyone else is having much more fun than we are. We just can't handle all the wonderful things we see others experiencing while we go about our hum-drum, boring Sunday.

We're driving away after dropping one daughter off at a fabulous party, and the other daughter sulks in the back seat of the car. Why doesn't *she* get those kinds of invitations? What about *her* day? Why isn't *she* having any fun?

Because I continue to meditate on Ephesians 2:6 and our special seat in the heavenly realms in Christ, I can say with confidence, "God has a perfect day planned for *you* that is entirely separate from—but not better or worse than—your sister's or anyone else's. God has good works prepared in advance for *you* to do today. God has blessings for *you* in store today. It might not be a party, but it will be something."

Can we believe it?

She sulks for a while longer but then something clicks inside of her. She announces, "I am going to make chocolate cupcakes from scratch from my own recipe." It's like the dark mood lifts and she's in a different spiritual place.

That's it, girl! There's a great day ahead that's *your* day.

Later, I ask her what advice she would give to other little girls who are having sad, empty days. She says, "Go bake. Make your own fun."

37. Run the Mile You're In

My sister always provides Runnerly Wisdom for me. Today she reminds me not to dwell on the past or focus too much on the future. "Run the mile you're in," she says.

It's a long race with many miles behind and many miles ahead. I run the mile I'm in right now.

38. Beautiful But Fatal

I'm relaxing in a neighbor's backyard, and she leans my lounging chair back to make sure I'm comfortable.

Then she exclaims, "Look! The delphinium!"

I turn to see the brightest blue flowers. What beauty! That blue shames even the sky.

Later, I learn that this plant's beauty comes with a caution: it's *poisonous*. It can actually kill a person if eaten.

Dr. Alice Russell, in the Department of Horticultural Science at North Carolina State University, reports that this gorgeous plant will cause "burning of the lips and mouth, numbness of the throat, intense vomiting and diarrhea, muscular spasms, paralysis of the respiratory system, and convulsions."[9] Her list concludes with a toxic warning: *Fatal.*

All from a tiny blue buttercup. I think about the nature of temptation. It always seems tiny, harmless—beautiful even—that thing we want that's outside the boundaries.

Remember the delphinium. It's beautiful but fatal.

39. He Will Follow You

This morning, the pastor explains that when the psalmist writes in Psalm 23 that "surely your goodness and mercy will follow me all the days of my life," we might translate this more accurately as "your goodness and mercy will *pursue* me, will *harass* me, will *eagerly chase* me."

The Hebrew words make me smile when I think about God appointing his mercy and goodness to chase me down. It's so eager, in fact, that it's like a kind of harassment: a harassment of goodness! I'd never thought of it like this before. The persistence of God to love me! The Hound of Heaven coming to bless!

I think of the whistling of God to find me to then harass me with goodness.

40. If Nothing Changes, Then I Don't Either

I hate change. It makes me anxious.

This morning at Saturday Morning Pancakes, my neighbor (the one who showed me the lady slipper orchid) reminds me that when I feel anxious, it's my opportunity to *have faith.*

I look at her as if she's just reminded me of my own name. *Of course.* It's so simple. When I'm anxious about anything, it's a bright flashing neon sign saying: Opportunity to Trust God Right Here!

I'm anxious because I have to travel. I'm anxious because I have to leave my environment and live in another one for a while.

As I explain all these anxieties, a boy beside me suggests that if the environment *never changes*, then a person cannot grow and develop. He explains it all using a video game analogy. You've got to move around! You've got to change things up! He tells me how *good* it is for my growth and imagination to have some change.

So this thing (whatever it is) that's causing anxiety? It's an opportunity to trust God. It's putting me in an environment for growth. If nothing changes, then I don't either. And I want to change and grow into the woman God wants me to be. That means welcoming situations that stretch me.

41. Suffering is Fertilizer

This morning, we have strawberry pancakes for Saturday Morning Pancakes. The neighbors come over, and the children pull back the netting to harvest the crop.

We have *too many*.

My husband flips pancakes with a neighbor's son, and soon, we have stacks upon stacks of strawberry-stuffed pancakes.

Everyone talks about this great harvest.

I offer up the secret: you plant in *compost*.

A few years back, we learned from our neighbors down the road how to compost. We let organic material decay, and then it becomes fertilizer. Our town lets you purchase a whole truckload of compost for next to nothing, but we also have our own composting bins outside the back door. After a year, we have nutrient rich fertilizer from the waste of our lives: eggshells, coffee grounds, paper, yard trimmings, fruit and vegetable peels.

All morning, I gaze at this bountiful harvest that comes about on the foundation of waste, decay, and brokenness. Compost provides exactly what the plants need. I'm in awe of the whole process.

I think about my own fruitfulness as a wife, mother, and friend. Isn't it true that any good thing God produces through my life needs *fertilizer*? I'll never look at hardship, suffering, or my break-downs the same way again. What I see as waste and decay just might be the fertilizer for next year's harvest.

42. A Huge Little Prayer

This morning I read a comment by Hannah Whitall Smith from *The Veil Uplifted*.

She writes, "We are made for union with Him, and union must mean oneness of purpose and thought, so the only pathway to this union must be a perfect harmony between our will and His."[10]

I pray for a "perfect harmony" between my will and God's. *Bring everything in my life into complete harmony with you, Jesus.*

I breathe the 11 word prayer and realize mountains have moved within me. Gears have locked, mechanisms have aligned. Whatever isn't harmonizing will tune itself to a holy note.

This is a huge little prayer.

43. Something to Gather Right Now

It's raining, but I know I have to harvest this day's strawberries. The whole time I'm out there in the mud and underneath the dark sky, foraging about for ripe berries hidden beneath the rich green foliage, I think about the blessing I might gather in *any* season, under *any* sky, in *any* circumstance.

Yes, it's terrible weather out here, but still there's something to gather.

Doesn't Isaiah 45 talk about how God can bring treasure from darkness? Doesn't Psalm 126 talk about how those who sow in tears reap a great harvest of joy? Doesn't Isaiah 43 talk about God making streams in the wasteland?

There's something to gather from this day and every day—some wisdom, some joy, some beauty, some blessing. Go and gather it! Go right into the rain and darkness and gather it up!

44. A Challenge

I'm listening to the Director of Operations for the International Justice Mission in Southeast Asia. He makes three statements that can reshape my purpose in my community.

1. Believe that the strong have a duty to the weak.

2. Identify the one in need of rescue.
3. Respond with courage and compassion to confront oppressors (spiritual and physical) and set people free.

I'm not in Southeast Asia, but I am in a *neighborhood*. Do I believe I have a duty to help others? Can I ask, "Where are the weak among us—those suffering, those oppressed by various sources—who God might send me to help?" And will I have the Spirit-filled courage and compassion to move into lives that need freedom?

Living with flair means going on rescue missions. Today, the verbs *confront* and *rescue* enter my list of actions I want to animate my life. Lord, give me courage.

45. The Marks of Emotional Maturity

Yesterday, a wise man explains that while we often exhibit spiritual and intellectual maturity, we forget to develop *emotionally*.

An emotionally mature person isn't controlled by circumstances. She can operate out of truth regarding God's love for her, His sovereignty, and His perfect provision. But how? No matter how much I learn or how much I grow spiritually, I still let my emotions dominate.

Something isn't clicking.

My wise friend suggests to begin by *charting the day*. I'm to make a list of everything that happens and my reaction to these events. I slow down, ask myself *how* I'm responding to my environment, *why* I'm doing this, and *what lie* I'm believing that generates the emotional instability. Then, uncover the truth about God I need to believe.

He remarks that most people behave inappropriately in reaction to their circumstances because there's a deep wound of abandonment or neglect. They lash out like caged animals because they want so desperately to have their needs met.

But we don't have to lash out or throw tantrums today. We can supply God's truth to this very moment and respond with peace, patience, and joy. We are not neglected animals. We are deeply loved and cared for by a generous and powerful God who heals us.

46. As Strong as This?

Yesterday, I examined the cattails by a beautiful pond. I've always studied cattails. As a child, I learned how the cattails hid the nests of mallards and geese. I discovered how you could walk between the stalks, nearly sinking into the marshy bank of the Potomac River, and find turtles as small as your thumbnail and bullfrogs the size of a dinner plate.

But I learned never to take a cattail inside the house. The seeds would disperse *everywhere*. So you left them alone—those tall soldiers guarding the ponds and rivers—and observed how, in late summer, great fluffy parachutes of seeds launched out over the water. They could overtake a whole habitat. Nothing could come against them.

I remember this, and I suddenly realize what the cattail represents: explosive, invasive, unmanageable, impenetrable *growth*.

You can't stop a cattail. The roots go deep and store massive amounts of nutrients. The tip of the plant constitutes innumerable seeds carried far and wide by wind. Bad weather simply aids the dispersal. A flood only makes the roots stronger. A drought just means the seeds leave sooner.

You can't stop a cattail. That's what I'm thinking about as my time in Colorado comes to an end next week. It hasn't been the summer I imagined. We've been more sick than healthy and more challenged than refreshed. But you can't stop a cattail.

Hardship can only aid our growth.

47. Fame and Fortune?

I'm listening to Vonette Bright speak about the days of co-founding a ministry in 1951 that now ranks as one of the largest missions organizations in the world. She mentions the moment she agreed to fully surrender to God. What would it require? What would it mean to submit to a calling?

I learned part of the answer I didn't know before.

I didn't realize that within an actual contract the Brights signed between themselves and God, the couple agreed *not to accumulate wealth or seek fame*.

I smiled when I heard her explain this. She knew something far greater and more satisfying than the world's most seductive paths. She knew what mattered most in another economy in another kingdom.

48. What You Set in Motion Today

I'm listening to Francis Chan speak to a group of 5,000 folks. He says, "Go do something that requires faith." I realize that every wonderful event in my life almost didn't happen because of my being too nervous, too insecure, or too self-involved. Marriage, parenting, writing, teaching, or moving to new places? These things aren't always easy, obvious, or natural.

As I thought about that quote, I suddenly realized that it's not just big and life-changing things that require enormous faith. What about knocking on a neighbor's door to start a friendship? What about writing this very sentence? What about even waking up this morning and choosing a good mood? (Now *that's* faith for me!) A very small act might create an avalanche reaction of beauty, joy, and change.

I'm going to do things that require faith today. It's not just big things. Waking up cheerfully might be my act of faith today. Who knows what I've just set in motion?

49. You Can Go Where Others Cannot

Today my daughter announces that she hates being so short. "Everyone else my age is taller than I am!"

I want to deny it. I want to comfort her. I want to tell her to get over it.

But she is rather short. So instead of denying the truth of her statement, I remind her that God has a reason *for everything*.

"Can you think of any reason why a loving God would let you be shorter than everyone else right now?" I ask her, staring deeply into those little girl eyes that will undoubtedly face a lifetime of the kinds of disappointments and heartbreak that come with the human experience. She will ask so many *why?* questions as the years unfold.

She tilts her head to one side and ponders the thought. "Well, I *can* get into places that most people can't."

This means she wins hide-n-seek. This means she has an advantage in finding hiding places that suddenly makes her stature valuable. What a change of heart!

All day, this statement resonates in my heart: "I can get into places that most people can't." I talk to God about this, and I imagine this conversation:

Yes. You can go where others cannot. That's what this confusion, this disappointment, this heartache is for. Your experience gives you access. It's a portal into a place others cannot—or will not—go.

I find myself welling up. God speaks to my own heart through my daughter's answer. Suffering allows you to "get into places that most people can't." I think about ministry opportunities, writing projects, insights, amazing friendships, communities, and blessing after blessing because I went into beautiful spiritual and physical places I could only enter through the door of suffering.

Living with flair means knowing that you can go where others cannot because of the things you've suffered.

50. "She was generous with her life."

Today, I hear a woman describe another woman by saying, "She was generous with her life. She expected nothing in return for what she gave of herself to me."

I dug into my purse to find my journal and pen to write down those words.

Something about the expression stung my heart. I normally think about being generous with money, time, or acts of service. But what about being generous with my own heart—giving my very self away—so others are blessed?

I want to be generous with *my life*.

51. Who But You?

As I prepare my writing seminar, I receive emails and comments from folks asking sadly, "What do *I* have to write that's worth reading? Why would anyone read what *I* have to write?"

In Mary Pipher's book, *Writing to Change the World*, she entitles a chapter, "What You Alone Can Say." She claims, "You have something to say that no one else can say. Your history, your unique sensibilities, your sense of place and your language bestow upon you a singular authority. Who but you can describe the hollyhocks in your grandmother's backyard or the creek outside of town that you fished as a child. . . ?"[11]

Who but you?

52. The Saggiest Wins

At the Denver Zoo, I become amazed with the number of animals who give prestige and power to other animals based on how much skin sags on their bodies. I'm serious. In a herd, the animal with the *saggiest chin* (dewlap) has the most power and prestige.

And another thing: Animals regularly make themselves *look larger* in this zoo. It's best to be wrinkly, big, and old. It's beautiful, powerful, and important.

The other day, I notice the thin little wrinkles that have formed around my mouth. I'm noticing all the sagging on my body and how nothing stays in its place. I notice my own hands as I type—leathery and sketched with crossing patterns in skin that's getting old. I notice that it's harder and harder to have a waist when you age.

But, oh, where these hands have been! Oh, the great conversations I've had with this very mouth! Oh, the places this body has taken me! I want these marks and sags to signify the beauty and prestige that they should.

I like the zoo. I like communities where old means beautiful. I want to foster that cultural shift in my own community.

53. Someone is Looking for You

Last night, my youngest asks me to tell her stories of when I was a little girl.

"What kind of stories?" I ask.

"The ones when you get lost and someone has to find you," she says.

I've never told her a story like this. But that's the story she wants to hear: *a little girl lost and then found.*

Sometimes I think we can tap into the one great True Narrative just by asking children the kinds of stories they want to hear. The story I tell her is the greatest story I know. A girl was lost—desperately and hopelessly so—but a great God was looking for her and wouldn't let her go. He searched long and far and wide. And He left clues and messages and little gifts along the trail to remind her of the way home.

I was lost but Someone was looking for me.

54. "All Seats Provide Equal Viewing of the Universe"

I discovered this quote at the public library yesterday. It's from the Museum Guide from Hayden Planetarium inside a novel by Lorrie Moore.[12] I read it out loud and it seemed to catch in my throat. All week I've wanted to go home to Pennsylvania. All week I've imagined a different life. It seemed, as I read it again, that some great voice of wisdom gently whispered in my ear.

I turned to my daughter and read it to her.

"Do you know what that means?" I asked. "It means that no matter where you are, you have an *equal chance* to perceive the beauty of God."

When I want to trade seats to find a better view, I'm going to sit tight and realize my equal chance to see—right where I am—the beautiful things God wants to show me. "All seats provide equal viewing of the universe."

55. The Best Hand Gesture

This morning during Sunday School, a mom found me to tell me that her daughter didn't want to be left alone in the room with the other children. But when mother and daughter entered the room, another little girl looked at her daughter and *patted the empty seat beside her.*

Problem solved.

Who wouldn't want to walk into a room, have someone catch your eye, and see that person's hand pat the empty seat beside her? It might be the greatest hand gesture in the world. It communicates this:

Be with me! I like you! You belong here! There's a spot just for you!

I want to live in such a way that I'm patting a million seats for everyone I see.

56. Higher Than I

This morning, I lean down to look at all the rocks by my apartment.

I remember the plea of the psalmist in Psalm 61:

"Hear my cry, O God;

listen to my prayer.
From the ends of the earth I call to you,
 I call as my heart grows faint;
 lead me to the *rock that is higher than I.*
For you have been my refuge,
 a strong tower against the foe."

I need a rock that is higher than I. It's a strange expression. To me, it's another reminder that God delivers me from myself. He's higher than self. I can hardly believe it, but I learn that God refers to himself as our Rock over and over again in Scripture. He's the rock that is higher than I! The Lord says in Isaiah:

"Who then is like me? Let him proclaim it.
 Let him declare and lay out before me
what has happened since I established my ancient people,
 and what is yet to come—
 yes, let them foretell what will come.
Do not tremble, do not be afraid.
 Did I not proclaim this and foretell it long ago?
You are my witnesses. Is there any God besides me?
 No, there is *no other Rock*; I know not one."

I need to remember that today.

For several days now, I've been complaining. Nothing's going according to plan out here in Colorado. As I walk around the apartment this morning, I know I need supernatural power to get out of this funk. Nothing corrupts living with flair like complaining, and I just can't talk myself out of my bad mood. And then I feel *guilty* for my mood because so many other women all over the world would trade their lives any day for the kinds of comforts I enjoy.

Oh, Lord, lead me to the Rock that is *higher than I!*

57. Sending Your Voice Into the World

While walking today, an extraordinary sight greets us. A beautiful hot air balloon hovers in the morning sky.

I race into the middle of the street, spread my arms wide, and wave at them. I'm jumping in the air, and I'm calling out, "Hello up there! Hello up there!" I realize I'm a colossal embarrassment. I realize this doesn't make any sense.

Someone on the ground beside me says, "They won't be able to hear you."

But still, I shout and wave. Then, I hear an faint, whispery answer.

"Helllllllllooooo!" They hear me! They *answer*. They wave and call down from inside the basket. I see a tiny arm waving to me. I hear the voice and smile. Our voices travel across this huge distance.

All morning, I realize how ridiculous of a notion it was to raise my voice and expect an answer. But my voice *was* heard, and an answer *did* come.

You just never know how far your voice will travel. You never know who might hear—from no matter how far away or in whatever unusual circumstance—the thing you have to say.

Living with flair means you go ahead and send your voice out into the world. You have no idea who can hear it and answer you.

58. I Wasn't Supposed to Have Even One

All year, I've waited for the raspberries. Finally, we have a single ripe berry on the bush this morning.

I complain to my husband about how unproductive the berries have been. "Look at the neighbor's berries! They have so many ripe berries! We have *one*!"

"We weren't supposed to have *any* this year," my husband—the gardening expert—reminds me. "The neighbor's plants are mature, and ours are young. Next year, we'll have our berries."

I wasn't supposed to have any. The truth of it resonates deep in my soul. I expect and demand so much. I look at all my worries on this Sunday: my daughter's possible gluten allergy, news of a sick friend in the hospital, my deadlines, my students. I place them all in the great lap of God. I'm humbled before that lap; I do not demand or complain.

His great blessing brought into my life the very things I now worry about. His great blessing—when I did not deserve even one of these things: children, friends, work or whatever it is means I cleanse my heart and rejoice in the very things about which I want to complain.

That one bright berry—when I wasn't supposed to have any—tastes sweeter than you can imagine.

59. Live Wide

My daughter tells me I must come to the garden to see another kind of butterfly. He's *golden*.

His wing pattern looks more leopard than insect, more African than Pennsylvania backyard. On top, he's a tiger, but on the bottom, he's a giraffe or spotted fawn. Up close, his compound eye reminds me that he can see in virtually *every direction at once*.

His wide angled eyes with miniscule sensors perceive the back, front, top, bottom, left, and right of him. There's something amazing about that kind of perception. He cannot see far, but he can see *wide*.

I'm reminded of my own limits when pitted against this marvelous creature. I cannot see *that wide*. My vision is basically limited to what's directly in front of me. Isn't it strange that humans can see far but not wide? We have to turn our heads to consider what's beside us. Unfortunately, I often race ahead into an imagined future—the one out there in front of *just me*—and I forget to widen my embrace to my left and my right.

I want to live wide.

I'm a girl who was supposed to *go far*. Remember my need for achievement? I'm so glad I decided to stop trying to go far and instead *live wide*. I pray I can gather whatever community I can in my life. I want to widely welcome, love, and encourage right here. I don't go far; I go wide.

I learn to turn my head. Living with flair means I live wide.

60. What a Child Needs to Hear from You

I'm visiting with my dear friend, the one who told me that the sign of a happy childhood is dirty children. This is my same friend who raises five children without a television set or computer games. I'm always eager for what new parenting advice she'll impart.

Today, I watch and listen. Over and over again, I hear her tell her children, "I just love to be with you." Her teenage daughter comes to sit next to her, and she says, "I'm so glad! I just love to be with you." She still walks with the teenager to school, she says, "because I just love to be with her *so much*." She says it so that daughter can overhear her.

The teenager's beaming face lights the whole kitchen.

Later, we leave to go on a walk in the neighborhood, and the oldest children want to come along. Their mother says, "Of course! I just love to be with you!"

That's the phrase I hear the most coming out of this mother's mouth.

I make lunch with my daughters later, and I tell them, "I just love to be with you." I walk outside and push them on the swing and tell them, "I just love to be with you."

Something's changed between us already.

I wonder if children would make better choices, grow in confidence, overflow with happiness, and connect better with their parents if we practiced saying, "I just love to be with you." I want my children to overhear me tell the neighbors this. I want my children to know I'd choose them. I want my children to know that those words reflect the boundless love of God who adores and delights in them.

I'm going to tell more children that I love to be with them.

61. The Nectar Made for You

We stand by the neighbor's flowerbeds and watch butterflies dance and skip across the petunias.

I learn that this butterfly tastes the flowers *with her feet* to decide whether she wants to drink the nectar here. The dance we observe is a taste test (who knew?). Next, she unfolds her proboscis (a straw!) to slurp up the nectar inside the flower.

Then she dives into the flower she wants and drinks.

I watch in amazement at the tasting dance. She's discerning—picky and sensitive—about where she quenches her thirst. I find myself remembering the dance and longing for the kind of sensitivity that would alert me to where and when I might *dive in.*

Our feet will take us many places during this new season, but I only want to dive deeply into places of real nectar. If it doesn't suit me, I rise in the dance and skip on to new openings. So many cups beg for our sipping. I want the nectar made for me.

62. Does He Really?

I'm reading the introduction to Immaculee Ilibagiza's memoir, and I'm overcome by this quote by Dr. Wayne Dyer: "The laws of the material world do not apply in the presence of the God-realized."[13]

I have no idea what I'm getting into when I read Immaculee's account. It's horrifying, shocking, and impossible to imagine. And yet, in the midst of this woman's battle to survive the genocide of millions—including the death of her own family—she forgives, loves, and experiences God in supernatural ways.

She hides in a tiny bathroom with 7 other women for 91 days while killers hunt for her. 91 days. In a bathroom smaller than a closet. With 7 women. What does Immaculee do? She prays. She receives comfort from a *real* God who *really* hears prayer, who *really* protects, who *really* directs, who *really* loves, and who *really* gives the power to let go of hurt and anger. This God *heals*.

Her material reality told her one truth, but God's reality was something totally different.

63. Why We Need a "Yes!" Day

It's only 7:30 PM, and I'm falling asleep. My oldest daughter climbs up beside me on the bed and says, "Mom, you really need a *Yes!* day. That's what you need! Remember the *Yes!* day?"

Oh, I remember.

A few years ago, I felt like every word out of my mouth was, "No." I'd scream that word about everything. *No* she couldn't eat this, touch that, go there. *No* she couldn't stay up late, sleep out in a tent, climb that tree, bake that thing, or visit that place.

I saw her little shoulders slump down further and further with every "No!"

So one day, I told her I was changing my ways. We were going to try out a *Yes!* day. For one entire day, I would say *Yes!* to every single thing she asked.

It was a very long and very strange day.

It involved brownies for breakfast, glitter, playgrounds, visiting neighborhood dogs, eating pizza, and watching movies. It involved baking, bubble baths, lip gloss, and dancing. It involved Polly Pockets somehow. I can't remember each event, but I remember I learned to say, "Yes!"

"Why do I need a *Yes!* day?" I ask her, rubbing my eyes and yawning.

"You need a break. You need to say *Yes!* to yourself."

(insert long pause as a mother sits up, tilts her head, and considers the wisdom of a child)

She's nodding with the words of an ancient soul. "You need to wake up and say *Yes!* to the stuff you want. You know, the things you love. Maybe just for a day, you could say *Yes!* to all the things you love and want." She furrows her eyebrows very seriously. "Like coffee. You could get the *best* coffee tomorrow."

I want to cry. Moms forget to say *Yes!* to themselves.

64. What a Change of Background Can Do

I realize today that I love experimenting with *background*. The word technically means the "scenery behind the main object of contemplation, especially when perceived as a framework for it." We distinguish objects and circumstances—understanding them properly—because we measure them against their background.

Live with Flair is my background. A different background changes how we understand and see.

I gaze into a deep, clear lake, and I have to capture the apple tree against that beauty. What's *behind* the object—the setting—fascinates me. It frames and contextualizes. It tells a story.

Just as in photography and writing, I think carefully about what background I'm choosing to view my own life against. What subtext, what ideologies, what memories, what conversations? Do these frame my life the way I want—in beauty, hope, and joy—or do they obscure, depress, and oppress?

I'm starting to wonder if I can identify sources of unhappiness and despair by asking folks what singular background they view themselves against.

I chose a different frame the day I started blogging. I decided to set my life against the background that I've been "blessed with every spiritual blessing in Christ" (Ephesians 1:3) and that nothing happens to me today that God doesn't use to "work out everything in conformity to the purpose of His will" (Ephesians 1:11).

God is good. All the time.

65. Where You Shouldn't Go and What You Shouldn't Do

A neighbor knocks on our door and begs us to come pick his peaches. "Take all you want!" They have so many peaches falling off their trees that the ground reeks of them.

"But beware of the yellow jackets," he says ominously and then departs for his travels.

I take my youngest daughter to the peach trees. I carry an epi-pen for my yellow jacket allergy, a bucket, and my dreams of peach ice cream and cobbler.

We cannot even approach the tree. Armies of yellow jackets fight over smashed peaches. Yellow jackets blanket the lawn. They suffocate the tree trunks and swarm aggressively. I look down and see masses of them sucking the sweet juice off of rotting peaches.

There's nowhere to walk without endangering ourselves. Finally, we gingerly travel in a wide circle around the tree and try to reach the luscious fruit by hanging far over the deck. As I reach for a peach above my head, I enclose a fist full of yellow jackets that were feasting on the other side of my peach. Shaking my hand free of them, I start running.

"Let's go!" I shout to my daughter. "This isn't a good place for us! It's not safe!" We race home. Suddenly the taste of peach cobbler isn't that appetizing.

Lesson learned: Run away from harmful environments. Flee! My epi-pen was no match for a swarm of yellow jackets. Living with flair means not being foolish. There are some places we should not go and some activities we should not do. That's what I want to tell my daughters and the incoming college freshmen. *Stay out of trouble by fleeing environments that are just not good for you.*

66. Mothers Who Get in the Way

I'm lounging by the neighborhood pool, and I notice a group of teenage boys wildly attacking one another, throwing one another into the water, and performing ever-increasing feats of manliness for all to see. I'm worried someone will get hurt, especially the young children trying to swim.

One mother gets up from her seat and positions herself *directly in their path*. She sits down, dips her feet in the pool, and reclines as water, sweat, and testosterone fall like grenades around her peaceful form.

"What are you doing?" I ask and join her while shielding my face from the onslaught of water and muscles. I know this mother has a teenage son, so I'm curious about her behavior.

"I'm putting myself in the way."

She's stationed herself between the teenagers and the young children. She whispers to me that one of her best parenting strategies is to "be in the way." Sure enough, those boys redirect their energy away from the young children trying to swim.

"Just be in the way," she says.

I nod my head and think of all the times I have already been "in the way" of family members, students, and neighbors. Something about getting right in the middle of somebody's business—being obviously in the way—could help avert harm. And I'm so thankful for all the mothers, teachers, pastors, and friends who stood in my way when I went about my own disastrous plans. "Get out of my way!" I'd think. "You're ruining my plan!"

Well, those folks who were *in my way* saved my life.

I love this pool mother's attitude. That tiny little woman got right in the mix with a dozen sweaty teens. She was in the way. And that's what mothers do.

67. A Dark, Sweet Pleasure

It's all poetry in my yard today:

The blackberries bring a joy I can't name. I don't need anything else but those warm berries in my hand. They deliver a dark, sweet pleasure.

Each one bursts with something rich and good.

It's a daily provision—just a *handful* of fruit—each morning.

We turn to the overgrown, unattended vegetable garden, and I send the girls within the tangled vines like jungle explorers.

The oldest sends up the offering.

Another handful—just enough—for lunch. I'd been thinking of the beauty of the Lord's prayer: *Give us this day our daily bread.* There's just enough today. We don't store or fret over this. We just open our hands and are filled with what we need for today.

68. Your Flying Leap

In the middle of the night, a raging storm rips through the valley. Loud thunder and blinding lightning wake us all.

Normally in such conditions, my youngest will race down the stairs, burst through our bedroom door, and take a *flying leap* to land right into the middle of our bed. She'll burrow down, wiggling and shimmying her way into a comfortable spot, stretch out her little arms and legs, and fall fast asleep in the security and satisfaction of it all.

Not my oldest. She arrives cautiously and stands by the door. She announces the obvious—the loud storm—and makes all sorts of excuses about why she's at our door. (Like the children in *The Sound of Music*!) I actually coax her to my side to let her receive comfort. Still, she's justifying herself, explaining her fear, and asking if I'm sure it's OK that she's bothered me at 3:00 AM.

All into the morning, I visualize the difference between that flying leap into my comforting arms and the cautious, justifying stance of the wise, logical older sister. So many times, my approach to God brings me cautiously to the door, making excuses, wondering if I'm a bother.

Doesn't scripture proclaim that we can come *boldly*—in a flying leap sort of way—to receive from God? I remember this from Hebrews 4: "So let us come *boldly* to the throne of our gracious God. There we will receive his mercy, and we will find grace to help us when we need it most."

When did my oldest abandon her flying leap? When did I?

Living with flair means we race, we burst through, we take a flying leap into the arms of God.

69. "They Received More Than They Knew to Want"

I'm listening online to Paige Benton Brown give a talk at a women's conference. I remember her from 1998 (back when she spoke at Camp Greystone to a group of us counselors). She always knew how to make the Bible come alive and apply it in ways I so desperately needed as a young woman.

So I tune in all these years later to hear her again. As she begins teaching from the Bible, she describes how when people encounter God, "they received more than they even knew to want."[14]

They received more than they *even knew to want*.

I write the sentence in my journal and stop listening to anything else. I'm just so amazed by the truth of it: God gives what we don't even know we want yet.

We don't know to want it.

Our hearts have been instructed by so many false narratives that we don't even know to want the great things of God.

God wants to give what I don't even know to want. The thought astounds me again. I entrust myself to this God who knows what I don't know.

70. You Just Can't Know

On our journey home from visiting family, we stop at a restaurant for a late dinner. Our waitress, an older woman with silver hair, might have been tired from her shift or just angry that yet another family with young children has come to her section. Whatever the reason, she seems impatient, frustrated, and just unpleasant.

I take a deep breath. *This is going to be a fun dinner*, I think sarcastically.

But as our meal comes out, the waitress starts asking questions about our children. She inquires about their ages and then tells us she has three grandchildren right in that age range.

"Oh," I say politely, still not liking her one bit.

"I'm raising them," she continues. "Right as I was about to retire, my son was killed, and I inherited his three little children to raise on my own by myself."

I'm cut to my core.

We learn her son was murdered. She raises her grandchildren. Alone. She works as a waitress when she wanted to retire.

It's the very end of her shift, and it's getting late. Nevertheless, she pulls up a chair and takes a seat because she remembers we said we were traveling back up to Penn State.

"How are you handling the news?" she asks, shaking her head and genuinely concerned for *us* because of the Sandusky scandal.

And so we talk for a bit. She wants to make absolutely sure I love my fried chicken. She wants to make absolutely sure I don't need more tea.

She shares more about losing her son, raising her grandchildren, and what it's like to live in this town.

We finish our meal and promise in our hearts never again to judge a waitress (or anyone!) in a bad mood. We just can't know what her life is like. We just can't know her story.

71. When You Find Yourself in Deep Waters

We drive to the beach to let our children see the ocean. Watching the sea creates that moment of awe I want them to experience; that sublime encounter when nature overpowers their imagination ushers in worship and joy.

Behold the great ocean!

We splash in the waves, dig in the sand, and collect shells. My oldest daughter and I venture out past the breakers into deep waters. *Could there be sharks?* Well, yes. *Could there be jellyfish?* Well, yes. *Will giant waves crash against me?* Well, yes.

In the midst of all the questions and real fears, we look down towards our feet and notice the sparkle of unbroken seashells scattered on the ocean floor. Here, they don't endure the assault of the waves. Here, they stay intact and beautiful.

My daughter runs to get a bucket and comes back out into the ocean. She picks up seashells (with her feet!) and builds a collection of treasures from the deep.

When I find myself in deep waters—amid real fears and assaults—I remember to build my collection of treasures from the deep. Certain gifts can only come from this deep and dangerous place.

72. The Where and the What Matter Less and Less

I finish a paragraph by Margaret Silf in her book, *Inner Compass*, and realize how much I believe it. She writes, "There is nothing on earth that doesn't reveal some fragment of the reality of its maker, nor any moment that I live that doesn't hold

God concealed within it. Sometimes this is obvious, as in a beautiful sunset. Sometimes it remains hidden."[15]

Every moment that I live, therefore, holds God concealed.

Here and now! It doesn't matter where I am or what's happening all around me. I can be assured that God is with me and *in even this*.

Sometimes, it does indeed remain hidden.

But if I seek, I will find. If I ask, the great door will be opened.

In even this.

I'm starting to consider this task as my life's work; the poetry of finding the concealed fragment that reveals God offers the kind of joy and meaning I cannot live without.

The older I get, the more I realize that the *where* and the *what* of my life matter less and less. The reality of God in and about me makes every place sacred, every person a mystery, and every situation ripe with glory.

Amen!

73. Like a Father

I'm reading another line by Margaret Silf that helps me understand something about God. She writes:

"Imagine yourself as a wounded bird savaged by a cat, or as an animal caught in a trap, or as a small child who has hurt herself. . . Now, without offering any excuses or justifications or reproaches against what has harmed you, just let yourself be gathered up by God and held gently in the palm of his hand."[16]

Just let yourself be gathered up. I think of how, when my daughters were toddlers, they used to scamper about the yard. My husband would swoop down, gather them in his arms, and lift them high into the air. They still beg for that game so they can be caught up in those arms!

I think of a Great Father, swooping down to gather me as I scamper about. After being gathered up, Silf says now to "Be still, and simply know that he is God, who loves you and desires your wholeness so much that he is ready to die for it."

A Great Swooping Father's Love.

74. Driven from a False Resting Place

I keep coming back to the same paragraph in Hannah Whitall Smith's, *The God of All Comfort*. In a chapter entitled, "Things That Cannot Be Shaken," she discusses the flimsy foundations we often build our lives upon rather than the sure foundation of God and God alone.

But these flimsy foundations seem *so very secure*. We rest in good things: ministry, productivity, family, kindness, orderly living, or intelligence.

How can we see what cannot be shaken? In order to gain the sure foundation of God and God alone, she claims we go through various "shakings" so that what remains is that which cannot be shaken.

These shakings come from a Loving Hand in order to make us strong, immovable, and fully secure.

Smith writes, "But there comes an upheaval, and all our foundations are shaken and thrown down, and we are ready to despair and question whether we can be Christians at all. . . If people have rested on their good works and their faithful service, the Lord is often obliged to take away all power for work. . . in order that the soul may be driven from its false resting place and forced to rest in the Lord alone."[17]

The false resting place!

Smith further discusses the false rest of good feelings, sound doctrine, prosperity, good reputation, secure home and family, accomplishment, and even mental clarity. So many things that we rely upon for a sure foundation—when shaken—reveal that they could never save us at all.

I'm left with God alone.

Praise God, I'm left with Him alone.

75. Places Within Places

I'm reading a line in Jamie Zeppa's memoir from her time in Bhutan about her love of secret places. As a child, she loved finding hidden places.

She calls them *places within places*.[18]

The line shimmers for me. I just can't stop thinking about it. Maybe it's because I'm learning how to dwell in the "secret place" of the Most High God. I'm learning about the inner refuge—the place within—of peace and joy.

Places within places.

I remember how my children love hiding under the Weeping Cherry. In that secret place, hidden away, they let the arms of that great tree fall around them.

I walk downtown with these little ones, and I remember a child's love of places within places.

I know about a secret pond that's tucked away right behind a building on campus.

"You won't believe it!" I tell my daughters. "Just wait!" We round a tall building, and there we find a little pond that I could cross in just five steps if I wanted.

We find newly hatched goslings, great turtles the size of dinner plates, and beautiful ducks.

We had to go deep within the campus, behind the structures, into the unseen. *Places within places.* No matter where I am, there's a place within this place full of wonder.

76. She Taught Me How to Love My Neighbor

When I moved to this town and showed up to retrieve my oldest daughter from kindergarten, a woman came to find me. She introduced herself, welcomed me to the neighborhood, provided her phone number, and immediately invited me over to her home for an after-school snack to meet her children.

I went. I had nowhere else to go and nobody else to talk to.

She connected me to all of her friends, cooked for me, offered to watch my children, and essentially did *whatever I needed* to help me transition to this new community.

Know this: She's a working single mother with three children, a busy schedule, and needs of her own.

And yet.

And yet she loved her neighbor. She took the time for me!

I think about this dear woman, Kristen Caswell, whenever a new family moves into the neighborhood. I find myself running to find the new families, providing a note card with my phone number, and offering to do what I do best: walk children to school and cook Italian meals.

My kitchen right now has all the ingredients for Chicken Parmigiana. I'll deliver a meal to a new family and ask, like Kristen did for me, "How can I help you? What do you need?"

She taught me all the simple ways to love a new neighbor. Since the Lord is teaching me to love in ways that are uniquely me, I'm going to love my new neighbor with loads of mozzarelle (I already discovered they love Italian cooking). And remember, the only reason I can do this is because the Italian Mama was a good neighbor to me last year when she taught me how to cook out of the goodness of her great Italian Mama heart.

I'm learning what it looks likes to help and to love. I'm going to love my neighbor, and I'm *so excited*.

77. A Day that Changed Me Forever

I've been sitting in my rocking chair by the Weeping Cherry and reading *The Hiding Place* by Corrie ten Boom. It's a cool morning, and I have my old green sweater around my arms, a fat cat at my feet, and coffee by my side. I feel older than I've ever felt in my life. I'm weighted down by more than age; I feel the heavy sadness and confusion of land wars, shot down planes, storms, suicides, and so much news of suffering that my heart cannot contain it. For a moment, I let God take it all from me, and I rest in my chair.

If you haven't read *The Hiding Place*, it's the account of how a Dutch Christian family helped many Jews escape the Nazi Holocaust. We follow Corrie ten Boom's imprisonment in horrific conditions and how she found strength, hope, and forgiveness in Jesus. You can also watch the movie made in 1975 based on Corrie's book.

This book is especially meaningful to me because I remember how one summer at Camp Greystone, I met the traveling companion to Corrie ten Boom, Ellen Stamps. Mrs. Stamps was a visiting speaker at camp who shared many stories of her time with Corrie ten Boom as they traveled the world together to share the message of Jesus Christ before Corrie died.

I scurry down to my basement and pile up all the old journals from that summer at Camp Greystone. I find the one that takes me back to this moment:

One day, Mrs. Stamps invited me to her little guest cabin, brewed me hot coffee (even in the middle of summer), and prayed with me about my own life and struggles. It was July 26, 1995, and I wrote in my journal everything I learned from this humble woman who had more wisdom stored in her than any person I had ever met. She talked to me privately—as the rain fell and the coffee brewed—to impart a few special lessons just for me.

I felt so loved by God that He would allow me to spend time with such a godly woman. I wrote in my journal, "I think my life began to change on July 26, 1995." I was young in my faith. I was confused and full of shame and worry.

I learned this:

Mrs. Stamps began by telling me that the Holy Spirit is a Spirit of Hope. *Anything else is wrong. Don't listen to any other voice but Hope.*

She also told me that the ups and downs of my heart are like the waves of the sea, but that the Holy Spirit is a *calm place within me.*

We sat in two chairs by a small wooden table with just a lamp and a Bible on it. It rained, and I could smell the mulch and the pine trees. Mrs. Stamps' wrinkled hands held onto mine. This woman who had spent so many years traveling with and learning from Corrie ten Boom held *my* hands in hers, and I wrote in my journal about all the hands those hands had comforted over the years. What would my hands do in my life? Why was God letting me touch what I felt like were sacred hands?

She spoke of forgiveness—of *forgiving oneself and receiving the Lord's forgiveness.*

She also spoke about a beautiful broken harp that no one in the village could repair. In this illustration, the only person who could repair the harp to make beautiful music was the one who built it himself. Mrs. Stamps reminded me that *God made me and knows how to repair whatever is broken in me.*

Those were powerful and important moments in my journey with the Lord as a twenty year old.

So I'm sitting in my rocking chair, now two decades later, and I go back to the lessons of Corrie ten Boom that she passed on to Ellen Stamps. I had forgotten my favorite lesson from Corrie's father after her first broken heart. He tells her this:

"Corrie. . . do you know what hurts so very much? It's love. Love is the strongest force in the world, and when it is blocked, that means pain. There are two things we can do when this happens. We can kill the love so that it stops hurting. But then of course part of us dies, too. Or, Corrie, we can ask God to open up another route for this love to travel."[19]

All morning, I think about when our love (our desires, our dreams, our hopes) is blocked and we experience pain. I'm filled with such overwhelming hope when I see the wisdom of asking God to open up another route for our love to travel.

If not this path, then that one. If not this, *then something else.* I pray for God to keep my love strong and to open up all the routes on which this love might travel best.

I look back on the wisdom of Corrie ten Boom, her father, and Ellen Stamps. On a single rainy afternoon twenty years ago, their stories intersected mine in a way that changed me forever.

78. Oh, How Quickly We Forget: A Confession

I'm rolling my eyes as I look out to the garden. I have to harvest the berries *again.*

It takes so long.

I get so dirty.

Then I have to store them.

Lord, why do we have all these berries?

Can you believe how quickly I can forget my *longing* for a berry garden? Can you believe how quickly joy and celebration turn to complaint and drudgery?

So very quickly.

For years, we lovingly cared for the soil, the new shoots, and the blossoms. We expertly staked and fed and watered and waited.

Now the harvest has come and is coming. Now the thing I've waited for arrives in my palms, and I just roll my eyes, exhausted by it.

Oh, how I need a Savior! The human heart wants what it does not have and balks at it when it gets it. We can turn every gift into a burden. We can turn every blessing into a complaint.

As I pick strawberries and see the red juice stain my fingers, I recall *how quickly* the thing we long for consumes us, becomes too much, and sours in our hands.

Even the berries carry the curse.

79. 65 Ways to Act Like a Fool

I'm reading the book of Proverbs and taking notes on what it means to be a fool.

My list grows long. (This is the shortened version below!) I have many ways to grow in wisdom. (The parts about eating, speaking, and sleeping too much always get me!)

I start to realize how much I long to be a *wise* woman, not a foolish one. I make my list and put it by my bedside table. I'm humbled as I think about it:

Foolish people
1. Are greedy for money
2. Hate instruction and don't enjoy learning
3. Have no fear of God
4. Are lazy and complacent
5. Take pleasure in evil
6. Are disloyal and unkind
7. Depend on their own understanding without seeking counsel
8. Plot harm against their neighbors
9. Pick fights
10. Envy others
11. Mock people
12. Cause others to sin
13. Chase fantasies
14. Speak with foul language
15. Commit adultery
16. Have no self-control
17. Love to sleep all the time
18. Lie
19. Kill
20. Sow discord between family members
21. Flatter and seduce
22. Cause grief to their parents
23. Talk too much
24. Squander their money
25. Irritate their employers
26. Harm their own city
27. Gossip and share secrets; enjoy listening to gossip
28. Are stingy and don't like to share
29. Act and feel self-important; they brag and boast
30. Are cruel to animals
31. Always think they are right
32. Trust in their wealth most of all
33. Are quick-tempered, easily angered
34. Waste

35. Use violence
36. Hang out with foolish people
37. Don't leave an inheritance for their grandchildren
38. Don't discipline their children
39. Have many unreconciled relationships
40. Believe everything they are told
41. Act recklessly because they love danger; they have no caution
42. Don't help the poor
43. Speak harsh words
44. Don't pursue godliness
45. Don't think before speaking
46. Love rebellion
47. Accept bribes
48. Hold grudges
49. Nag
50. Don't keep their word
51. Love pleasure
52. Love to drink alcohol
53. Accumulate debt
54. Exploit people
55. Rejoice when others fail
56. Show favoritism
57. Want the highest seat of honor
58. Eat too much
59. Argue with foolish people
60. Conceal their sin
61. Fear people other than God
62. Complain
63. Abandon friends and family
64. Impulsively spend money
65. Act with selfish motives rather than serving

I'm so glad God doesn't give up on me!

80. The Smallest Act Sanctified

Today I remember the beauty of small, humble living. I'm reading Thomas a Kempis' *The Imitation of Christ*, and I'm reminded of simple acts of love that reflect the glory of God.[20]

And it just so happens that both my daughters are sick today (one with a stomach bug and the other with an infection), and I find myself going about the unglamorous tasks of cleaning a toilet, serving tea, and simply pressing a cool hand against a hot forehead.

Nobody sees. It's quiet here. We're all alone.

But suddenly it feels holy—like Jesus is here with me. It feels like His love is here, and I'm to extend it to these little ones with every whisper of comfort and act of service around them. That's the grand calling for today, and I accept it gladly.

81. Unconditional Positive Regard

I learn from a former nurse about the concept of "unconditional positive regard" for every single patient. Something about the phrase resonates with me because it's about believing the best about people and treating them with respect regardless of what the person says or does. It's about giving equal chances and equal care.

I know this idea has necessary limits in the case of law-breaking or when being harmed by someone, but generally speaking, it's about kindness.

15 minutes before learning this concept, I witness a woman screaming at an employee in a coffee shop because he doesn't get her order correct. She stomps her feet, pounds the counter, and begins humiliating the employee in a loud voice. I want to run to that tired worker, throw my arms around him, and comfort him. (I actually do intervene and encourage him briefly; he ends up giving me a free coffee!)

I find myself favoring the employee—showing *him* unconditional positive regard—because it's easy. But what about the angry woman? What if I had gone to *her*, put my arms around *her*, and comforted *her*?

I'm learning to go beyond my natural, first response judgments and see new perspectives. What if I found the person hardest to love and went to *her*?

I'm thinking about that angry woman this morning. I wish I had loved her.

82. By the Time I Finished, I Came Out New

This morning, I read a post by Judy Douglass on *going low*. It's about motherhood, but it's also about choosing the "lowest place" in all things. Judy writes about what it means to "go low": you go last; you give up your plans to defer to others; you sacrifice sleep; you forfeit your own time.[21]

I need to read it. I need it like I need air. I wake up with the little ones bouncing around me wanting to bake cookies, play dolls, read, and swing on the swing *with me*. But I want to be alone. I want to sleep. I want to read poetry.

They need hair brushed, sunscreen applied, laundry folded, emotions soothed. *All day long.*

Once, before children, I slept until noon. I strolled downtown to a coffee shop and drank a leisurely cafe mocha while reading poetry books and composing thoughtful poems of my own.

The whole day belonged to me.

Then I became a mother, and I was depressed for years and years. I wrote this in the midst of one of the hardest days, and by the time I finished it, I came out new on the other side.

Steadfast in Motherhood

Split-pea soup on the stove;
chicken pot-pie in the refrigerator;
ingredients for morning waffles made ahead;
laundry, folded; bed, made.

I'm here, God, with candles lit
in the middle of the day.
Just me, with a steadfast heart,
like some pebble thrown out across
a pond, settled in generations of silt.

I still believe and wait for wonder to seize me
in the midst of flour, sugar, and peas.

This morning at 8:00 I drove
to get groceries. The check-out line
was long enough for me to read every headline,
study a hundred other women's lives,
wrapped in silk and chocolates.

I kept thinking of my soft, warm bed
where once, I slept in
for hours, then sipped cocoa, reading poems
in the middle of the day. Maybe here and there
a light-hearted phone call.
Me, pampered, but with a lost heart
wanting freedom
with only myself to please.

God, you have saved me from myself.
You recreated me in a new recipe.
I'm the pebble that shines because of the
elements that cover and consume it.
You let others dine on me and be satisfied,
and I let myself wash away with the dishwater.
You have come, in the midst of myself,
and saved me.

83. Led, Not Driven

Today I remember to calm down with all my *driven* tendencies to do more, write more, plan more, build a better platform, etc. etc. etc.

I read Twitter, and I feel bad about all the ways I'm not being influential or important.

I start to feel driven again.

Driven folks feel forced to succeed, produce, and excel. *Led* people respond to the gentle whisper of God's spirit. They accept specific, simple instructions and go exactly where they're led. Everything comes after that—the planning, writing, doing, and building.

Seek first the kingdom and *then*. . .

When I'm driven, I'm fearful, frantic, and frenzied.

When I'm led, I'm full of faith, peaceful, and ordered.

My prayer today: *Lord, let me be led and not driven. Your yoke is easy and light. Mine is hard and heavy. When you lead, you bring me to paths of peace and joy. When I'm driven, I find disorder and unrest. I want to be led by you to accomplish the good works you've planned for me. No more, no less, at just the right time. Led and not driven. Amen.*

84. My Biggest Writing (and Life) Struggle: Point of View

All week, I revise a novel's point of view. It's hard! The narrator tells the story through the lens of just one character, so I have to be sure his knowledge comes from what only he experiences. Even though I know *everything* as the author, I can only reveal to the reader what comes from the main character's point of view.

It's limiting! It binds me to dialogue and observation. I just want to tell everything quickly and obviously, but this would be no fun at all for the reader.

Studying point of view alerts me to exactly *how limiting* it is. There's a whole larger story that I deliberately don't let a character—or a reader—access yet. The narrator exists within clear boundaries of a chosen viewpoint for a very specific reason:

It makes a better story.

I have to remember my limited point of view. It's just one character's lens.

I love thinking of God as an Author who knows the whole story. I'm sitting here within those boundaries—accepting what I cannot know and cannot do—and surrendering to the joy of the *whole story*.

One day, I'll read it.

85. A Thorough Repentance

Last night, the fireworks show begins with a reading of the Declaration of Independence.[22] I'm listening to the voice boom over the loudspeakers across the valley, and I'm deeply aware of the verbs for the first time in my life: *dissolve, throw off, absolve*.

I'm hearing it again: We totally dissolve this. We will not tolerate this oppression. We will not. We throw it far away from us.

I think of how *very thorough* the breaking away is. There's no going back.

It's a declaration against what comes against the human spirit. It's a declaration against tyranny. As I sit there in the darkness, I consider my own declarations against that which tyrannizes and comes against everything of God in me. I think about repentance and all the ways I want to turn away from sin and move towards God.

I consider the *thorough* language of the Declaration of Independence—the great care, the attention to every detail of oppression—and how strong and forceful it becomes. I want to be that thorough when it comes to anything oppressing me and my family and community.

I feel courage rising in me. I feel another call to battle, but this time, *thorough*. I look at encroaching sin, and I sever ties; I dissolve, throw off, absolve, and declare a new allegiance.

86. Too Much Too Soon

I harvest the beautiful cherry tomatoes today.

I'm disappointed by how many have split open. All but a few are ruined. I learn that split tomatoes are breeding grounds for bacteria and generally aren't good for eating.

Why do they split and crack like this? Most gardeners agree it's because of irregular watering that causes the tomato to grow so fast that the skin cannot accommodate the growth.

Too much growth too soon cracks us wide open. I consider the value of *slow* growth. Things come about in time. There's no rush.

I love fast and big. The split cherry tomato reminds me that slow, even growth wins the day.

87. If You Have a Child Who Talks Too Much

First of all, I was a child who talked too much.

My older sister and parents don't laugh about these memories; they *agonize* over them. If you ask them about how much I talked as a child, they'll close their eyes and step back as if they are trying to distance themselves from the terrible memory of my talking, like people shielding their eyes from the glare of the fiery sun. My mom will say, "You have no idea. You have *no idea* how much she talked."

It was all this as a child: *Heather, stop talking. Heather, please, please be quiet. Heather, let someone else talk. Heather, will you please just stop talking? Please? If you don't stop talking, I'm going to go crazy.*

My talking single-handedly caused more migraine headaches in my house than any other trigger.

I had such serious articulation needs (isn't that a nicer and more medical way to say it, like it wasn't something I chose?) that *talking* wasn't actually enough. Not at all. I *wrote* in journals, voiced stories inside my head to myself, and maintained an ongoing glitzy parade of words all day long. I remember walking around my backyard, reciting the Gettysburg Address or a speech I wrote of my own, just to hear the rhythm of the words.

Everything I learned, I had to teach someone because I loved them that much. Besides, everything I thought, I had to export somehow or it corrupted inside of me, festering.

As an adult, this need never waned. I've written a thesis, a dissertation, six novels, thousands of blogs, and twenty journals full of words. And I talk. Oh, Lord, I talk. And then I talk some more. And more. I talk to God most of all. He's the best listener.

Words, words, words. I can't stop. The words are just so sweet and juicy and must be shared. The thoughts fill up my head and have to escape or else I go crazy inside, like steam screaming on the kettle.

So I both talk and write too much. I generally *am* too much.

My oldest daughter inherited my too-muchness. So at dinner a few nights ago, she asks the table guests, "Am I talking too much?"

We *gently, gently* suggest that she might want to let others talk, too. Just like her teacher *gently, gently* told her she might want to let other students answer in class. Just like her youth pastor *gently, gently* reminded her that other people have thoughts to share, too.

So we're doing all that gentle training. It's good. She needs to learn, like her wise father says, that there's a time and place for things—like fire in a fireplace is good, but fire outside the fireplace harms people. She has to control the fire a bit to right times and right places. Who doesn't?

But something overcame me this morning. I called out to my daughter to come to me immediately, in a voice like something was on fire or that *I* was on fire and needed rescue (it felt like I was).

"What, Mom? I'm here."

"Do you know when you asked if you were talking too much last night? Well, listen to me right now. Listen as hard as you can: You are absolutely perfect. You are absolutely amazing. You have things to say." I think of her thoughts bubbling over like the caramel you melt for candied apples in autumn. "You just keep being you, all the time."

I said this because I have found people who love me and who let me talk and write because I must. They don't silence me or shame me. They fold their hands under their chins, refill their coffee mugs, and let me talk and talk and talk. I suppose I could have stopped talking because it was so annoying (and it often is), but it's also part of who I am.

A man fell in love with this talker and thanks the good Lord that for every introverted, quiet man, there's a boisterous, extroverted woman bushwhacking her way into social settings and paving an easy path for him to follow. (One neighbor said it's more like I'm a Marine storming new territory, and my husband is like the Army coming in after, quietly maintaining peace and order.)

The point is that my husband has been listening to and reading my words for 15 years.

And, to give you hope, dear parent of a talker, I've learned to meet all of these articulation needs in more unselfish ways that don't require people to just sit and listen, but *I've never stopped getting the words out.*

It's because at just the right —when I was exactly my daughter's age—a teacher told me to write speeches and compete in oratory contests because I just had so much to say and people needed to hear it. I didn't lose one word during those years. I wrote them all down and spoke them on stage. In high school, I went straight from oratory to Policy Debate where the goal was to speak as many words as possible in the shortest amount of time.

As many words as possible! There were prizes given for this sort of bliss. I was home. I found myself. While other girls were riding horses or shopping at the mall in the summers, I went to debate camp with all the other talkers who were so happy together we were like young wizards finally using their wands at Hogwarts. My sister and parents fully supported this competitive speaking, and they drove me all over the United States to debate things I can't even remember now.

It could have gone differently. I could have listened and stopped talking like all the precious, orderly, appropriate, silent daughters of the world who speak only when spoken to. These children, I fear, turn in on themselves, closing tightly shut like sea anemones who open for no one.

But I didn't.

I just don't want my daughter's words lost because she's been shamed one too many times or made to feel like she's too much, exhausting, selfish, or annoying.

I don't want to silence children; I want to fan the flame of all their glorious word seeds and let the whole thing rage on.

Someone wants to listen. There's a stage waiting for her like there was for me.

So when she asks again, "Am I talking too much?" with those wide, tearful, insecure eyes, I'm going to say, "No! In fact, tell me more. Tell me so much more."

I'll sit back and watch that blaze of glory.

88. Just Because It's Hard Doesn't Mean God's Not In It

I'm reading Genesis again, and I'm struck for the first time with God's great call on Abram's life. He asks the man to leave everything and "go to the land I will show you." There would be blessing! There would be greatness and prosperity!

So Abram follows God into a new land, and instead of prosperity, he finds a *great famine* there. I'm not kidding. It's right there in Genesis 12:10. This doesn't sound delightful or promising to me. This doesn't sound very glamorous. This sounds hard and unfair. Where's the blessing, greatness, and prosperity?

So I keep reading, and then I find that wonderful truth we've all been waiting for:

"After this, the word of the Lord came to Abram in a vision: 'Do not be afraid, Abram. I am your shield and your very great reward'."

I am your shield and your very great reward.

God himself is the very great reward. That's why, even in a great famine, we still have our shield and great reward. We still have our blessing, our greatness, and our prosperity. It's *God*. No matter what kind of scarcity—whether resources, relationships, insight, or health—we have a great reward in the midst of the famine.

And perhaps that's the only way we know it to be true. Perhaps that's why God called Abram—not to glorious abundance—but to famine.

89. As You Want It to Be

Lately I've been thinking about the ways we bring life and joy to people and our circumstances. I am learning how to speak about people and circumstances and envision the very best. I want to envision the glory of what *could be*—even if it's not quite there yet.

It's the same with teaching and parenting. I speak into what could be, as I want it to be, as I know it can be. I learned this technique back in my camp counselor days when the wise director trained us to *shape a particular reality* for our campers. You simply tell nervous or homesick children what's coming and how they will feel. Children, I learned, sometimes don't know how to feel unless we tell them.

It's a strange thing to observe an influential voice tell a child how awful or inconvenient something is, and then see another voice proclaim the beauty and blessing in the very same circumstance. Two children in the same situation will feel differently based on whose voice they allow to shape their reality.

I'm learning that I shape a reality by my words and demeanor for my children, their friends, my students, and my peers. I look out from here and see the glory of God, indescribable hope and joy, freedom, and strength to overcome. I see healing, wonder, rich community, laughter, and blessing.

This is how I'll speak of it. This is how I want it to be. This is actually how it is and will be.

90. You Have Authority

Today at an intersection, I see a central point around which tentacles of cars line up to wait their turn to go. So many "lane closed" and "detour here" signs dot the landscape that nobody really has any idea what to do or where to drive.

Then I see him. A thin old man complete with a white beard and weathered face stands in the middle of it all. It's like the government called in the oldest and wisest to handle this mess.

The man waves his arms to one group, directing with pointed figures exactly where to turn. Then he holds another hand to stop a line of cars. Then he changes direction, challenging cars that try to sneak on. *Oh no you don't!*

He's so *small* in stature against the onslaught of cars, but so very large in authority.

As he continues this full body workout of directing us, I notice that he doesn't seem self-conscience or worried in the slightest. It's because he knows he's been put there for such a time as this. He's been placed right in the middle of a complicated mess—with work to do—so he doesn't question himself.

So small. Such authority.

It doesn't match up. He's so powerless-looking and yet has ultimate power here. It makes me think about all the complicated places God sets me down to accomplish his work. The obstacles might be huge and threatening, but I don't have to think about them or myself at all.

I have delegated authority, so I don't worry.

91. Within the One, Two Thousand

I climb on a chair to peer inside.

The sunflower is really *in there.*

My youngest is amazed that a seed no bigger than her fingernail is making *this.* And that one seed will turn into as many as 2000 seeds (they are really called the "fruit" of the plant) once the sunflower blooms and continues to grow.

One seed into two thousand? How can it be?

I love this simple truth that some things we plant do multiply into more than themselves. Within the one, *two thousand.* We just cannot know.

Living with flair means we remember that one good thing sown in faith can multiply beyond our imagination.

(I need to learn how to harvest the seeds to eat. Hopefully, this will be easier than my acorn flour experiment.)

92. "You can't see me; I'm kneeling down."

This morning in church, the pastor kneels down in worship during his sermon. Practically speaking, nobody can see him. Folks strain their heads, and he calls out, "You can't see me! I'm kneeling down!"

That's right. In a sermon on taking the lowest place, on humbling oneself, and on exalting the name of Jesus instead of our names and platforms, that moment of *invisibility* in worship isn't lost on me.

I've spent all my life trying to make a name for myself. I thought Christianity might save me from this, and yet, I find Christians all around me climbing the same ladder to stand out, be heard, be named. I'm not sure where *I* fit in. Wouldn't it be lovely to be free from that race?

I think about the great children's book, *Charlotte's Web*. I was thinking about Charlotte and the phenomenon that she could write. Nobody thinks about the spider; they think about the pig she writes *for*. Wilbur gets the attention. It's so strange. A spider can *write*, but Wilbur becomes famous.

God, if nobody can see me in this crowd, let it be because I'm kneeling down.

93. Even If It Means Less

I see a black swallowtail in the garden. By the two rows of spots and the fast wings beating (females have one row of spots, apparently, and they beat their wings slowly), I know it's a male.

And I know what he wants: the purple *buddleja* flowers. We grow light purple and dark purple, and I'm learning that butterflies and hummingbirds simply can't resist them.

But why? And why do they stay so long on these particular flowers?

I discover that this unique flower has one of the highest levels of sucrose in the nectar compared to other garden flowers. The butterflies go after *quality*. And they stay so long on this plant because it actually doesn't produce much nectar. *Fascinating*. A butterfly will go for less nectar of higher quality than tons of nectar of low quality. He'll risk capture. He'll risk death.

He knows he's got the best, and he simply won't compromise.

I want to be both the *buddleja* and the butterfly. I want to give my best, even if that means less. And I want to go after the best, even if it means a longer journey with less.

Even if it means *less*.

Living with flair means we aren't seduced by bigger and more. We produce less but better. We feed on better but less.

94. I Stand Corrected: Emotional Well-Being Isn't the Goal. Intimacy with Jesus is the Goal.

This summer, I'm speaking on emotional maturity and well-being in leaders. I've accumulated over ten years worth of research in therapeutic settings on how people can achieve well-being and happiness.

But something doesn't seem right as I talk about boundaries, creativity, toxic relationships, balance, and all the other tricks one learns to protect oneself from anything distressing or negative.

I've gone too far. I realize how much I miss out on in the name of "emotional well-being." I realize what I won't allow, what I resist from God, where I won't go, and what I won't do in the name of my own emotional health. It's too self-protective. It's too self-exalting.

It's an idol, really. At least for me it is. Emotional health trumps everything these days, and it feels wrong.

It's good—in moderation—to apply boundaries and techniques for balanced, happy living, but when it comes right down to it, that's not the primary goal of my life.

The primary goal of my life is to know and love God. It's to learn the secret of being content in every situation (which, I'm ashamed to admit, isn't the happiness philosophy of the day). The secret is that we can "do all things though Christ who strengthens [us]."

If God leads us to distressing places, we don't resist to protect our emotional health. If God leads us to a hard-to-love person or a difficult circumstance, we don't shy away in the name of our own need for comfort.

If God leads us to sorrow, a lack of balance, depression, anxiety, or pain, the first question isn't, "How do I get back my emotional health?" The first question is, "How can I be with Jesus in this? How can I find the strength of God here?"

I have so much more to learn.

95. The Best Definition of Freedom: 4 Things

I'm reading Ruth Haley Barton's *Longing for More: A Woman's Path to Spiritual Transformation in Christ*. She writes in the introduction that "the whole spiritual journey could be characterized as a journey into freedom."[23]

I've got my pen poised above the book as the early morning sun shines on me. I'm ready for this. I want to learn more. I love the pause in summertime when I ask questions towards my own spiritual growth.

The writer considers how when Paul writes in 2 Corinthians 3:17 that "where the Spirit of the Lord is, there is freedom," this means something *deeply profound*.

It means, according to Barton, "the freedom to be completely given over to God and to others in love in any given moment. It is the ability to live from an inner security, freed from self-interest, self-consciousness, and self-protection. This is the freedom to live a life of utter responsiveness to the Spirit of God within us."[24]

Completely given over to God and others in love.

Living from inner security.

Free from self.

Utterly responsive.

This is my prayer in my journal today. This is the best definition of freedom, and I'm excited for God to work it out in me. At any given moment, I pray for utter responsiveness and that kind of authentic love.

96. What Oprah's Harvard Commencement Speech Taught Me

Yesterday, I read Oprah Winfrey's commencement address at Harvard University's 362nd commencement ceremony.

I learned that in all of Oprah's interviews with famous people from all over the world—presidents, celebrities, businessmen, even criminals—she discovered they all shared one thing in common: *they needed validation.*

After interviewing both the famous and the unknown, Oprah reflects, "They ask, 'Was that OK?' I've heard that from President Bush, I heard that from President Obama. . . I even heard that from Beyoncé in all her Beyonceness. . . They all want to know one thing: Was that OK? Did you hear me, did you see me, did what I said mean anything to you?"[25]

Was that OK? Was I OK?

All of us share that need, and today, I remember the profound importance of validation. I hear you. I see you. What you share means everything to me.

You are OK.

(And Oprah concluded her speech by asking the crowd, "Was that OK?")

97. An Extraordinary Find: The Secret Resonance Chamber

This morning, my youngest finds the shed exoskeleton of a cicada. She can hardly believe it. She's heard the news about the seventeen year wait for such insects to emerge. She's heard their songs—haunting, loud, and strange—across the landscape. But she's never seen one.

We examine the abandoned shell and marvel at the tiny hole by which the cicada exited. Such an interesting insect!

We talk about that distinct cicada sound, and I learn that it's actually one of the loudest of insect-producing sounds. But how? We discover that the hollow inside of the cicada's abdomen acts like a resonance chamber to amplify that song.

"What's a *resonance chamber*?" she asks.

The very term delights me. It's an enclosed space where sound waves combine, reinforce, and intensify one another. And it's all happening inside that little insect. I begin to think about the space inside of *me*.

Just the other evening, a dear friend talked about her "mind space" and whether or not she makes room for lovely, noble, and pure thoughts. We talked about godly thinking that we allow to occupy our spacious minds.

It's like my own resonance chamber up in here. In the enclosed space of this life, I want to allow the Good, the Noble, the Lovely, and the Pure to combine, reinforce, and intensify. And I want the resulting music to be as loud and invasive as the cicada's song. Against a complacent and compromising culture, I let another song resonate, haunt, and confront.

You cannot escape that kind of song.

98. Let Things Be

I return to my blackberries after a summer away. What I love about blackberries is that they thrive when you *let them be.*

Nobody looks after them in the summer. They just do what they do until they ripen and nearly burst off the vine.

Some assignments from God are like this. You set something in place and let it be. You send off a prayer and let it go. You sow something deep and go about your life. One day, you look out the window and find the fruit of your labor that you neither tended nor worried over.

99. What You Give Away Comes Back to You

On my walk today, (I wish we had been together, so I'll just share everything I would have told you!) I think about the verse from Acts 20:35 (when Paul quotes Jesus) that claims, "It is more blessed to give than to receive." I start to wonder *why* this might be so. As I think about my life, I know that everything I've given of myself freely, purely, with love, *expecting nothing*, has come back to me abundantly.

It's a spiritual law that I'm starting to understand. I look back on all those times I behaved in order to get something—whether more money, more attention, or more *anything*—and I realize that these things have all disintegrated. They do not last. They do not bring a blessing.

Things that truly remain and bring all the joy are things I've given *just because of love*. When the motivation is love, something changes. It's a key to unlock unimaginable blessings that far surpass the lesser goals of money, attention, prestige, reputation, security, comfort or any goal that ultimately builds a kingdom made of vapor.

Dig even deeper into this spiritual economy, and you'll find that not only is giving more blessed than receiving, but giving *in secret* earns a special reward from God (Matthew 6).

What will this reward be? What comes back into your empty hands? I have found that it's always joy, peace, community, and a richer relationship with God. This is more precious than anything you could earn or enjoy on earth.

100. Scatter Far and Wide; Some Will Take Root

The visit with the Bakers was wonderful! A special moment for me was when the daughter (the one with freckles who reminds me that "a face without freckles is like the sky without stars"—that one!) shared with me the list of my blogs she had personally saved to a file over the past four years. She's a rising 9th grader now, and she's been a faithful blog reader all these years. She read on my blog that I wanted to compile my favorite blogs for a little devotional book, and she figured her list might be of interest to me as I build my chapters.

I was so touched! I was so honored! I didn't realize she not only read them but *saved* them. All this time, when I think I'm doing no good in the world because publisher after publisher rejects my manuscripts because I'm not famous enough, I have before me an amazing young woman who reads my writing and gains courage and hope from it. I didn't know! I will keep writing for you forever and ever and ever!

So she pulls out her handwritten list of her favorite 25 blogs by title, and I smile for so many reasons. I smile because she chose some blogs that I thought resonated with *no one*. I smile because she put little stars by her favorite blogs within the list.

What did I notice? I noticed she loved blogs about courage, strength, hope, and risk taking. She loved blogs about family and authentic living and Jesus. Teenage girls want these things in their deep, intelligent hearts!

I also noticed that there was *simply no way* I could have predicted which insights mattered to her and for what reasons. I wrote what I felt like writing, and God did all the rest. I scattered my writing far and wide, and some of it took root in her heart.

I was amazed and thankful.

As the days passed, email after email came from readers who wanted to share their own lists of favorite blogs. Some told me that they reread the ones about the gift of celebration or the one about words that sound like what they mean (Effervesce! It sounds like it's fizzing over.)

My friend in Texas told me how she and her mother cried together when they read the blog about my time with Corrie Ten Boon's traveling companion. She told me they read my writing together at their kitchen table every night.

I read a note from a woman who kept all my blogs about how to thrive when you're in an in-between time in your life.

As I began to compile the writing for this book, I remembered one of my favorite letters from a reader. All her life she wanted to take a class from a college professor, but her family could never afford to send her to college. She hungered to learn, and her favorite college was Penn State. She prayed and prayed that one day, she could go to Penn State. The years passed, and this young woman grew into an older woman who gave up that dream. One day, she was reading my blog about a writing lesson, and it occurred to her that God *did* answer that prayer. Here she was in her old age, learning about writing from a Penn State writing professor! She wrote to me that my blog was God's answer to her prayer. Because I wrote every day, she felt like she was taking a course from me as she daily read my blog. I laughed and smiled for days about this.

I read that email over and over again. Now, she has the textbook to hold in her hands.

Finally, I was learning the truth of Ecclesiastes 11:6: "Cast your bread upon the waters, for after many days you will find it again." I cast out my words into the silence, and I found them again through the love and encouragement of readers all over the world.

I scattered. Some took root. Thank you, Lord.

Autumn

The trees are bearing their fruit;
the fig tree and the vine yield their riches.
Be glad, people of Zion,
rejoice in the Lord your God,
for he has given you the autumn rains
because he is faithful.
He sends you abundant showers,
both autumn and spring rains, as before.
The threshing floors will be filled with grain;
the vats will overflow with new wine and oil.
 "I will repay you for the years the locusts have eaten. . ."

Joel 2:22-25

1. I'm Taking You With Me

This morning, I dread that one student who looks me in the eye and says, "I just don't care." He's required to take this class to graduate, and so far *nothing* interests him. Not even short stories. Not even poems. Not even *semicolons*. He actually responds to a question I have about a story with, "I really just don't care."

You could hear a piece of chalk drop from my hand and roll back towards the chalkboard.

It happens every semester. Some students just don't care. And I can't make them. I can just showcase the wonder of the subject matter and pray that they connect.

And I can bring donuts. This is my secret weapon.

So this morning, I burst into the classroom bearing treats. It's going to be a great class. I'm going to inspire! I'm going to make that student fall in love with poetry! I'm going to fight apathy!

And that student *doesn't show up to class*. I deflate and wilt at my desk.

My secret weapon mission fails.

I'll try again on Friday. I'll have a new strategy that might involve Starbucks.

Whatever it takes to get students enthused, I have to try. There's so much to experience; there's so much to learn and *do*. I can't handle apathy because I've lived in that land. It's a partial death.

Generating enthusiasm means I continue the pursuit of that one person who doesn't care. With indifference, lack of emotion, and lack of concern ruling the day, nobody moves. Nothing changes. We ignore others and lose the passion in our own lives. I can't go back there. And I'm going to drag students, family members, neighbors, and friends with me back toward the light.

If I have to tempt you with treats, I will.

Living with flair means we fight apathy with whatever weapon we can.

2. Is God Like This?

This morning before church, I have a moment to relax with a cup of coffee at the kitchen table.

I put a dollop of whipped cream in my coffee mug. (I like to pretend I'm at Starbucks.)

All of a sudden, the little one flits over, skirt twirling and finger pointing at my mug.

Then she does it. She actually does it. She sticks her finger straight into the cream, pulls it out, and licks away.

The audacity! How *dare* she? I'm feeling. . . something. As she completes another twirl around me, I see her pointed finger approaching my mug. But instead of punishing her, I tip the coffee mug so she can get the most cream. I'm *encouraging* this atrocious behavior.

I'm so overcome with love for that little child.

The image of the little one dancing about me with inappropriate manners and audacious finger-pointing requests delights me. I should have been angry. I should have scolded her, but I cannot. That little twirl! That little finger full of cream!

Later in church, the image stirs up within me. It wasn't an audible voice; it wasn't a boom of thunder from the clouds. But as I recalled that child and how I couldn't help but tip the mug so she might enjoy more of what I could offer, I felt that Spirit-whisper saying: *I feel this way about you. I'm overcome with love.*

Dance about. Make audacious and inappropriate requests. Point the finger and dizzy yourself with twirls. God tips the mug, *delighted.*

3. Thank God for Friction

Yesterday, I hydroplane.

It's terrifying. One minute you're driving along the slick wet road, and the next minute, you're flying. The tires lose their grip on the road. The steering wheel seems disconnected from the car. The vehicle swerves recklessly.

It's out of control.

But just as quickly, the tire rediscovers the road. That clash, that beautiful resistance, keeps you centered in your lane and attached to the road.

I don't want a easy life. I don't want *smooth sailing*. It's the friction that ties me to my path. It's the clash against me that makes me function best. This sticky situation, this disappointment, this complaint reminds me of my need for God, of my absolute dependence, and of the reality of danger apart from that grip. It's humbling and it's uncomfortable sometimes. But it's safe.

Those things I don't want in my life just might be the friction I need to get to where I'm going.

4. Losing Something You Can't Recover

My student bursts into the classroom. "I've lost my paper! I didn't save it properly and the whole thing is *gone!*" The exasperation in this student's face is one I've seen many times before.

My student can't get that paper back. He stands in front of me, small and hopeless. *I've been there.* I remember the first time it happened to me. I remember the discouragement, the anger, the desperation, and the embarrassment of it all when I forgot to save a term paper.

It's not fair; it's not right. But I told myself I had to move beyond what's fair or right. I had to move beyond the anger and the shame.

I had to start again.

Students tell me that what they produce after the loss turns out stronger, more authentic, and more concise than the original paper. They build on the memory of what they once wrote and make something *better*. It's not easy, and it never seems fair. Losing stuff is like that. I'm learning to take a loss and build on it somehow to create a marvelous new thing.

Otherwise, I get stuck in the anger.

This won't be the last time we lose something that can't be recovered. But beauty does arise from the ashes. I see it every semester with every lost paper. I see it in my own life with every thing I've ever lost. There's a way to start again on the fresh page, remember what you had, and press your fingers down on the keys. You start letter by letter, word by word. Soon, you're not just back where you started. You're *beyond* in a beautiful far country that you never imagined existed. And the loss got you there.

5. A Mistake We Make

Our acorn stockpile—the one we stored up by the tree for the squirrels to find—wasn't such a great idea after all. A few days ago, I learned that acorns contain bitter tannins that interfere with a squirrel's ability to metabolize protein. That's why they *bury* them!

Burying acorns and letting them sit underground allows moisture to percolate through them to "leach out" the tannins.

Our stockpile circumvented this process. We'll have to bury them or let them sit in groundwater for days.

How could I not think of ways I seek short-cuts, of ways I stockpile and fret, when all along, I'm preventing a much needed process? When my plans rest dormant underground, might I see them as percolating in the moisture needed to make them nourishing and not destructive?

God is leaching out the bitter thing—the thing that might harm me.

Squirrels surrender to the process. They don't resist the truth of their circumstances. They gather, bury, and then feast only after that secret underground process completes. Might living with flair mean we watch the squirrels and understand something about our own journey with God?

I can't circumvent what *needs* to happen.

6. True Snapshot

School pictures never go well for us. Over the years, they always return with faces that more resemble mug shots than happy school pictures. One year, it actually looked like my daughter was growling at the photographer. Another year, the oldest daughter's eyes were half shut, and she had a haunting smirk on her face.

That year, our photographer friend rescued us. We met her at the studio in the mall, and for a comparable price, she created the most fabulous photo shoot for my daughters. They could choose all sorts of fun backgrounds, use props, and relax while the camera clicked away. Even better, this great photographer stopped and combed hair, adjusted clothing, and worked to capture the most authentic and vibrant smiles. We left an hour later with a package of prints to send to grandparents and aunts and uncles. And we could display two "school photos" in our living room that didn't look terrifying.

Telling my daughter she wasn't ordering school pictures that morning nearly sent her into a fit. That's when my husband said, "You're right. I want to make you *miserable*. I don't love you *at all*."

What she didn't recall (and couldn't know) was that his "no" meant a great "yes" and a trip to the mall later. And instead of 3 dull backgrounds, she would choose from a wide array of whimsical ones.

I throw fits in private to the Lord of the Universe about that cosmic "no" (whatever I'm not getting). But that "no" always, always ends with a better, more authentic and more vibrant "yes." The things I want might just be bad set-ups—as torturing as school photos compared to glamorous photo shoots. When I see it that way, and when I hear that voice chuckling, "You're right. I want to make you *miserable*. I don't love you *at all*," I realize how absurd my thinking is.

Do I really believe God withholds something to make me miserable? Because I'm not loved at all? Listening to my husband tease our daughter in the kitchen—and her delight in hearing the absurdity of it—made her actually beg for him to say it again. Even my older daughter wanted a reprise.

I want to make you *miserable*. I don't love you *at all*. We giggled. We hugged. We realized the truth.

7. How We Made Acorn Flour (A Lesson in Bitterness)

We gather the acorns from our oak tree.

Then, we carefully crack the shells and remove the nutmeat (I use a little hammer and a pick).

We shell about 2 cups worth of nuts because this is our first experiment.

Then, it's time for the long process of removing the tannins. I learn that tannins can harm you; they inflict stomach distress and kidney problems if you consume large amounts of this bitter substance. Removing the bitter tannins requires *time* and a steady flush of *fresh water*—either cold (like in a stream over a week-long period as the Native Americans did) or boiling hot (the quicker way).

When boiling, the water turns a deep brownish-black. Every 20 minutes, I change the water. After several hours, the water boils clear, and that tells me the tannins are gone. To be sure, I'm told to taste a nut. If it tastes like a sweet pasta—bland and not bitter—I've successfully leached the tannins. Since my acorns are from a Red Oak, they taste supremely bitter (as opposed to a White

Oak), so removing these tannins takes nearly 4 hours. If I had finely chopped the nuts, I could leach them faster.

The verb leach, by the way, means to drain away and remove. Here I am, *leaching bitterness* out of acorns, and the spiritual parallel rises up as surely as the sweet smell of acorn nutmeat. Those nuts submit to the process of cleansing, of uncomfortably stressful temperatures, over a long period of time. No wonder life seems hard sometimes.

Perhaps I'm being leached.

Finally, I take the leached nuts and grind them in a food processor. I want a coarse grind for a hearty, nutty bread.

I add a few cups to a regular bread recipe (flour, yeast, honey or sugar, oil, egg). I knead the dough, let it rise for one hour, and bake it at 350 degrees for 40 minutes. I've heard you want to use equal parts acorn flour and another flour or even cornmeal.

The bread tastes absolutely delicious. It's a warm, nutty, rich bread that the girls spread with sweet cream butter for breakfast. I'm not an expert in acorns, but the research claims that as long as you leach out the tannins, your acorns can provide muffins, breads, pancakes, cakes, and a whole variety of baked goods.

But you need that fresh water, boiled for a long time.

Lord, leach me. Remove every bitter thing in my heart.

8. Darning a Hole in Your Community

Last night, our neighborhood launched the second year of autumn Monday Night Neighborhood Fitness Group in the parking lot. We had children and adults jumping rope while others biked, skated, threw football and Frisbee, walked a circuit around the perimeter, flew the big turtle kite, or raced up the steep hill beside the parking lot.

From above, I wondered if we looked like one huge mass of criss-crossing elements filling in the space. We wove in and out, passing one another.

I thought of *darning.*

Darning is the technique one uses to repair a hole in fabric or knitting. I learned that a knitter makes a framework around the hole and then uses a crisscrossed pattern to fill the gap. My friend alerted me to this concept two days ago when I mentioned that the beautiful socks she knit me last year were beyond repair with two gaping holes in the heels. She says, matter-of-factly, "I'll just darn them for you."

Darning reminds me of how scabs form on the body. Platelets, fibrin, and plasma all work together to form a web around the wound—filling it in and sealing the hole.

There's something beautiful in the webbing and criss-crossing that must take place to repair a hole or a wound. It happens when we repair fabric or our own bodies, but it also happens in our *lives*.

I thought about my community and all the ways we hold each other in place, all the ways we intersect, gather in, unite, and fill each others' lives. We choose to deliberately criss-cross. We are wound healers when we come together like this.

Something was darned in my heart last night—some gaping hole I hadn't remembered was there. I only played for an hour. The sun set upon us, shining gold through the trees in the distance, and there I was, jumping double dutch (making a fool of myself) with these folks I'm living life with. We aren't related by blood. We were strangers a few years ago—some a few days ago. Now, we are something else. I'll gather on the asphalt every week with these people: platelets, fibrin, and plasma that circle, web, and heal.

9. Draw Out Your Inner Teacher

The Latin root of the verb *educate* means "to draw out" or "bring forth."

Teachers illuminate the subject matter, but they also bring something forth from the student. They draw knowledge *out*, not dump it in.

It's a different way of understanding the verb and a teacher's role in the classroom. It changes *everything:* how I teach, what I expect, and what constitutes the goal of our interaction. Drawing out means there's some glorious and wonderful thing inside a mind that I want to bring to the light.

I'm on a treasure hunt; I'm on a deep sea dive; I'm on a fishing expedition.

"To draw out" a person—to bring them to the surface—means I cast the line, linger patiently in those deep waters of the mind, and wait until the nibble comes. It's not a perfect analogy, but it reminds me of the work of drawing any person out. Marriage, parenting, friendships, work relationships, and even encounters with strangers might be deep sea fishing and diving expeditions.

Wouldn't our dates, our dinner conversations, our seminars, and our book clubs be richer if we were all deep sea divers into the mind of another person? What a privilege to learn from you! What a privilege to draw something out of you!

I suppose that's why I want to be a teacher, not just with students, but with every interaction. I want to draw out and not dump in.

10. A Message From God in My Vacuum

Yesterday, I vacuumed my entire house.

We recently had the carpets cleaned, and the kind cleaner suggested we needed a new vacuum. He said to get a "multi-cyclonic" system with a canister I empty out—not the bag kind.

I like my old vacuum. It's been with me all these years. To me, the carpets look great: clean and soft with little lines from where the vacuum travels. We don't *need* a new one.

But late in the afternoon, my husband suggests we purchase the "multi-cyclonic" vacuum (it was on sale!) to help keep our carpets clean. With his fall allergies, our three cats, and our Grand Central Station lifestyle of game nights, parties, and meetings in our home, I agree to see what the big deal with multi-cyclonic vacuuming was.

So I test it. I re-vacuum the entire house.

Apparently, multi-cyclonic means "miracle" in Greek. From the view of this different mechanism, the carpets I think are clean are actually filthy. The new vacuum removes so much unseen debris from my carpets that I literally sit on the floor and admire it in the canister.

I even call two friends to tell them about this vacuum.

Today in church, I think about that different mechanism that could remove what the old one couldn't. I ask God to come in multi-cyclonic form into the depths of my being to lift the stain and invisible dirt *that I can't see*. God removes it thoroughly, and for me, that's the beauty of the gospel.

The *unseen violations*—pride, criticism, judgment, favoritism, self-focus—sink deep in my fibers. Let me not just be clean on the surface. Let me be multi-cyclonic clean.

11. What Were You Thinking?

Yesterday, a particularly thoughtful student said she wanted to start a blog. She's been thinking about this for a long time. As we walked together, she said, "I wouldn't have anything to say, though. What would I write about?"

I wonder if what she really means is: "What would I write about that anybody would *care* about?"

The desire to make our internal thoughts external immediately comes under attack. We often stay supremely private because we feel we have nothing worthwhile to say. Our observations aren't valuable contributions, so we stay quiet and unheard.

We think that nobody would care anyway.

If only we would share! If only we all could talk openly about our thoughts and have others *honor* them. Not because they were clever or wise or funny. Not because they were politically or socially popular or trendy. But because it's you!

Sometimes I ask my daughters to tell me what they are thinking about. My oldest reveals she's been wondering why in the world garlic wards off vampires.

When I ask students what they are thinking about, the weight of silence in the room unsettles me. I ask them to write me something instead. Just a paragraph. Just a few sentences.

That evening, I burst into tears at my desk as I read paragraph after paragraph of "what they were thinking." Such depth! Such complexity! Such unique viewpoints! Why don't they share these out loud? Why don't they proclaim these things?

Might I change the climate in that classroom (and in my home) to have them speak up? *I want to hear everything you are thinking about.*

Even if it's about garlic, I want to hear it.

12. What You Have to Set Free

Walking to my classroom today, I passed a cluster of pines. Beneath their branches, a perfect circle of pine cones posed like ornaments shaken from a Christmas tree.

I stopped to consider what it might mean that a tree would drop all of its pine cones. It seemed like loss; I felt longing in my heart.

I know that the cone is just the protective cover for hundreds of seeds housed within it. Once a year, a pine tree drops its pine cones to the forest floor. If you pick one up, you can gently shake it to release tiny seeds—black dots in thin paper—that might not have yet flown free.

Normally, the pine cone stays on the branch, opens up when the weather is dry, and lets the wind disseminate all her seeds. Then, she'll drop to the forest floor. The whole process takes about a year.

Something about opening up, releasing those seeds, and then dropping to the ground like that made me wonder about the gifts we disperse, the creative acts we protect and then finally circulate, and the offspring or relationships we let loose. It's all part of the process—shaking our pine cones free—emancipating things that we need to release and no longer control. A pine tree forest's survival depends upon the ability to protect a seed and then send it out. The remnant of that cone on the forest floor is proof that it *let something go*.

If I were a pine tree, I'd want thousands of cones beneath my feet. I'd gaze upon the cones to remind myself of what I released into the world and didn't keep for myself. And I know there's something we lose with every release. There will always be that vessel in our hearts—that tiny cone—to remember what we wanted to hold onto but knew we had to set free.

13. A Way to Stop Fighting

We woke up to screaming. All week, we've been listening to our daughters work out their conflicts. Lately, they've been fighting over *everything*: Whose turn? Whose portion? Whose toy?

In church this morning, I asked another mother how she handles sibling fighting. Her answer surprised me.

She said to teach my children that they aren't special.

Is this mother *American*? Has she been hiding underground all her life? Aren't I supposed to be training my children to believe in their absolute specialness? Aren't I supposed to be telling my little girls how wonderful, how amazing, how special, special, special they are? Of course they deserve that turn, that portion, that toy. I've trained them to expect nothing less.

I think I've been raising narcissists. Something's gotta change.

That mom told me to ask one sister if her other sister were any less special than she.

So I did. Without that sense of "I'm uniquely special," it was hard to justify who deserved that turn, that portion, that toy.

Who is more special? Me or you?

As I'm worshiping God in church this morning, I think about what causes so much distress in my own heart. So many of my own internal and external conflicts arise out of a sense of entitlement. I'm so special, God, so don't I deserve this thing? I'm so *special*, God, aren't you going to do this wonderful thing in my life? It's my turn, God. It's time for my portion.

The problem isn't that I'm not special. *I am.* The problem is that *you are too*—just as much—and I don't see it. If I did, I wouldn't fight for my personal story, my turn, my portion, and my toy. I'd see you as equally deserving of every opportunity and every bit of joy.

It was a sobering thought for someone like me (a recovering narcissist of sorts). I looked around the sanctuary at hundreds of folks on their own spiritual journey. Might I give up my turn, my portion, and my toy for them? Might I reengage with people, recognizing a profound sense of how special they are?

Selfishness might stem from an exaggerated sense of my own specialness.

Are others special enough (as special as I am?) that I might defer to them, sacrifice for them, and lose my place in line? Living with flair means admitting (though it's painful!) that I am not *more special*. That's one way I can love others better, even when they get the biggest portion and the best toy.

14. Flabbergasted! (A Student Laments Being Over-Scheduled)

Yesterday I had lunch with a college student who looks back on her grade school years with a certain regret. She won awards in three different sports, had a full schedule of activities, made great grades, and got into a wonderful college. She's a triathlete. She's a straight A student.

I look at that life and see how many parents in my community make extraordinary sacrifices for their children to have that kind of portfolio. Even in elementary school, children are in multiple sports, multiple classes, multiple shows.

If I'm honest, I want to be that parent. I feel so badly that we can't afford to have our children in more activities. I feel like I'm depriving my daughters of all the good things in life. But talking to this college student changed my attitude.

"I feel regret when I look back," the student said. "I spent all that time developing my skills in all those activities, but I did *nothing* for my community. I did nothing for the world."

She challenged me to put my girls in one or *maybe* two activities and let the rest of our days be spent engaged in community service.

"Did you know that right now children are enslaved in sweat shops?" The student leans over the table in disbelief. "Should I join the Peace Corps? Should I start an awareness campaign?" She asks the question with tears nearly filling her eyes. "Nobody is reflecting on anything because they are all so busy doing their activities!"

She spent hours in clubs and activities that bred a self-focus she laments. Her perspective left me as flabbergasted as when the mother at church said I should teach my children they are not special.

I went home and looked at the list of possible activities for my children. *And then I looked at my own personal calendar.* I could book gym classes, lunch outings, shopping trips with girlfriends, Bible studies, dance classes—all for me! What if I put a stop to everything and took a look around my community? What if I gathered my family together and asked my girls to change the world and not their dance shoes?

There's nothing wrong with sports and activities. Children and adults learn vital life skills in extracurricular activities. There *is* something wrong with cultivating a self-focus that excludes community, nation, and world. I want to raise compassionate citizens trained in community organizing. And as a citizen, I want to forgo my devotion to self-improvement (hours at the gym!) and think about how I can serve someone else. What a hard paradigm shift!

Living with flair means we live in a community and serve that community even if it means giving up another sport, another club, or another performance.

15. Am I a Husky or a Collie?

I recently walked in the woods with my neighbor and her Siberian Husky. While other owners let their dogs run free in the woods, she keeps hers tight and close on a strong leash.

"I wish I could let him run free," she says sadly.

"Why can't you?" I ask, watching other dogs bounding off into the distant cluster of pine trees.

"Because Siberian Huskies have a strong urge to run but no homing instinct."

If she let him off the leash, he'd run and run with no regard for traffic or danger. *And he'd never return home.*

Unlike other breeds, the Siberian Husky wants to run away and lacks that inborn, mysterious, and often astounding ability to return home. Other dogs can find their way back to you even if you drop them off *hundreds* of miles from home. Tales are told of Collie dogs, for example, who, when adopted into new families, have to be kept inside because their homing instinct is *so strong* they will return to wherever their previous home is even if it's in a different state.

Collies have an urge to run, but they always know how to find their way home.

Let me be more Collie than Husky! The urge to run—to follow the whims of an adventurous life—makes me dash off to fulfill that career possibility or that dream. I'm a Siberian Husky racing off into the wild.

Praise God for the leash!

I wonder if when I feel most restrained by my circumstances that it's really the firm hand of God not letting me loose. He knows I'd run straight into danger with no ability to find my way back. That tether on my life that I think keeps me down is actually the lifeline that keeps me safe, loved, and *home.*

16. Trusting the Process (without Peeking)

I'm a horrible disaster in the kitchen. But God seems to teach me things in this place of flour and butter. This morning, I tried my neighbor's delicious "popover" recipe. Their family loves popovers. They sprinkle lemon juice and powdered sugar atop the fluffy dish, and *voila!* Breakfast joy!

Yesterday, she scribbled the recipe for me on the back of my daughter's "She Had a Wonderful First Day in Kindergarten" card. You melt 2 tablespoons butter in an oven-safe skillet at 475 degrees. Meanwhile, you whisk together 1/2 cup milk, 1/2 cup flour, and 2 eggs. When the butter melts, you pour your batter in the skillet, close the over door, and wait exactly 12 minutes. No more, no less. *And you cannot open the oven door.* The popover won't puff up if you do.

I do everything according to the instructions. But when it comes to the "no peeking" part (and my oven has no glass window for seeing inside), I can hardly bear it. Was it working? Was my batter fluffing up?

12 minutes seems like an eternity. I'm dying. I have to peek. I have to make sure the process is working.

I bite my lip and wait. I actually count down with my timer—aloud—those last few seconds. Finally, I can open the oven door.

It worked.

Why was it so hard to trust the process? Why did I have to bite my lip and restrain myself from needing proof that something good was actually happening inside that hot oven?

Oh, me of little faith! As I enjoyed that delicious treat with my family, I remembered that I can trust the process even if I can't see what's happening. God works in secret within what often feels like an emotionally dark inferno. But if I trust the process, I'll turn into what I'm supposed to become.

Living with flair means I'm OK with not peeking. What's supposed to happen *is* happening. I'll see the product when it's time.

17. Breathing Deeply in the Froglet Phase

When you aren't a tadpole anymore, but you still aren't a frog, you're a *froglet*. I'm reading a book about frogs to my children on this chilly evening (how could we not after chasing a toad on Saturday?), and I read that, on the way to becoming a frog, the tadpole endures a curious in-between phase.

The froglet phase.

She has lungs but must stay in water. She has feet but can't yet manage the land. Now a foreigner in the place once her home, she cannot even breathe. Her gills betray her, and her tail that helps her swim disappears.

She doesn't quite fit in her environment because she's made for a different one.

I read the text with my daughters and look at pictures of frantic froglets, fanning a worthless stub of tail, bursting through the water's surface to gulp that breath of air.

Something about coming to the surface like that resonates deeply with me. I saw myself in that froglet. I saw myself gulping for spiritual truth, for spiritual refreshment, because the physical environment wasn't—and couldn't—be my satisfaction.

As spiritual beings made for communion with God, how do I manage in the grime and slosh of daily life when I'm made for a different environment—a heavenly one, a spiritual one? We toggle like froglets on the rim of two environments. I need to rise, fast and direct, to the surface of the water and take the deepest breath I can *from the environment I was made for.*

When a frantic froglet realizes her gills and tail won't work—and shouldn't—she propels herself up and out of that murky underwater world and up into the light. She breathes in what she was made for.

It helps me live with flair to think of myself as a froglet. My environment wasn't *meant* to sustain my life. There's a whole world outside of the dark water. I need to swim up, breathe deeply through a life of prayer and connection to God, and look around.

There's *glorious land* ahead. And once I see it, the weight of this world doesn't hold me down.

18. Embrace Mediocrity

Sometimes I go around the room and ask students to introduce themselves by telling me what they were known for in high school. I learn so much about how students perceive themselves through the lens of *other people.*

Valedictorian. Lead role in the school plays. Class President. Eagle Scout. These students have been groomed from birth to be the *best.*

A few days ago, one incredibly bright student said:

"I was known for being good and not great. I was known for being mediocre."

When I asked for more information, he said he played every sport but was never the star. He did well in all his classes but was never the best.

He didn't mind. He didn't have to be the best.

I couldn't help but smile. He was *exceptionally* mediocre. We laughed and affectionately call him "Mediocre Man." Everybody likes this student. He makes us all feel relaxed and lighthearted.

I thought about the philosophy of life already governing this student's attitude. He wants to excel, but he knows his limits. He rests in what he can do well, even if it won't win a Nobel Prize or put him as quarterback on the team. He's thinking of who he can serve in his career, what he can contribute, and what he can change—even if he's not the star of the show. His identity has nothing to do with rising to the top. He's already outside of that paradigm.

He could have quit back then. Why bother—some would argue—if you can't be the best?

Not him. He's working at top capacity despite the odds. Despite the label.

I like that. I *love* that.

As I look at my life and the lives of my children, I know we'll have days upon days of just being good and not great. But we can be exceptional in that. We can be the best at being who we are, within the boundaries of what God allows for our lives, and not despair when we aren't winning the prize. We can be exceptionally humble, exceptionally loving, exceptionally willing to serve and change our world. A mediocre life may seem ordinary, average, or even inferior. But to whom? Who decides?

Let me be exceptionally mediocre today. Let me excel in leaving the spotlight and embracing a humble life that wins the sorts of prizes God doles out at another time, in another economy, that values *who I am* and not what I produce. In that land, the mediocre folks might just be the ones with the most flair.

19. You Weren't Alone Today

Do you remember when I cried while mopping my kitchen floor because I was thankful for the filth? Well, today I bring out my mop to clean the floor once again, but this time, I think of a different narrative.

I imagine who else in the world is mopping a kitchen floor at this *exact moment*. Of the 6 billion folks living on the planet today, chances are good that somebody is also mopping a floor. Maybe thousands of us are.

And then, I start imagining you fellow moppers: your countries, your lives, your particular sorrows. I can't help what comes next: I start praying for unnamed, unknown people. I pray that you would find joy in the work; I pray that whatever happens on your floor today would be a *good thing*.

Then I go about my morning. But something has changed in me.

I wash dishes, and I imagine other people who are scrubbing breakfast dishes at this exact moment. Next I fold laundry and wonder who else of the 6 billion of us are folding underwear right now. I smile and giggle to think of this community of underwear-folders. And then I say a prayer for the people folding underwear out there.

I'm not alone in these tasks. I'm never alone at all. We are all in this together— you, me, and people all over the world—mopping floors, scrubbing dishes, and folding underwear. We did it together today. So if you felt alone, you weren't.

20. Would We Have Done This?

Down the big hill and towards the school, some new neighbors moved in last spring. I met them once, and since then, our paths have not crossed. Nobody on my street really knows them.

Our community holds Trick-or-Treating on Thursday night, and as we approach this new family's house last night, we are already freezing in the darkness as wind whips underneath our costumes. Then, I see a sign in the yard. It says: "Welcome! Come in for Hot Chocolate, Cider, Coffee, Tea, and Donuts." Like a beacon of warmth and cheer, that house glows from the sidewalk.

We can't resist. We swarm the place. We stay a spell.

The family nobody knows cleaned out their garage and turned it into a little barn with tables and chairs for neighbors to rest during Trick-or Treating. The couple dressed up as farmers, and as they pour cider and pass out donuts to us— strangers—they laugh and smile and introduce themselves.

The family none of us knows is now the family that *everybody* knows.

This family models how to enter a community with flair. The next time I feel lonely, left out, or unknown because I'm the new kid on the block, I'm not going to wait around for the Welcome Wagon. I'm going to make a sign, clear a space, and offer the kind of hospitality that folks can't resist. This kind of hospitality that makes people stay awhile.

I love my neighborhood.

21. Your Most Memorable Act

Last year, my daughter's teacher asked me to provide some healthy Halloween treats for the 2nd grade party. Everyone knows how terrible I am at anything involving baking, crafts, or decorating. I try, but when it comes right down to it, I'm just not good at these things.

I am good at *words*, though. And I recalled the wisdom of my friend in Texas who says firmly, "Heather, God gave these children to you. You are the *perfect parent* for them. Your gifts are perfectly matched to their needs." So this time last year, I arrange some vegetables in the shape of the word, "Boo." I have no idea what I am doing. I take some foil, make a pattern, and fill it in with vegetables. That's about as crafty as I get.

Despite my anxiety about this platter (was it cute? would the children love it?), I bring it to the school party. My daughter beams. Children come over to read the word, and they laugh and eat vegetables because they are in the shape of a word.

Story over. A year goes by.

This week, my daughter bursts from the school doors and calls out, "Mom, I signed you up to make treats for the Halloween party. Everyone wants the Boo Platter! Let's make another Boo Platter!" She's holding my hand, staring up into my face, and talking about this Boo Platter like it's become a public school *legend*.

I wake up this morning and arrange the foil in the shape of a word. It might be the most important thing I do today, the thing that matters as the years go by. God made me a certain way, and when I act out of that authentic self, I leave a beautiful mark. A simple embellishment—in my style—to a platter created a memory—a tradition—that children remembered and needed. These small acts that I think make no mark, that make no *difference*, that seem silly and awkward and out of place, actually embed themselves in neighborhood memory.

Living with flair means pressing on in small embellishments *that flow from my personality* that help shape a family and a community. Sure, some other parents made more creative and impressive things, but what my children remembered and love was a word. Because that's *me*.

22. Be Careful What You Pray For

This afternoon, a group of children practice their instruments together in my home. One girl drags in an enormous baritone horn, another assembles her flute, and still another positions herself at the piano.

These brand-new musicians (two being my daughters) all want to practice their first song: *Hot Cross Buns*.

It's loud, squeaky, and all out of sync.

I'm listening to it all, and I remember how I prayed that God would fill my home with music. I know nothing about music. I don't even know how to read music. But I knew I wanted to raise musical children; it seemed right and good and wonderful.

That year, I said in despair to a friend, "I don't have a piano, and we'll *never* be able to afford one." My friend said, "Well, you need to ask God to send you a piano and to fill this home with music!"

So I did. And He did. The next day, a friend texted to tell me the church down the road was giving a perfectly good piano away because they were getting a new one. Did I want it?

Within an hour, I had a dolly and a truck from U-Haul, several strong students, and a piano entering into my living room.

And today I have a concert happening before my eyes.

I think about that prayer as my house explodes with music.

I've never heard a more beautiful sound.

23. A Glorious Death

I'm looking up into the autumn leaves, and I realize I'm watching a *glorious death*. These colors—this vibrant display of glory—come at the point of death (technically the disintegration of chlorophyll). This beautiful moment represents the end of life for these leaves. I don't name it as tragic. I revel in this autumn landscape. I take a picture and marvel.

What forms of death are *glorious*? When, like these leaves, is death a moment of glory?

I think of when the will bends to God in a moment of surrender. I think of what it means to become absorbed in divine purposes—letting my right to my own life, my own plans, and my own demands disintegrate like chlorophyll. Like autumn leaves, I am most beautiful when I'm at the end of myself. The Christian life might be seen as a glorious dying—a surrender of self—to become a child of the one whose Glorious Death wasn't tragic but victorious and radiant.

Later, I hike through a forest and come upon a massive decaying tree. I think of this as a glorious death as I imagine the refuge and nourishment such a dying tree provides for the ecosystem. Might I see my own life as a fallen tree, bowed down, dead to self, so that I might find the life that's truly life?

A life surrendered might feel tragic and painful. But not for long. It's nourishing, radiant, glorious. We see and marvel.

24. When "Plan A" Fails

We hear that a frost will come this week. It seems so tragic: dozens of beautiful tomatoes that never had a chance to ripen.

But all is not lost. As novice gardeners, we take advice from a master gardener in our community. She tells us to harvest our green tomatoes, wrap them in newspaper, and tuck them away in a closet. In several weeks, we'll have a bounty of luscious, deep red tomatoes.

I've never ripened tomatoes this way. It seems unusual and unnatural. It's an entirely different means to a harvest.

We eagerly wrap tomatoes like little gifts and hide them away to ripen. We'll peek in on them every week and watch their progress. It's not the way it's *supposed* to happen, but it works. It's exactly right for this season.

I'm up to my elbows in unripe tomatoes that *will ripen* in an unexpected way—a way I didn't imagine existed. No God-given dream in my life has turned out in the manner I imagined. The right process, the plan that was supposed to unfold in a particular way, veered off into orbit and produced a harvest in a different way, under different conditions. I've learned to trust this concept. I've learned to accept, trust, and then rejoice when Plan A fails.

I hold my dreams loosely—gently wrapped and tucked away. God knows *when* and *how* they'll come about.

25. Your Best Habit

On the walk to school, my rurally-raised neighbor (who knows everything about the land) comments upon the beauty of various trees' *habits*. She informs me that a tree's *habit* refers to its overall shape.

She identifies trees by their habits. Some trees squat and spread lower to the ground.

Others rise tall into the sky as perfect vase shapes.

Some grow into beautiful ovals.

And some unfold against the sky like Japanese fans.

But as I look around me, I notice something astounding. Some trees in the forest don't squat or unfold. Some don't rise up and spread their arms wide.

I learn that if other plants or objects crowd a tree, the intended habit changes. It diminishes. Stunted and pressed upon, the tree loses potential somehow.

I think about the simple and natural need for space. We have an *intended shape*— our best habit—but when crowded and pressured, we change.

I think about making room for my husband, children, friends, students—and myself—to unfold, to stretch wide. Do I stifle? Do I crowd? What would it look like to give everybody some breathing room?

Today, I'm making space for my best habit to take shape. I want to unfold like a bright yellow fan.

26. The Beauty Always There

Autumn alights on my kitchen table as neighborhood children unload this gift of leaves. We configure the apparatus: one leaf, a white sheet of paper, and a broken crayon stripped of its packaging.

We smooth the crayon against the clean page. As if by magic, the unseen leaf appears.

The children hold their breath, amazed. One of them looks at her paper and then up at me. She exclaims, "We didn't even need the Internet to do this!"

My youngest is overcome with the impossibility of it—a crayon pressed to her page reveals a pattern that's *there* but could not previously be seen.

All night I press my mind against this event. The leaf represented a reality we couldn't see but that made itself evident when we rubbed against it. Was I encountering a truly beautiful thing in that moment, the kind of beauty philosophers pause for, the kind of beauty that poets claim can break your heart (and repair it)?

It's always there, underneath.

27. The Bored Student Speaks!

My *I-Really-Just-Don't-Care* student hands me some of his writing to read. He's typed *eight* single-spaced pages. I didn't assign him this project. He wrote something on his own, and he wants to meet today to talk about writing.

He gives me permission to tell you this:

It's a personal memoir about watching his brother leave for service in the Marine Corps. It's about the first letter he receives from him.

It's about the first time he sees his face again.

At one point, the student recounts the moment when he's about to see his own brother. Mid sentence, he includes in parentheses: "I've stood to type this section because I can still feel the excitement."

I can't put it down. The writing is so good, the story so profound. I'm overcome with the fact that a student has to *stand up* to write because the emotion is that great.

I thought he had no feeling. He actually had too much. The ones that seem the most bored are the ones thinking more deeply than I can even imagine.

I have to remember that. I have to remember that the reclusive soul sitting before me who doesn't care about anything might actually *care too much*. The silence, the frown, or even the bored comment masks something underneath. Something so thrilling he has to stand up to write it.

I ask him again if I can write about him today. He says, "I really just don't care." Now I know what he means.

28. Your Adventure

I glance at the morning sky and spy a hot air balloon drifting across the valley. This part of the country displays the most vibrant autumn colors, and hot air balloon rides provide a terrific (although terrifying) vantage point.

I'd never do it. A balloon? A basket? Me in *there*, high above the earth? *Never.*

Moments later, I stand in front of college students who do remarkable things despite fear. They visit Egypt on archaeology trips; they study Latin American countries so they can travel and negotiate border disputes; they enlist in the Army and await deployment; they go into prisons and practice rehabilitation methods.

Unsafe things. Terrifying things.

Yesterday, my neighbor tells me her oldest daughter is mastering Arabic so she can spend a year in the Middle East.

"Isn't that really unsafe? Aren't you so *scared*?"

"Of course," she says.

Of course it's unsafe. Of course she's scared. But something else matters more than her fear.

Later, I'm talking with a friend about her husband's new job offer. A huge unknown. A huge gamble. She's terrified.

I tell her to surrender to the adventure of it. If you know what's going to happen, that's not adventure, that's a *script*. That's a high-action drama with a plot-spoiler. Don't give the fear power. If there's fear, it just means the adventure is *that great.*

No fear, no adventure.

The spirit of adventure I see in younger folks challenges me to move ahead in the face of fear. *Of course it's scary.* Most adventures are. That's what makes them adventures.

29. The Fence Around Your Life

I'm driving with a friend who flew all the way from the West Coast to see me for the weekend. This friend knows how to get to the point, say the right thing, and change your reality. 5 years ago, she looked me in the eye during one of my darkest days and said, "God is not against you. God is *for* you."

That conversation was a turning point for me.

So I'm showing her around my little town. I'm thinking of the glamorous lives people live in California, and I start apologizing that there's not more to do. I point to the tiny excuse for a mall and say, "There's no retail here."

She says, "Less choice means it's *easier*. You don't have to make so many decisions all day."

Her commentary reminds me of the story I once heard about the school children who were let out into a schoolyard with a fence that surrounded the large play area. With the fence in place, children enjoyed the freedom to explore, play in safety, and run free. One day, a researcher took the fence down. Without the fence in place, the children huddled together near the school building.

What looked like freedom actually paralyzed them. They didn't play. They didn't run free. They needed the boundary—that fence—to experience freedom and safety.

When I look at the narrow parameters of my life (small town wife, mother, part-time this and that), I feel tempted to rage against that fence. I think there's *more* out there. As my friend and I drove all over town (it didn't take long), celebrating the good things that God had accomplished in our lives, I found myself saying, "the *more* is right here." The smaller my life becomes, the more abundant it seems.

That's why it says in Psalm 16 that "the boundary lines for me have fallen in *pleasant places*." The boundaries I want to fight are the very ones that keep me in the right place to experience God and all that's in store *here*.

30. Try This at Home

I'm standing in the freezing cold, tapping my foot and sighing.

Finally, both daughters emerge from school. As I herd them away from the building, I list out all the things I want them to do when we get home. *Hurry! Let's move, girls!*

We get inside, and I'm scurrying around to empty backpacks and neatly replace them on their hooks.

My oldest (the one whose fame lasted till lunch) pulls me aside and whispers, "Mom, what happened to the Warm Welcome?"

The Warm Welcome? Please, child. It's been a long day.

But she's right. I love these children. Why can't I just give a warm welcome? (My mother was fabulous at this!) As we talk about what we could do to welcome each other into the home, she makes this list:

The Warm Welcome
1. Smile and say, "I'm so glad to see you."
2. Offer a snack and a refreshing beverage.
3. Play soft music or light a candle for a peaceful mood.
4. Please don't ask questions or give orders.

That's the *Warm Welcome*. It turns out that even asking how somebody's day was can feel like pressure. My daughter tells me to wait until she's *settled in* before asking her questions.

I seem to recall marriage advice along the same lines.

How many family and neighbor entrances have I clouded with my impatience, my demands, and my agenda? When a family member returns home, what if I didn't ask questions, give orders, or rush?

I stop my scurrying, put on some music, light our pumpkin candle, and pour a glass of orange juice as my daughters transition from *out there* to *in here*.

Living with flair means I learn the *Warm Welcome*. You've been out there. Come inside. We are so glad you're here.

31. How to Enter a Room with Flair

I walk into a room and wonder *who's going to talk to me*. Inevitably, I spiral into a self-conscious moment.

I'm waiting for my daughters to finish a gymnastics class, and I look around the waiting room. The lively chatter of mothers all around me makes me feel terribly alone. I don't belong in this group; I'm an outsider to this world of sequin leotards, glitter hairspray, and the flurry of little girls trying to finish their homework before the coach calls them in.

Nobody is paying attention to *me*!

Sulking in pity, I overhear a little girl ask her mother the difference between a homophone and a homonym.

My specialty! I can't resist such questions. I have to assist. For the next 5 minutes, I find myself helping a 4th grader think of words that sound the same but are spelled differently (homophone) and words that sound the same and are spelled the same but mean different things (homonym).

You can't help somebody else and also think about how neglected you feel. It's a strange phenomenon. It doesn't matter that I'm supremely out of place here. I'm serving somebody, and then, *everything feels right.* And in a powerful turn of events, the mother who once seemed so cliquish and perfect starts telling me about her life. Over homophones, I'm learning about a lifetime of heartbreak.

Each of those mothers might have their own story of loss. The room isn't what it seems; *it's nothing like it sounds.* Beneath the clique and chatter, there's somebody who needs attention.

Perhaps when I feel most alone, most forgotten, I need to look up, find a way to help and bless (even if it's through homophones), and stop focusing on myself. I want to enter a room, take my eyes off of myself, and find the one who needs help. Surely, that's one way to live with flair.

32. The Ridiculous Ritual

Last night, the neighborhood children gather in our basement for Monday Night Fitness Group. It's cold, dark, and dreary in the evenings now, so our alternative to biking and double-dutch is Dance Party and Jumping Jack Challenge.

I don't *want* to do this. I want to change into my pajamas and watch television. Earlier in the day, one child races out of school and asks, "Is tonight the night?" Children are calling my cell phone, begging. My own daughters are already in the basement, ready. We've started some fitness revolution, and I can't stop now. Soon, I'm texting families to invite everybody to dance in my basement after dinner.

We're in a circle dancing to whatever comes out of my iPod. At one point, the "Hamster Dance" song comes on, and 10 of us crawl around like hamsters. Then we skip in a circle.

I'm too old for this.

A hula hoop rests in the middle of our circle, and each child takes a turn standing in the hula hoop and doing whatever dance move he wants. The rest of us copy him. As we rotate around each child, dancing and hollering, I start to feel like I'm in a tribe doing a ritual dance.

I think of Native American dances designed to strengthen tribe members spiritually and emotionally before battle. Perhaps each of us, in our own way, fights something. Each child needs us here, circled around him, *seeing him*, celebrating him, strengthening him for the fight.

This ridiculous dancing suddenly turns to ritual right in front of my eyes.

This is my *tribe*. I need this. We enact these rituals that, on the surface, represent fitness. In a deeper sense, we build our tribe when we gather like this. Deeper still, we prepare each other emotionally and spiritually for tomorrow's battle.

We rally and fall, out of breath, only to rise up in a brave dance.

It doesn't take much: a space to move, people, and a song. It cost me nothing, and I went to bed more satisfied than I'd felt in months. I have to remember that living with flair means I build my tribe. We gather up because we need that strength, that ritual, that dance.

33. When You Start to Feel Old

After church, I'm chopping vegetables to add to my pasta sauce, and I remember my garden. I haven't harvested in weeks because the season's over. The peppers are surely past their prime, so why bother? Those peppers are old, withered, and *done.*

It's cold outside. The leaves are changing. The garden is no more.

But something nags at me to check the garden *just in case.* I run out into the crisp fall air, doubtful. I can't believe what I see.

Whoever said a season's over or that something (or someone) is past her prime hasn't seen my peppers.

I'm out there, knee deep in glorious peppers, and I'm laughing about all the hope out here in my garden. I recall the verse in Psalm 92 about folks "planted in the house of the Lord." The psalmist writes: "They will still bear fruit *in old age*. They will stay fresh and green."

And these peppers aren't finished. They still blossom! They still send out new leaves! Defiant! Prolific!

Living with flair means I know nobody's too old or past her prime. Things can happen and *hope can live* no matter what season, no matter what age, and no matter how long it's been.

34. One Little Cane, Passed On

This morning, a neighbor comes by with a shovel to uproot several of my raspberry canes to plant in his own garden. I want to offer a bit of what was originally given to me.

Two years ago, I was that neighbor taking raspberry canes from another garden down the street. That neighbor was so generous, and I planted five of her canes that multiplied from a single plant.

Two years from now, I wonder who will take canes from the neighbor who came today. The five he takes from me will multiply and cover his whole backyard.

All throughout the neighborhood, folks harvest raspberries. I realize the beauty of how interconnected this harvest has become. All this produce came from *just one little plant* that multiplied and spread.

I think about my own life's work. I want my words and actions to nourish a family, a neighborhood, a city, a nation, a world. I offer bits of what was originally given to me—loving, encouraging, teaching—and pray the roots go deep and pass between generations. One *little cane*, over time, can cover a whole community.

Let it be beautiful fruit. I think about the bitter fruit of a negative, discouraging, damaging presence passed on between generations. Equally prolific, I fear this fruit also stays within a community.

May our raspberry canes be a blessing and not a curse.

35. The Ache You Need

My little one's molar has been hurting her for months. She's already had a root canal (we definitely needed to invoke the Bad Day Slogan on *that* day), and still, the tooth pain won't relent. Yesterday, the dentist prescribed an antibiotic to ward off infection.

"But we can't pull that tooth," he explains in his office. My daughter listens, wide-eyed. "That tooth is a *space-maker*, a place-holder. If you pull it, every other incoming tooth will crowd toward that space, and her mouth will really be in trouble. Nothing new will come in right. I'd like to keep that tooth there for as long as we can."

I nod. The little one nods.

"It's about timing," he says. "I can pull it, but then we'd have to design a spacer for her mouth, and it won't ever be as great as what God made naturally."

I smile. He's talking Dentist Theology now. He tells me it's often normal for molars to ache while the new teeth underneath emerge. *Just wait. A good thing is happening.*

The sore molar as a "place holder" to keep everything in line, to make things work as they should, stayed with me the whole day and into the night. That troubling sore point in my life—whatever it is—might just be the place holder to keep things right until the new thing comes. Could I begin to see those dark years as space-makers and place-holders that ushered in present joy in the right space, at the right time?

The ache keeps things aligned. It makes a space I need.

36. Am I Willing?

Driving through central Pennsylvania, I gaze with wonder at the work of Amish families on their farms. Through the warmth and convenience of my car, equipped with music and movies, I watch the dance of their laundry on lines between trees; the long pants kick up in the wind, and the crisp white shirts wave as we pass.

A farmer works his field by hand, tilling the soil with pleasure. Barn cats leap up around a little girl's feet as she pushes her wheelbarrow through the family's garden. A mother collects sticks for her fire. We have to slow our pace to give a horse and buggy room on the road.

How inconvenient this all is. How strange this work.

As I think about the labor of living in my own very convenient and very comfortable life, I'm suddenly aware of my stubborn heart. I want ease and comfort. I want the smoothest way out of *work*. But when I look back at my happiest days, the ones full of joy and peace, I realize those were days when I surrendered to the work.

I had a *willing spirit*. I submitted to tasks, to people, and to my circumstances with joy. I got up and worked the way a farmer works a field and wipes a brow. I worked the kind of work that makes you so hungry you eat with a different pleasure and so tired you relish sleep like it's a precious gift.

Will my children know this kind of work in my culture?

The convenient and the comfortable, the lazy and the entertained life, may seem like pleasure, but it doesn't satisfy the way work does.

Lord, give me a willing spirit to do this work. Let me labor hard and enjoy the tasks before me. Living with flair means I sweat and wipe my brow. I meet the tasks assigned with pleasure.

I want to be *willing* for my whole life. As the psalmist writes, "Lord grant me a willing spirit to sustain me."

37. A Clog in My Heart

Yesterday, I'm walking alone in the woods behind my house.

It's not a very big forest, but it's big enough to get lost in.

I'm looking up through the pine trees, taking photos and moving forward with a grand plan: I want to see the sun set through the pines, and I want to find beautiful pine cones.

A chill settles on the forest, and a strong wind snakes around the trees like it's coming for me. I know if I keep walking in one direction, I'll hit a road, but I'm not sure which road or how far it is from my home.

By this time, I find myself taking a winding path and tumbling out onto a foreign road like I'd been spit out from the forest's dark mouth. I'm in some strange neighborhood now. It's getting colder, and I'm sapped of strength.

Finally, I clench my teeth and call my husband because I have no idea where I am. He's so loving about it, so gentle. But I'm angry at myself that I have to call him for help, and I *refuse* to have him drive to pick me up. Instead, I walk the mile home along a road with no sidewalk. I'm too smart to be lost. I'm too capable to need rescue. If you saw a hopeless woman without her coat, tripping along and nearly falling back into the forest, you were looking at me.

What is this deep resistance in me? What ancient sap inside of me keeps me proud and unyielding when I know I need rescue? I refuse for anyone to come find me and just take me home.

This morning before church, I review my photos: The pine trees and these cones aren't oozing sap like they do in the warmer months. In the colder seasons, the sap thickens and hardly flows. There's a clog in the heart of those trees until the summer sun comes and warms it, changes it.

As my husband pours warm syrup over snowman-shaped pancakes this morning, I pray that God would unclog the cold, hardened things in me. Otherwise, I'll stay lost and wandering in that dark woods.

38. More Than Enough

A long time ago, a friend of mine remarked that you can see things more clearly in the late autumn and winter. She said that the contrast of empty, colorless landscapes makes anything vibrant stand out that much more. There's a focus you gain when you find yourself in stark places.

I like that. I like that because when it looks desolate, maybe it's because there's something I'm supposed to *see*.

Yesterday, I leave my house to walk to pick the girls up from school. It's 2:15 PM, and here I am, trudging through my own bleak landscape. I take my camera because I'm learning photography. It's nearly winter. Few leaves hang on the trees like lovers not ready to depart. There's a desperation in the air and a sadness as I crunch all these dead leaves under my feet. Everything mourns. But then, I remember the feature on this old camera called "Digital Macro." I fumble with the camera, punch the button, and look around—differently this time.

I'm exploring with hope on this mile walk to school. Two acorns survived the fall from their tree, and as the sun shines through the bare trees, I lay down on the path and take a picture.

I rest a minute in the stillness of it all. It feels like flair to be a grown woman stretched out on her stomach on the ground like this with her hands propped up to steady an old camera.

What else can I find out here? What beautiful thing awaits?

All of a sudden, the view isn't *barren*. It's absolutely *abundant*.

This grim landscape has gifts to offer.

And even in the starkest landscape, there's more than enough.

39. The Next Step

My one-eyed cat, Jack, has taken another important step.

Remember how wounded and sick Jack was? How unattractive and miserable? We brought him home and gave him all the love we could. He'd lost his ability to purr. He couldn't even meow. His whole kitty identity seemed withered and dying.

Then one day, he found his purr again, deep and rich and wild. We were petting him, and we heard the slow chug, like some distant train coming from a far-off country. He's *purring*! Then, nearly a year into his recovery, that kitty self was back.

It gets even better. Yesterday, I walk into my bedroom, and I see the once lonely and wounded kitty in a warm embrace. He's *holding another cat. He's holding her still and bathing her face and the back of her ears!* As I watch this display, I realize that Jack's journey has reached yet another point of healing.

I snap a picture of him and think of what it means to care for somebody. The once-wounded cat is now serving others.

Living with flair means that we don't stay wounded. We press on, find ourselves again, and discover where we might serve. Even if you've had a loss that changes how you see everything (and limits you), there's hope towards a journey of healing-turned-ministry. Maybe that's the best kind. Maybe Jack is *particularly good* at caring for other cats because he's come back from the worst.

Maybe I'm *particularly good* at helping folks live with flair because I lived without it for so long. How could I not offer an embrace, hold you still for a moment, and speak out whatever words might help make today meaningful?

40. I Have an Announcement!

Last night, for Monday Night Fitness Group, we had 15 children and their parents gather to dance and jump rope in my basement. The space isn't fancy— it's just big enough to let a group of children dance for one hour. As we finish up with jumping jacks and a game of "Little Sally Walker," we pause for "Community Announcements."

So many little hands go up in the air. I have an announcement! I have an announcement! We sit in a circle and share our most *important news* for the neighborhood to know. I begin with a challenge to walk to school—even in the snow—so we can celebrate our 100th mile with t-shirts and dancing. I have more weight to lose and more health to gain, and I need this neighborhood to help me.

Then the children go around the circle with their most important announcements:

One child has her first loose tooth. We cheer and clap. She's growing!

The next child reports that there's a new student at school. She says, "We have to talk to him and make him feel very welcome." Another child pipes up that there's another new student who only speaks Portuguese, so we have to pay attention and help that new person.

Then one boy announces that he "played outside the whole afternoon, ate dinner quickly, and rushed back outside to play." We clap because it's a fitness achievement for him, and our neighborhood is on a mission towards *fitness*. The next child claims she danced for one hour in her basement with her friend. Another fitness win.

Then, we hear of new badges earned in scouts. We cheer more.

And then, we are alerted to a *neighborhood emergency*. Earlier in the afternoon, some of the children discovered a tree that had a rock embedded in the trunk. They perform surgery and remove it. When they examine this tree, they find that too many acorns are taking root near it and within the hollow between two limbs. They proceed to clear away the acorns and water the tree. And then they observe that it's all solid clay around the trunk; no water seeps in. So they grab shovels, till the soil, and mix in compost to save the tree. 2 hours they work. *Emergency averted.*

Our announcements show me what our neighborhood values: our growth, our community, our fitness, and our environment. We celebrate each other and press on toward our goals—together. We also value *announcing* our lives, living them out alongside one another. A loose tooth, a new student, a tree in danger— these things must be noted and marked in our annals. We chronicle lives lived in this little neighborhood. We hear you. We love you.

41. The Danger of Inviting God In

Last night, my youngest daughter and I read together from a book, and it occurs to me that she's actually reading. She's actually reading *words*.

She'll never be the same. Once you learn to read, you can't undo it. You see a word, and you *must* read it. You can't refuse. The effects of learning to read are irreversible.

And involuntary. Try it. Look at a word and try not to read it. You just can't help yourself. You've cracked a code; you've escaped from a labyrinth and nothing will ever look the same.

It reminds me of a life of faith. The Teacher shows you how to crack the code; you're out of the maze.

A life of faith irreversibly alters the way a mind sees the world. It shimmers with the radiance of God's glory, and you interpret everything through the lexicon of God's love, goodness, and power. At first, like for a young reader, the process is slow and basic. You recognize God in obvious ways, perhaps recounting answers to prayer, emotions felt in worship, or wisdom gained through Bible reading. But then, you find you're really *reading*. You can't help it. You read God in the tiniest moment and see into the life of things.

You'll discern the truth about this world. Your heart will break, and you'll want to hug strangers in grocery stores. You'll start worshiping God when you see an acorn, a seashell, or a cat's missing eye. You'll see a spiritual narrative behind even the garbage in the parking lot. You'll write a blog every single day because you can't contain the worship and keep it all to yourself.

You'll want to *proclaim* things.

That's the danger of inviting God in. You will learn to read, and you won't be able to undo it.

42. It Really Works!

I was a doubter about the whole ripening-tomatoes-in-the-basement plan. Everybody said they would rot. Everybody said they wouldn't taste the same.

My daughter and I journey to the basement late yesterday and sit cross-legged before a box of tomatoes wrapped in newspaper.

She unwraps the first one.

It's a juicy deep red. It's a brilliant and fragrant *red*.

We can hardly believe it. My daughter and I unwrap each red treasure. The experience is better than picking them off the vine. Add the element of doubt and surprise, and all of a sudden, we have a celebration on our hands.

We carry our produce to the kitchen. Outside, the cold wind blows. There's a chance of snow, and the gray sky announces winter. But my kitchen says it's summer—the kind with fresh tomatoes and a counter top full of vegetables.

We get to work. The little one decides we must make homemade. . . *something*. We chop each tomato and roast them with cloves of garlic. Then we remove skins and seeds and blend the whole thing into a delicious soup. We've got grilled cheese sandwiches crisping and homemade garden tomato soup simmering.

I'm so thrilled that those tomatoes never ripened this summer. I'm so happy for that particular disappointment.

When Plan A fails, Plan B often turns out better—more magical—because of the unexpected, against-all-odds sort of outcome. The truth of it all hits me like the cold wind against this window. Plan A has to fail sometimes because God's got a surprise in mind that I'll unwrap when the cold wind blows, in the sorrow of a dark basement. That's when I'll need it most.

43. What We Think and Do Not Say

Yesterday, I write an unusual email to a friend who lives in a different part of the country. We rarely talk on the phone. We haven't seen each other for *years*. But this week, I think about her several times for interesting reasons. So I write a numbered list of all the times her face came to mind.

She's the friend who introduced me to the joy of cooking on a baking stone, and whenever I bring it out, I think about her.

I think of her when I order elaborate coffee drinks because we did that together years ago.

I think about her when I see pistachios because she once told me about a delicious recipe involving a pistachio crust.

Random things. Fleeting things.

But I was *thinking* about her. And it occurs to me to tell her this. How would she know otherwise?

Later, she emails me back to tell me she printed out my list and put it in her journal. I think about that little list—baking stones, coffee, pistachios—that seems silly and unimportant.

It matters *so much*.

44. Does Happiness Have a Sound?

Lately, I've been amazed at how *loud* the autumn leaves are. They crunch underfoot, and those left in the trees chatter as the wind blows. And then there's the haunting whisper of a leaf as it descends—barely audible—but still vibrating whether I perceive it or not.

I stop everything and gaze at that leaf. It arrives on the ground soft and silent.

What beautiful sounds never reach my ears? If I stop and think about it, I'm hearing so many things at this exact moment I'm surprised I'm not crashing from auditory overload.

I know I'm growing older. Movie soundtracks seem too loud and assaulting. I can barely handle the frenzied circus beat of a video game. I've been known to scream out, "Can't we just have some *quiet?*"

I want enough quiet so I can hear beautiful sounds: the purr of a cat, the clink of ice in a tall glass of water served to guests, the hush of wool socks on the hardwood floor. I want to hear the gurgle of homemade sauce simmering and the teasing fingers of the first drops of rain on the roof.

And the measured sigh a page of a book exhales when I turn it.

I take my hearing for granted. One day, I might lose it all together.

I want a beautiful soundtrack to accompany this day. I want to be still enough—aware enough—to hear it. Living with flair means I *manage* the auditory track. Might I be a gatekeeper for my ears and my living space? Might I create a culture of beautiful sounds in my home—the kind of sounds that delight and don't disturb?

45. Love is a Tornado

This morning, my daughter hands me a little card that says her love for me is like a *tornado*. She drew a picture of a tornado and wrote, "It's like this."

I turn to her and say, "You mean it's powerful and destructive?"

She smiles and pretends she's punching me. She tries to explain the comparison: "It gets stronger each day like a tornado gets stronger with each spin."

Her tornado is a giant mess of scribble that looks terrifying.

Love is a tornado?

That can't be right.

My husband adds at breakfast that a tornado is like love because you "never know where it's coming from." It can take you by surprise (like how I met him when I least expected it).

I look at this little family. I think of the kind of love that breaks the heart and repairs it simultaneously. I think of the terrifying surrender of it, the giant mess of living lives intertwined. I think of the powerful destruction that love's wake leaves on the landscape of a heart. It's a tornado that rips you apart.

But it's the kind of devastation you endure because there's no other way to have it. It's the most beautiful storm you'll ever experience.

I hug my children—these little tornadoes in my heart—and think about the kind of love I want in my life. Let it be giant and powerful. Let it get stronger each day.

Let it destroy what in me needs to be leveled and remake a pure landscape.

46. When Everything Aligns

I'm driving to work, and I pull up beside a yellow school bus. The children inside wave and giggle. I motion back with an exaggerated wave.

I notice one cute little girl in the backseat. Her ponytail bobs and her head tilts back as she laughs. I look again. It's my *own daughter* on her way to a field trip at the marsh. She doesn't know that I can see her. I watch her for a few seconds and then have to exit. As I pull away from that school bus, something rises up in my heart. It's the strangest and deepest kind of joy.

I can't explain it other than to say watching a group of laughing school children is good for the soul.

I'm so happy for the warmth and safety of a little yellow school bus that takes children to a marsh. I'm so happy for my daughter as she rides on that bus, laughing with all her friends. God bless that bus. God bless that teacher. God bless the whole elementary school, this whole great state of Pennsylvania, and the whole wide world for that matter.

For at least a few minutes, something aligns. Everything, at least right here, is just as it should be.

47. My Encounter with a Turkey Vulture

My minivan nearly runs over a turkey vulture today. A *turkey vulture*. On my street! I watch this bold bird swoop from tree to tree.

I learn that turkey vultures can smell a dead creature from miles away.

These birds detect death by smelling the special gas released once something begins to decay. I pull over to the side of the road and approach this turkey vulture. He's surprisingly calm, and I figure it's because turkey vultures have no natural predators; why should he fear me?

I watch him feeding on road kill. Rarely will they kill their own food (that's good because what if he wanted to feast on *me?*). Instead, they seek out what's already dead and rotting and stinking.

I don't like this bird. I don't like him at all. He's not very attractive, and he can't even sing. He just grunts and hisses. I also learn that turkey vultures cool off by urinating all over themselves. And if I make him mad, he'll spew semi-digested meat into my eyes. Finally, if I would have happened to harm this bird (by running him over, which I nearly did), I would have to pay $15,000 dollars and go to prison for 6 months.

I do not like this bird.

Why would this bird appear in my lovely blog? Apparently, whether I like this bird or not, he plays a vital role in the ecosystem. He cleans up rotting things and prevents disease. We need him. Maybe I could like him, even love him, after all.

48. Can You Make This Unfamiliar?

I'm teaching my students how to de-familiarize themselves from their own writing in order to find errors. It's a strange phenomenon of writing: when you write a paragraph and then reread it, it's as if the brain knows how it *should* read and somehow blinds us to mistakes.

We need to make the text unfamiliar again.

I invite them to read their paragraphs in reverse order; I encourage them to change the font; I have them read words on paper instead of on a screen; I challenge them to give the writing a 48 hour break. I knew a man in graduate school who placed a ruler under every line of text in order to detach it from its context. He could find errors every time.

All day, I remember the beauty and power of the unfamiliar. I remember why I need to detach from the old familiar contexts. In familiar settings, coping mechanisms, dysfunctional relational patterns, and spiritual blind spots set in. But remove me from my settings and get me away from the familiar? Suddenly I have clear focus. I can see all the junk. I think this explains the importance of weekend retreats, marriage date nights, travel opportunities, and simple changes in routine. This explains why I need to get on my knees, away from my life patterns, to listen to God.

We makes things *unfamiliar* in order to see again.

49. In Great Deeds Something Abides

I'm walking on the battlefields today. I'm deeply moved by Joshua Lawrence Chamberlain's words spoken at the dedication of the Monument to the 20th Maine on October 3, 1889, Gettysburg, PA.[1]

He says, "In great deeds something abides. On great fields something stays. Forms change and pass; bodies disappear, but spirits linger, to consecrate ground for the vision-place of souls. And reverent men and women from afar, and generations that know us not and that we know not of, heart-drawn to see where and by whom great things were suffered and done for them, shall come to this deathless field to ponder and dream; And lo! the shadow of a mighty presence shall wrap them in its bosom, and the power of the vision pass into their souls."

Something abides. Something stays. Certain places—thin places—where the boundary between flesh and spirit disappears and we can peer into eternity, realign me to *great ideals*. Gettysburg does this.

297

We ponder and dream here.

50. A Lesson from the Wise Big Sister

Today, my Wise Big Sister offers another bit of wisdom. This is the Wise Big Sister who wrote me letters in college with Bible verses in them (when I was very far from God). This is the Wise Big Sister who prayed for me through every break-up, every bad haircut, and every rejection. When I didn't get invited from the sorority sisters to pledge their sorority as a freshman, she sent me flowers with a card that said, "From Your *Real* Big Sister."

My Wise Big Sister continues to mentor me:

In March, she instructed me to *do the thing I don't want to do.*
In June, she reminded me that *when you're having a bad day, there's always the hope of flair.*
In July, she taught me that *to get a great thing, you have to lose a great thing.*
In August, she sent me *a message in a bottle to remind me of wonder.*
In October, she encouraged me to *go to the gym.*
In November, she challenged me to *be my own competition.*
Later that November, she explained that *one can be spiritual and stylish at the same time.*

So I text her that I feel burnt-out. She simply says, "Train hard. Rest harder." She calls to explain my situation using a running analogy. She repeats: "Every good runner trains hard but *rests harder.*" She explains that when you're resting, *you really have to rest.* "No running. You can cross-train, but you can't run."

She diagnoses my burnout as a metaphorical stress fracture. "You ran when you should have been cross-training. You didn't rest *completely.*" Cross-training means you engage in completely different and even opposite activities. Runners will swim instead, for example, when they rest but still keep active. In my life this means solitude instead of company; a movie instead of writing; a walk in nature instead of being plugged into technology; or being taught by a mentor instead of being the teacher.

Different and opposite activities.

We have to train hard and rest harder.

51. Things That Make Us Humble

I'm learning to give thanks for things that make me humble. What a blessing in disguise when we experience failure, sickness, less-than-perfect children, a rebuke from a boss or superior, moods we can't manage, laundry we can never finish, schedules we can't control, or any host of things that cry out: *You are not capable—in your own strength—of living your life! You are not as great as you think you are!*

I'm sitting in church, upset about all the hard things happening. I'm skimming the first chapters of the book of Isaiah, thinking about my own proud heart. I find the most unusual verb: *whistle*. God *whistles* twice in the book of Isaiah. The prophet Isaiah says God whistles for us—getting our attention—so we'll turn to Him. I start chuckling in my seat. I picture myself running off into the distance, into all my own plans and in all my own prideful independence.

Then, I hear that long, sweet whistle calling me home.

That's what these disappointments mean. I need God. He's calling me home.

52. What Our Elementary School Principal Calls Herself

Our elementary school principal manages *extraordinary tasks* like learning the first and last names of all 495 students in the school.

That's nearly 500 students. Last September, I wrote about observing her in action in the hallway.

Last week at Back-to-School Night, she introduces herself, not as the principal, but as the *Lead Learner*. She signs all her correspondence this way as well.

The Lead Learner!

For some reason, I want to cry right then and there. No wonder she's been at this school for over 20 years and has the best reputation of any school principal I've ever known or heard of. No wonder the students at this school love learning so much. The leader of this school is a *learner*. How could we not follow her with that attitude of curiosity, humility, and reverence for this sacred act of learning?

I recall Parker Palmer's quote, "We teach what we most need to learn."[2] I want that truth to shape my teaching philosophy and the ways I interact with other instructors, my students, and the material I teach.

I'm not the teacher, I'm the *Lead Learner*.

I'll think about this tonight at Neighborhood Fitness Group. The children will learn to jump in and out of the double dutch ropes, and *I will too*. I'll try to get a picture of me in action (Lord, help me!).

Living with flair means being the Lead Learner.

53. The Hidden Harvest

I'm out in the autumn rain in over-sized rain boots to dig around in the garden. I glance at the raspberry stalks.

Nothing.

But then—because hope dies slowly—I venture deep inside the raspberry patch and stick my head underneath the wet stalks. Tiny barbs on the stalks scratch my fingers, but I keep going.

A *hidden harvest* greets me!

Afraid they might disappear like some desert mirage, I frantically start gathering berries. There's too many to carry in my hands. Hidden on the underside of every stalk, I find more and more.

I return with a bowl and finish the work. I'm amazed at this hidden harvest. We feast until we've had our fill.

The whole time, I'm wondering about this *hidden harvest*. What harvest awaits, hidden from public view—from public consumption—because it's a deeper, internal sort of fruit? I think about all the quiet, hidden things I harvest from the Lord's work in my life. I think of character traits like perseverance, humility, courage. The world might not immediately see it, and it might not be obvious to anyone else.

But I know I'm changing.

Living with flair means thanking God that He produces fruit in our lives of good character. When there's no obvious fruit on the vine, it just means the harvest might be internal—deep within—on the underside.

54. "Mommy, Today Was a Small Day"

My six year old whimpers beside me, "Mommy, today was a small day."

"What made it small?"

"There were not enough play dates or friends. This was not a big day. I need *big days*."

Already, I think about what kind of big life this little girl will lead. She's challenging me to wake up to big days. I don't want to ever have a day that's too small.

I'll never have this day again. Lord, let it be a big day.

Living with flair means we don't have small days.

55. How to Survive the Waiting

This morning, a boy turns to me and asks, "Can you give me any tips on how to wait for something?"

I'm stumped. I'm floored. I'm overcome with how sweet (but so important) this question is and how many years of his life he'll be waiting for *something*. Here he is—just a boy—already waiting and needing to know how to survive the wait.

I'm overcome with how much of life is about waiting. I think every person I know has something they are waiting for. My own waiting—for the dreams of my children, for the plans I've made with my husband, for my own novelist longings—are equal parts delight and despair. Waiting is the *not yet*. It's a yes and a no at the same time. It's the impossible focus on two dimensions: hope and the reality of now.

It's the grand universal Maybe.

I tell the little boy (he's not so little now—we're on our 4th year of walking to school together) that all I can offer is this: Focus on the great things right in front of you today. But then I correct myself. I remember the beauty of longing, the joy of waiting because *something is coming*. I run up beside him and tell him that it's a great thing to wait. It's the best thing in the world.

Something is coming. It's just around the corner. Living with flair means we delight in the Maybe.

56. "The Higher You Go, The More Sap There Is"

My daughter climbs high into the pine trees and returns to me covered in tree sap. It's everywhere: hands, feet (she climbs barefoot!), arms, and all over her new white pants. They're *ruined.*

The next day, she climbs again. More sap. More ruinous results. What can I do? Do I ban tree climbing? I imagine her high within those limbs, smelling the sweet pine oil, and enjoying the wind on her face. Once, I climbed so high into a pine tree that I could see the top of my own house. Something about that vantage point gave me confidence as a little girl. Marked by sap, I returned to the earth happier.

That horrible sap! But I know this: Just because there's sap doesn't mean she shouldn't climb. *And the higher you want to go*, she tells me, *the more sap there is.* Perhaps every truly great pleasure brings its own form of darkness—its own trouble and cost—and we learn to account for it and manage it. We learn to battle it because the higher we go, the more trouble comes. I find this true spiritually and emotionally especially. The more we embrace God, the more the enemy pursues. The more we love, the more we risk.

But we're ready. We are willing because the vantage point we gain delivers a certain joy. What's a little sap in light of this joy?

Besides, we discover that Pine Sol cleaner really does remove tree sap from white pants.

57. The Trap Set for You

Today I read in Proverbs 13:14 that "the teaching of the wise is a fountain of life, turning a person from deadly traps."

I think about the wise teachers in my life who turned me away, at just the right time, from traps of all forms: bad relationships, risky behaviors, poor business decisions, or any other potentially ensnaring situations.

I read throughout scripture of the ways idols, evil desires, our own words, the pursuit of wealth, drunkenness, and even religious people can seduce us away from the fountain of life.

I also read in Psalm 31 the plea that God might keep us free *from the trap set for us* as we take refuge in Him.

Is there a trap set for us? I read in 2 Timothy 2 about coming to our senses to "escape the trap of the devil."

I pray that God brings wise teachers into my life and that I might become one of those wise teachers for others. Traps wait all around us, but wise words turn us from them. We need great wisdom and discernment to avoid traps because I realize *how hidden* they are. They don't look like traps; they masquerade as freedom, happiness, pleasure, fame, and wealth, but they ensnare us in the end.

58. "Stress Comes from Assuming Responsibility for Things that Are Not Your Responsibility"

15 years ago (I remember the day!) a wise, older woman took me by the hand and said, "You experience so much stress. Sometimes stress comes from assuming responsibility for things that are not our responsibility."

What could she mean? She explained that *God* is responsible for it all. I'm not. Have I taken on responsibilities that are not mine to take? Oh, yes I have.

"You assume responsibility for things that are not your responsibility."

If I'm not responsible for this or that, but God is, then everything changes.

Everything changes because God can handle it.

I think about this conversation multiple times a year.

59. "The Harder You Fall, The Higher You Bounce"

I'm telling my woes to my hairstylist (the one who told me last year that it's better to *be* the spotlight than be *in* the spotlight), and he says, "Well, the harder you fall, the higher you bounce."

He advises me to go ahead and fall hard and fast into whatever pain or sadness each day brings. Then, I'll rise up into joy.

I'll bounce. Remember: *The harder you fall, the higher you bounce.*

He's cutting my hair (adding bounce, of course, because everything's a hair metaphor). "Don't avoid pain. Don't be afraid of it. Sit with it and go ahead and fall. Then, you'll *bounce.* The point is not to say 'cheer up' to anyone. Instead, go right into the pain and wait for the bounce."

I love getting my haircut.

60. What I'm Learning About Self-Acceptance

Yesterday, I learn about how to help children love *who they are*—who God uniquely made them to be. I'm observing the problems of conformity, popularity, social acceptance, and rejection all played out in my daughters' (and my own) lives.

We cry a lot around here. It's painful to not fit in.

It's painful, but as my great friend in Texas reminded me this week: "If you're rejected by the popular crowd, it's probably because you're doing something right." This is the woman who regularly reminds me that I'm the perfect mother for my children.

So instead of thinking about all the ways we're rejected, we're thinking about self-acceptance. We're delighting in the unique, quirky, totally awesome things about us.

It's working. My prayers are working. I find that when children are being themselves—creating, imagining, playing freely—they stop thinking about popularity. They remember they are made for something great, and this probably means they won't fit in.

That's OK. We're really learning that's OK around here. I tell my friends it took me 30 years to really accept myself and believe in God's complete acceptance of me. Living with flair surely means we relish in God's unconditional acceptance of us in Christ. When we know this, we run across the playground freely without a care in the world.

61. Encounter with a Writing Spider

This morning, we see an enormous brown and yellow spider on the walk to school.

I learn that this garden spider commonly holds the name "Writing Spider."

She constructs and deconstructs this web daily. She builds a fresh web every new day with that distinctive zig-zag through the center of her web. Nobody knows for certain why she creates the series of X's in her web. Called *stabilimenta*, this silk structure inside a web confuses arachnologists. It seems to serve no purpose at all other than decoration. It doesn't necessarily stabilize or reflect light a certain way. It doesn't serve to attract prey or warn birds.

It's just writing in the web. It makes it beautiful; it's *artful*.

The arachnologists want it to serve a great purpose and to aid survival. But it doesn't.

It's just there for beauty.

Perhaps even the spider writes just because it's beautiful.

62. It's Not a Constraint; It's "Creative Pressure"

I read last night in *InGenius: A Crash Course on Creativity*, by Stanford neuroscience professor Tina Seelig, about the importance of pressure in the creative process.[3]

She talks about "building up creative pressure" that motivates us to produce. Without *pressure*, creativity actually wanes.

High pressure leads to *high creativity*, especially when there's a mission. Seelig cites numerous examples of how constraints (time, resources, support, energy) fuel genius acts of creativity. She explores the Apollo 13 crisis, eBay's Auction for America, Twitter, the Six Word Memoir project, and others.

The tighter the restrictions, the more creative people became.

What if we saw daily constraints as *creative pressure*? We don't have the time to write a novel. We don't have the space to design this new thing. We don't have the energy. We don't have the money. We don't have the support of others.

Maybe these things aren't the end of the world if we saw them as building our creative pressure.

Maybe our creativity requires these restrictions.

I like thinking of it this way.

63. "This Is Where We're Going."

Every few weeks, I stop in the middle of class and remind students of the whole narrative of the course.

"This is where we're going. This is what we're doing. This is why we are doing it." I reiterate the whole thing again.

We'll have the same conversation in a few weeks (then again a few weeks after that).

If we don't pause to remember where we're going—what it's all *for*—we lose the narrative of the course. If we lose that narrative, students choke upon the details. They don't move forward.

Often, I find myself assuring students that it doesn't make sense now, but it will.

It will. One day soon, this will all come together, and you'll see.

Since I've been teaching so long, I can make this promise. I know what they don't know. I see what they can't see. All the pieces will fit beautifully because I designed this course.

Suddenly, I remember the importance of connecting to that Larger Narrative— the one true story—that guides my life. If God designed it, then I'm pausing to consider the narrative: Where are we going, God? What are we doing? Why?

If I lose these answers, I lose everything. I choke upon details because I forget where we're going.

64. How to Avoid Heart Rot

My youngest and I examine a tree trunk by our home. Once, it stood tall over the neighborhood, but experts knew something wasn't right.

The tree suffered from *heart rot* and had to be cut down.

The entire inside of this externally beautiful tree *rotted*. (And yes, the heart rot possesses the shape of an actual heart. I feel like Someone's trying to get my attention.)

How did this happen? Why? When? How could such an enormous and wonderful tree actually reveal nothing but hollow decay?

Both my daughter and I need to know. (I'm really asking about myself and my own heart. I'm really asking about my own internal states.)

We research a bit and discover how heart rot results from decay caused by fungi that enters from *wounds* cause by storms, improper pruning, and insects or animals. These wounds will come, but we learn how to prevent or minimize the rot.

Yes, tell me! Teach me how to minimize heart rot when the wounds come!

Apparently, you want to make sure you have *deep root feeding* and properly sealed wounds. You have to make sure toxins cannot continue to enter. You also need to remove—by pruning—those parts of you that allow the harmful things in. I learn about *clean breaks*. I learn that if, in fact, heart rot begins, a tree knows how to *compartmentalize*. The tree knows how to grow around the decay and form a border so it can't harm the rest of the tree.

In my own spiritual life, I consider deep-root feeding on God, clean breaks from toxic things, and creating boundaries against decay. I think deeply about the "root of bitterness" that can defile our core. I think about love and forgiveness and unity and acceptance.

I don't want heart rot. Living with flair means we're beautiful and strong, inside and out.

65. "Comfort in Everything"

I read this morning a quote from Hannah Whitall Smith. She argues that "the soul who gives thanks can find comfort in everything; the soul who complains can find comfort in nothing."[4]

I realize the truth of it, especially when she later writes this bold statement:

"There can be nothing in our lives that lacks in it somewhere a cause for thanksgiving, and no matter who or what may be the channel to convey it, everything contains for us a hidden blessing from God."[5]

How different my days could be if I only believed that every moment has within it a cause for thanksgiving and a hidden blessing from God!

Training the heart towards such truth—remembering it each and every day—changes everything.

66. From Worry to Watching

This morning, I read some beautiful words in Paul Miller's *A Praying Life*. He says that when you "stop trying to control your life and instead allow your anxieties and problems to bring you to God in prayer, you shift from worry to watching."[6]

I love it. I love that when I go to God, I'm then invited to *watch*. I'm watching for God's amazing answer and work on my behalf. I'm watching for His power and presence.

I'm watching, not worrying.

Miller says that I'm looking for God to "weave his patterns in the story of [my] life." As I see God work, Miller insists that my life will begin to "sparkle with wonder."[7]

It does. It really does. I'm not worried today. I'm *watching* for God's intervening hand.

67. Are You Truly Content?

This morning in church, it occurs to me that much of my thinking involves wanting some aspect of my life to *change*. I pray in this direction. I hope in the direction of *just make this all different*.

Wait. Stop!

I remember that *contentment* in our circumstances represents one of the greatest gifts given by God. Contentment means happiness and complete satisfaction. The apostle Paul writes in Philippians that, "I have learned the secret of being content in any and every situation, whether well fed or hungry, whether living in plenty or in want. I can do all this through Him who gives me strength." Later, I read that "godliness with contentment is great gain."

I need the wisdom to know when to stop praying for change and to start praying for contentment.

Maybe I can do both. I don't know.

I choose today to ask for contentment, and I feel myself rising out of the darkness into glorious light.

68. If You Know How to Use It

I read this morning a fascinating quote from E. Stanley Jones:

"A young army officer said this, 'Weather, in war, is always favorable, if you know how to use it.' That is the point—if *you know how to use it*. The fact is that everything that comes to you in life is favorable—if you know how to use it."[8]

I look at the day before me and grimace over the tasks, but then I wonder, *Is everything favorable if I know how to use it?*

I look out at the icy rain and frown over the weather, but then I ask myself: *How can I use this?*

Beautiful things are coming; I'm already choosing joy. Over these last hundreds of blog entries, I'm learning to use *whatever* comes in order to learn, grow, and find beauty. That's God promise, and I find that He keeps it.

69. Hope for the Out-of-Tune

Today, the Piano Tuner comes to tune the piano.

We have to be *very quiet* so he can listen.

I learn that the Piano Tuner makes minute adjustments to the tension of the piano strings. He's listening for how the notes on my particular piano interact and tunes my piano based on its unique features.

The piano will not, on its own, stay in tune. The whole instrument experiences continual stress from both internal and external sources. Even slight changes in atmospheric pressure can undo my little piano within just a few weeks.

So we call the Piano Tuner, and he sets the instrument right.

I listen, watching him work. "Is it hopeless?" I ask, embarrassed for how long it's been.

"Not at all!"

When he's finished, he plays *extraordinary music*—warm, beautiful, rich, and resonant—that I didn't realize could come from this piano.

There's hope for the out-of-tune! There's hope for me yet!

Lord, come and set me right today. Make any adjustment you need; apply or undo any tension. Let music flow out of me that's tuned perfectly to your perfect ear.

I know how quickly and how thoroughly I go out of tune (not just with my horrible singing voice!) in attitude, ambition, and action. I remember the great hymn and sing out: "Tune my heart to sing Thy grace."

70. "You Make Me Feel Smart"

In class yesterday, I try to make the point about just how difficult it is to be *kind* in argumentative writing. I'm teaching ancient truths like the rules of civility and the lost art of listening. We're learning about how to defer to others, to believe the best about them, and to persuade them by finding common ground and acknowledging when an opponent is actually right.

To demonstrate, I ask students to give two *genuine compliments* to the person on their right. It's so awkward. It's so embarrassing. But they do it. We end up loving it. We end up laughing and nodding our heads in agreement with each compliment given.

At the end of it all, a student calls out from the back of the room to me: "*You're* on my right, so I have to compliment *you*."

"OK," I say. "Go for it."

He's quiet for a moment, and then he says carefully and clearly, "This is my favorite class because you make me feel smart."

I nearly burst into tears. It's because I'm suddenly aware of the narrative he's fighting; someone told him he wasn't smart, that he couldn't do it, that he didn't have anything to offer.

But not here. You're smart. Your particular intelligence matters deeply here.

71. The Beauty of Disintegrating Things

I'm walking through the autumn leaves, and I realize how much I absolutely love the smell of dead leaves. That warm smell brings such longing with it; I think of fall school days as a child and jumping into leaf piles. That unmistakable leafy smell just *makes me happy*.

Then I realize I'm actually delighting in decomposition (rot, if you will). I'm loving the smell of a disintegrating, dead thing.

Yes, yes I am. There's a particular beauty to what dies in this season. I celebrate it by jumping about, crunching into it, smelling it deeply.

I wish I could approach my own life that way. When things naturally and rightfully have to fade away because a new season is coming, I want to embrace it as eagerly as a child jumping into a leaf pile. New things always come about from old things falling away. I love the disintegrating leaves of Autumn. I pray I can welcome whatever disintegrating work God wants to do in my own life. Let the leaves fall and nourish whatever comes next.

72. Pull Through

I find myself talking to a woman who has suffered through chronic pain and fatigue for most of her life. She tells me all the ways she's adapted; mostly, she's learned to *rest well* and accept her limitations. This means she doesn't live the way others live. This means she lives with the acute reality that while others live very productive, fast, and high-capacity lives, she has the energy for maybe two or three good hours a day.

That's just how it is.

She doesn't push herself. She listens to her body and swims in a completely different current than all the rest of us. She doesn't push against the current; she leans back and lets God pull her through.

Sometimes, I think that's what our bodies are telling us, and we don't listen. We don't know how to lean back into the arms of God, rest well, and let Him pull us. We're too busy pushing through.

73. Why the Wilderness?

My husband reminds me of Deuteronomy 8 this morning, in particular this part beginning in verse 2:

Remember how the Lord your God led you all the way in the wilderness these forty years, to humble and test you in order to know what was in your heart, whether or not you would keep his commands. He humbled you, causing you to hunger and then feeding you with manna, which neither you nor your ancestors had known, to teach you that man does not live on bread alone but on every word that comes from the mouth of the Lord.

I spend a few minutes this morning recalling all the ways God "caused me to hunger" in my life. I remember all those things that humbled me and forced me—out of real desperation—to cling to and depend upon the Lord because I had no where else to turn. I remember the wilderness of my own heart. I remember those years of wandering.

All these years later, I can thank God for those times of humbling and hungering. Does God want to teach us how to need Him? Out of that Great Mercy, he allows the wilderness of the heart so we turn back to the One who loves us and truly meets our needs.

74. Catch

This morning I read a verse I don't remember reading ever in my life. Deuteronomy 33:27 offers this wonderful promise:

"The eternal God is your refuge, and underneath are the everlasting arms."

I try to imagine God's everlasting arms underneath me.

Even if I fall (or am falling), the everlasting arms are underneath me.

They will catch me.

75. A Most Extraordinary Piece of Art

An incredible artist, Ted Cantrell, sends my family a piece of his original artwork for our home. From the moment I remove this piece from its shipping box, I know I'm holding something extraordinary in my hands.

This Texan Artist once found an old tree that had grown up through a barbed wire fence on his grandfather's farm. He examines the dying tree with barbs running through it, and he sees something that we don't see. Taking discarded copper from a scrap metal yard, he shapes beautiful roses with barbed wire stems with the tree's wood as a base. He titles this piece, "Love Will Find a Way," and describes how it's about "beauty from ugliness" and "value from worthlessness."

We can't stop exploring this amazing creation. The Texan Artist knows that when a tree grows up against a barbed wire fence, it eventually incorporates it into itself.

I think about suffering—about all the painful barbs in life—and how we *take it all in*. It becomes part of us. We can't escape it. But I think about how under the hand of a skilled artist, this reality turns into something exquisite. All the parts we deem worthless suddenly become *so beautiful*.

We talk about symbols, and my children and I see a wooden cross, a crown of thorns, and the beauty of Christ in the roses.

I see the strength of a tree that won't be stopped.

I see perseverance, joy, and beauty despite any obstacle. In fact, I see how the obstacle *becomes* our greatest meaning and our greatest raw material for beauty.

This is what God does.

76. The Interview Game

My youngest daughter tells me today that her friends at school never ask her anything about herself.

"I ask about *them*, but they don't ask about *me*," she explains.

"I know what you mean," I tell her. "Hardly anyone knows how to ask good questions of one another. We might need to learn how to do it."

So after school, I ask her and her friend all about it: "What kinds of questions do you like people to ask you?"

Her friend says, "I want people to ask me about what it's like to have brothers or what I'm thinking about my pets."

My daughter insists that she wants people to ask her about her fashion (of course!).

"You might tell your friends what you want them to ask you about since nobody seems to know."

I suddenly realize this is a great idea. Instead of stewing about how friends aren't asking enough about us, why don't we just tell them the kinds of things we love being asked about? Later, I hear my daughter ask her friend, "How many pets do you have, and what are their names?"

Her friend tells her and then turns to my daughter and says, "So what's your favorite style of clothing?"

I think we're on to something. Telling people what you like to discuss could certainly help build friendships. (Don't ask me about weight loss, grading, or holiday shopping. Ask me about God, writing novels, teaching, and blogging.)

"It's like an interview game," I tell them. "And the first question is always, 'What do you want me to ask you about?'"

77. Read and Be Inspired: An 8-Year-Old Dresses Up as Her Greatest Insecurity

My friend calls from Texas to update me on her life and children. She shares this incredible story and gives me permission to share it with you.

Her sweet daughter has had to wear hearing aids these past few years. This little girl doesn't want *anybody* talking about them; she hides her hearing aids with her long hair, and she just wishes everybody would ignore them.

For years, she hides them.

But this year, she asks her dad to make her into a *giant hearing aid* for her Halloween costume. She asks him to cut out ear holes so she might point to her hearing aids and explain to everybody at school how they work, where the battery is, and where she hides the wires.

I repeat: A little girl dresses up as her greatest insecurity and essentially says to the world, "Ask me about this."

Tears fill my eyes as I think about all of us parading around, showcasing our greatest insecurity. I think about walking around in freedom, coming out of hiding, and amplifying the thing we hate the most about ourselves in order to turn it into a beautiful thing.

I share the story with my college students, and they are moved and inspired. I ask them about their greatest insecurities. Would they do what this little girl did? Would anybody?

I'm amazed. Living with flair means we come out of hiding, show the world our greatest insecurity, and boldly say, "Ask me about this."

We'd be free.

78. Miriam's Tambourine: The Song You Would Sing

This morning I read in Exodus 15:20: "Then Miriam the prophetess, Aaron's sister, took a tambourine in her hand, and all the women followed her with tambourines and dancing. Miriam sang to them: 'Sing to the Lord, for he is highly exalted'."

Something about this woman challenges me today. She takes up a tambourine and leads those following her into a great song of praise. I thought about women in my life who remind me of Miriam; they go before me and invite me to worship a great God. They lead others with the song their lives sing.

I thought about the younger women in our lives who we might lead into worship. If they followed us, what song would they hear? What song is my life singing? Would it be a dirge, a complaint? Would it be an exceedingly joyful proclamation?

I'm thinking about the song my life sings today. Living with flair means we lead women into praise.

79. Go Now, Write It on a Scroll as an Everlasting Witness

This morning, I consider the strange call to . . . blog. *Blogging?* What a weird little genre of writing! I remember in Isaiah 30:8 that simple command to "Go now, write it on a scroll so that in days to come it may be an everlasting witness." I know this command was specifically for the prophet, but something about it rings true today. Something about recording the Lord's work—actually *writing it down*—matters so much. I think about creating a document for my children that's an "everlasting witness" to the Lord's work.

I think about Psalm 102 and the words, "Let this be written for a future generation, that a people not yet created may praise the Lord."

What if I simply recorded it all? Here's what God is doing. Here's what God has done. I don't want to forget. I don't want my children to forget.

I especially don't want to forget the nuggets of wisdom I find during the day. For example, on Thursday night, my husband and I took a missionary couple to dinner. They had been in Eastern Europe, raising their family and faithfully serving the Lord for decades. After all this time, their passion and love just oozed out of them.

"What's your secret to persevering all these years and keeping your joy? What's your best advice for us?" we ask them.

I learn three things that I want to pass on. First, they tell us to be certain of our calling from God and to not expect others to understand this special assignment. Second, they advised us not to compare ourselves with others—either falling into the trap of superiority or inferiority—and to press on into our *specific calling*. We don't have to look like other families look. We don't have to do what other families are doing. And we don't expect them to behave just as we do.

Third, they said the big secret to perseverance was "understanding the Biblical definition of rest." They counseled us to "rest well" since there will always be too much work to do in a day.

Be certain of your calling. You don't have to be like other families. Rest well.

There, I wrote it down to remember it. I wrote it down for you and my children as well.

80. The Greatest Temptation in the Christian Life

I've been a Christian a long time—since 1985—and I find that *one thing* tempts me more than anything else.

It's the temptation to live a life of self-effort rather than one of spirit-filled dependence.

I rely on *myself*. I do it in *my own strength*. I am filled with anxiety with all *my micro-managing*. I work harder in *all my power*. I attempt my spiritual disciplines with all *my energy*.

Aren't you tired just reading that sentence? I am. It gives me a headache.

I remember the day in 1997 when a woman shared with me about spirit-filled living. It seemed too good to be true. We looked at the scriptures together (mostly Romans 8 and Ephesians 5), and I learned that I can ask the Holy Spirit to control, direct, and empower my life.

I turn from self-effort. I do this by faith.

I can surrender control of my life and invite God's spirit to live a supernatural life through me. Otherwise, the Christian life isn't just hard; it's really impossible. It's really not good news at all if I have to work harder, in my own power, to do anything.

With God's power in me, I'm increasingly filled with the "fruit of the Spirit" (Galatians 5) and have a mind "governed by life and peace" (Romans 8).

Really? Is it that simple?

Yes. The good news of Jesus is really *good news*. But I find that every few months, I'm tempted away from this reality back into the drudgery and enslavement of working harder in my own power.

So today I remember this simple and joyous truth.

81. I've Gone to Seed

Today, I consider things that *go to seed*. The expression, "go to seed," normally refers to loss; things that deteriorate, worsen, devitalize, or fall apart have "gone to seed."

It's a funny expression, especially when you think about gardening.

In gardening, allowing plants to "go to seed" means you let them enter into a new phase: seed production. The plants direct *all their energy* into a new generation. The resulting seeds will scatter and take root. Some gardeners claim that these seeds create the strongest, most durable plants. Going to seed, in this case, isn't terrible; it's wonderful and necessary. What looks like loss for the plant is really multiplying (too many to count!) growth.

I think about John 12:24 and how the seed that falls and dies produces many seeds. If it doesn't fall, it just remains a single seed.

If we seem to the world that we're deteriorating, falling apart, and losing our productivity—especially in these tasks of parenting, community care, and teaching young people—we think of it as *going to seed*. We're directing energy into a new generation.

As we should.

82. How to Stop Comparing Yourself: You're Appointed for That

I'm learning another path to freedom from comparison, jealousy, insecurity, and even fear. Two Bible verses inoculate me against these kinds of temptations: 1 Corinthians 3:6 tells me that "the Lord has assigned to each his task." Ephesians

2:10 reminds me that "we are God's handiwork, created in Christ Jesus to do good works, which God prepared in advance for us to do."

I realize that some of us are simply *appointed* for certain externally beautiful, prosperous, joyous things, while others seem *appointed* for suffering, disappointment, loss, or failure. Is God not still in charge? Is God not still assigning—with great care, specificity, love, and purpose—our task (whether pleasant or challenging)? Is our prepared "good work" suddenly less meaningful because it looks different from another's?

I'm reminded that we're sovereignly appointed for our tasks and our good works. No one has the same tasks. Externally, we compare and measure ourselves against one another and end up in places of jealousy, insecurity, and sometimes fear. But the way out (at least for me) is to always remember *what I'm appointed for*.

It might be harvesting raspberries, walking with my neighbor, writing, cooking dinner, leading a quiet Bible study, helping my daughters with their homework, making snacks, grading, and teaching. I'm filled with peace when I realize this is what I'm appointed for today.

And I pray that I enter into the path of freedom where I receive my specific tasks with joy and confidence.

I'm appointed for this.

83. What Could Be Better?

My youngest daughter always says exactly what's on her mind. There's no beating around the bush, equivocating, or flattering.

So when she invites my dear friend to dinner (who is also her most favorite person in the world), she's flabbergasted when the friend declines. My friend has other plans.

My daughter puts her hands on her little hips and says, "What could be better than *me*? What plans are better than *me*?"

She's laughing at her own sassiness, but I see that sparkle in her eye that tells me she also sincerely can't imagine her favorite person missing a dinner date with her.

Oh, to have that self-confidence and assurance of your own awesomeness!

Later, she wants to recount a dramatic story from school. She stands in front of me and says, "Now, Mother, don't be distracted! Put down your phone! Stop cleaning dishes!" In other words, she has that same sparkle that says, "Nothing's more important than what I'm about to tell you."

Our silly demanding banter—What's better than *me*?—reminds me so much of God's voice in my heart. Why would I ever decline an invitation or keep up my distracted multi-tasking when there's something to hear from God?

Nothing's more important. Nothing's better.

What's better than me?

84. It's OK to Ask

This morning, I read the simple prayer of David when he was being persecuted by Saul. He prays: "I call on you, O God, for you will answer me; give ear to me and hear my prayer."

Don't you want to know what he asked? Don't you want to know what this great request might be?

It's this: "Show the wonder of your great love."

Show the wonder of your great love for us today.

Show means to "make visible," to "display," or to "allow to be perceived." Essentially, David needed to see a tangible demonstration of God's love to encourage his heart.

Yes! Make it visible to us. We need tangible today, God. We need to perceive you. It's OK to ask this.

David asked for this, and so shall I.

85. A Reminder from Tozer: "No Common Act"

I find an old quote in one of my journals from A.W. Tozer:

"It is not what a man does that determines whether his work is sacred or secular; it is why he does it. The motive is everything. Let a man sanctify the Lord God in his heart, and he can therefore do no common act."[9]

I like to remember this. Sanctified, even the folding of laundry and the washing of dishes, even the picking of raspberries, the making of beds, the cleaning of toilets, and the shopping for groceries elevates from common to extraordinary.

Why we do what we do matters more than what we do.

We do no common acts today.

86. The 10 Glorious Verbs of Psalm 65

I read Psalm 65 as someone obsessed with verbs.

My students know my great love of verbs; they weasel "grapple with" and "fritter" into their papers because they know such verbs send me clapping.

So I'm reading Psalm 65, and I discover glorious verbs about God:

He *answers* us with awesome deeds of righteousness.
He *brings us near.*
He *calls forth* songs of joy.
He *enriches* us abundantly.
He *drenches* furrowed places.
He *levels* hardened ridges.
He *softens.*
He *crowns.*
He *clothes.*
He *mantles.*

Our God *does* things.

I ask for Him to answer; to bring me near; to call forth songs of joy within me; to enrich me; to drench any dry and withdrawn parts with His love; to level all my hardened spots; to soften me; to crown my year with bounty; to clothe me with gladness; to mantle me with fruitfulness and joy.

I love the pure verbs of God.

87. "An Ideal Far Beyond Yours"

This morning, I read in Hannah Whitall's Smith's, *God is Enough,* an interesting assignment for the soul.

She insists: "Realize to yourself what your ideal shepherd would be—all that you would require from anyone filling such a position of trust and responsibility—and then know that an ideal far beyond yours was in the mind of our Lord when He said, 'I am the good shepherd'."[10]

What would I require of such a Shepherd? What would I want Him to do for me? After I make that list of *every single thing* that might signify I'm truly cared for, God exceeds this in ways that are "immeasurably more than I could ask or imagine."

We are truly cared for, beyond all we could ask or imagine.

88. "Because I'm So Loved"

I'm unloading grocery bags into my car. It's unseasonably warm and sticky outside, and I'm dreading the walk to return my cart to the store. Then, an older man (gray-haired, wobbly, and adorable) asks if he can return my cart for me. He has his own cart in one hand and grabs my cart with the other.

"Yes!" I call after him as he trudges away with my cart. "Oh, thank you! *Thank you!* Why are you so kind? Why would you do this?" I continue to call after him, so thankful and pleased that kind people exist in this world.

"Because I'm so loved," he says.

I stand there, car keys dangling, amazed at the truth of it.

He's so loved. He has nothing to gain and nothing to lose. He lives his life differently, and I noticed it. He's so loved, so he knew just how to love *me* at that tiny moment that came and went in the grocery store parking lot today.

When we know we're so loved, we overflow with it.

I'm so loved by God that I have nothing to gain and nothing to lose. I do everything because I'm just *so loved.*

89. The One Who Does the Most

My colleague and I conclude today that the student who often appears the most disengaged can be the very student thinking the most deeply.

Maybe, just maybe, the more silent and separate the student becomes, the more her brain works. We cannot assume that silence or staring off into space means what we think it means. We favor the talkative, energetic, busy, over-producing student because we misunderstand what's happening inside a student's mind.

I hear the story of a challenge presented to a group. Three group members tackle it head-on with eager involvement while one sits aside, apparently bored and consumed with his media. As the other three try and fail to solve the challenge, the disengaged student calmly announces the solution the others cannot see. He'd been thinking all along. He'd been problem solving even as he stared at the screen.

His way of thinking looked different from what we praise in the classroom.

I remember that sometimes I do my best thinking when I'm doing something else. Sometimes I have to talk and talk to get to a solution, and other times, I have to watch television and let my mind work on its own in that mysterious process where thoughts roam without pressure. It might seem like someone's "wasting time" when really, the brain's working in its own way.

Maybe the one doing the most is the one doing nothing at all.

90. Protecting Your Friends

Today, a friend asks me to protect her from over-scheduling herself. All morning, I think about a friend's function as *protector*.

"Yes! I will protect you! I will help you say 'no' and not ask too much of you!"

Friends should indeed work to keep one another from harm, but I seldom think of friendship like this.

I want to ask my friends this question: *How can I help protect you? From what or whom?*

I realize we all need protection—spiritually, physically, emotionally, socially, financially, or in any other way.

I need protection from desserts containing coconut.

I also need protection from trying to micro-manage my children.

I need protection, like my friend, from doing too much. I need protection from discouragement and burn-out in my teaching life. I need protection from afternoon coffee that keeps me up all night.

I need protection from watching too much news and obsessing over it.

I need protection from pride, anger, impatience, and gossip.

I'll stop now.

I love thinking about friends as *protectors.*

91. Releases Easily

I've learned to pick only the autumn raspberries that release easily into my hands. I know they're ripe and ready to enjoy this way.

I enjoy the morning sun, the glistening dew, and the smell of wet grass.

I think of all the things in my life that come easily when they're *ready*, when God *appoints* them, and when *I'm* ready. I remember Proverbs 4 and how the "path of the righteous is like the morning sun, shining ever brighter till the full light of day."

I pray for God to put me on the that clear, bright path and that I'll wait for the kind of harvest that releases easily, in perfect timing.

92. The Big Goal: Participating in the Divine Nature

This morning, I glance at a new study guide called *How People Change*, by Timothy Lane and Paul David Tripp.

I'm struck by the governing question of the text. It's this:

What hopes and goals give direction to your life?[11]

Well, I'm so glad you asked.

I realize how easily I veer off course in my ambitions—whether writing, parenting, teaching, or even emotional well-being. The authors present the idea that the best hope and goal for a life is to "participate in the divine nature and escape the corruption of the world caused by evil desires" (2 Peter 1:4).

Can I really say that the singular hope and goal of my life is to "participate in the divine nature" and to help others do the same? Is becoming more Christ-like my hope and goal above all else?

If so, then I realize all my experiences, both good and bad, function as stepping stones toward this goal if I allow them to. When filtered through this lens, I experience joy I never thought I could have. I know God is working to help me participate more and more in the divine nature.

If this is the hope and goal, then what happens to us doesn't paralyze us with fear or insecurity. We realize that God has the power to bring everything under His control to complete the good work He began in us.

He uses everything to help us participate in the divine nature.

93. "Who Can Show Us Any Good?": Encouragement for Sad Days

This morning as I sat in my minivan after another night of comforting sad children over the death of our beloved cat, I felt the weight of sorrow in my heart. So much sorrow! Not just for pets that die, but for all the other sorrow in my own community and across the whole world. I realize that losing a pet is a small thing compared to other sorrows that potentially await us all. What if things actually don't get better? What if they get *worse*?

A wise pastor told my husband that *life gets harder, but joy gets greater.*

I'm having a hard time with it. I can't muster up the hope today. In fact, I feel Creeping Cynicism. I don't want to pray. I don't want to read my Bible.

But a phrase keeps repeating in my mind as I sit in my minivan. It's the question in Psalm 4: "Who can show us any good?" When life weighed the psalmist down, he asked the question I feel myself asking on my worst days. *What's the point? Who can show me any good today?*

I remember the answer from my own childhood when I memorized Psalm 4. The answer is this:

Lift the light of your countenance upon us, O Lord.
You have put gladness in my heart,
More than when their grain and new wine abound.
In peace I will lie down and sleep,
For you alone, O Lord, make me to dwell in safety.

I ask God to put the kind of gladness in my heart that doesn't depend upon what happens to me. I thank God that He gives peace and helps me dwell in a kind of safety I cannot comprehend. He does it. He puts it in there. Who can show us any good? Even in the midst of the distressing question, God puts gladness, peace, and safety there.

94. Catching Words As They Fall

All of a sudden today—right in the middle of daily life (when there's no time at all)—I sit to write the paragraph I've been mulling over for a month. It's as if it just overflows out of me naturally and easily. I'm just catching words as they fall.

Why can't it always be this way?

I think about overflowing things. Overflow, as a noun, denotes excess or surplus that the available space can't accommodate.

Maybe, the thing I'm thinking about must become *so large in me* that it runs over. If the writing's not flowing, maybe the thing isn't large enough to me yet.

95. The Terrible Danger of Efficiency

I've had a major life course correction these past few weeks.

Imagine the old me *efficiently mastering the tasks of the day in a frenzied zeal of productivity.*

Efficiency governed my life.

In fact, I judged the success of each day by how much I could squeeze in. I relished advanced preparation, shortcuts, multi-tasking, checklists, and all the other trappings of a Type A, High I, ENFJ type of woman.

More, more, more! Faster, faster, faster!

But why? *Why?*

I was cutting up chicken for tomorrow's pot pie, and I thought about all the time I was saving. *But was I really saving time? What was I doing with all this hypothetical time?* I was just cramming in more stuff, being ever more efficient, in a stifling, exhausting, and never-ending cycle.

What would happen if I simply weren't efficient anymore? What would happen if I stopped trying to maximize my productivity?

In a strange and beautiful moment, time froze as I put the pot pie away for another day. I rested my chin on my folded hands and took a deep breath.

There's no benefit to efficiency if it only keeps you on a treadmill. There's no benefit to efficiency if it keeps you so future-oriented that you're never actually enjoying the present moment at all.

Lately, I'm enjoying my tasks in a slow, focused, and present manner. I'm not interested in saving time. I'm interested in living my life fully and joyfully. Efficiency steals that kind of life from me. Efficiency steals peace from my heart.

Besides, it all gets done anyway—at least the important things. Try abandoning efficiency, and you'll see what I mean.

(I actually don't see Jesus as *efficient* in scripture, by the way. Do you?)

96. Final Harvest and In-Between Living

I think I've picked my last bowl of raspberries for the season. The snow is coming. The cool autumn days end.

What a great harvest! I think about that lovely routine of gathering all the ripe things in life. The summer and early fall felt so abundant and juicy.

But now? I look at all the withered things about the garden. I know it's a necessary ending—that wintering in order to grow fruit again next summer and fall—but it *feels* so empty.

The feeling only lasts a moment because I know this: with a freezer full of berries, I'll feast on sweet things all winter. I've stored up, like those who recall God's great faithfulness in seasons of emptiness, so it's not empty at all. We feast on what we've stored up of Him.

Maybe that's what winter is for. It's a deeper enjoyment, a deeper feast.

97. An Emotional Mom Learns a Drama-Free Way to Talk to Pre-Teens

I'm learning how to better communicate with my family and friends. Most recently, I learned how often I like to *rescue* and *react* when someone comes to me with distressing emotions.

So, hypothetically, when my pre-teen begins to share about her day, I go into *rescue* mode. Then, I *react* with all sorts of dramatic emotions (not surprising!). I want to solve the problem, help by my intense emotional reaction, and immediately provide smart strategies. I want to enter in to her emotional states.

No! This doesn't help her!

I learn that instead of rescuing and reacting, *responding* and *rejoicing* serve the other person best.

I'm invited to respond with empathy (You seem confused, worried, sad, or angry). I might even share how one might normally feel to help the person clarify how she's actually feeling. (I can imagine someone feeling jealous, lonely, or scared).

Then, and this is the missing piece for me, I learn to ask, "What did you do? or How did it go?"

How did you handle that?

Then, I remember to *rejoice* with every decision the person made on their own. This kind of conversing empowers others, releases them to feel in control of their emotions, and keeps the drama to a minimum. It tilts the emotional drama back to peaceful rejoicing.

For those of you moms out there who share my emotional intensity, remember the 2 R's: respond and rejoice. Instead of react or rescue, we *respond* and *rejoice.*

98. You Missed Everything

My least favorite emails from students include these kinds of sentences: "I wasn't in class this morning. Let me know if I missed anything important." Or this: "I'm going to miss class Monday. Will I miss anything important?"

Yes. Yes, you will miss *everything* important. What will you miss? I'm so glad you asked.

You will miss that moment that will never come again, with people who will never gather in this same configuration again, with words spoken by us all that won't leave our lips again in that same way.

You will miss a comment by a student that could have changed your mind; you will miss talking to the one girl about something that might just make her your new best friend; you will miss a lesson on writing that might have inspired a novel or memoir that the world needs. You will miss writing something in your notebook that you'll keep for forty more years and read again when your own daughters take a writing class.

You will miss this. And we will miss this.

We will miss your voice answering a question that unlocks something for someone else. We will miss the tilt of your head as you think about something and the way you tap your pencil like that. We will miss your insight. When you miss class, you miss *you* being you at that moment, in that place where verbs and semicolons dance in some spiritual place where students gather with coffee cups and bagels and notebooks and pens with a teacher whose entire life culminates in this moment when she holds the chalk and begins.

So yes, you missed something.

You missed everything.

99. He Will Rescue You

As I read Psalm 35, I'm suddenly struck by the repetition of one word: *rescue.*

I learn afresh that God rescues us from what comes against us. I recall all I've been rescued from, and I can hardly contain the joy inside of me when I remember.

But today, I ask God to rescue me from ways of thinking and being that violate and disable the sweet peace He offers. I ask God to rescue me from fear that keeps me in a state of hyper-control and anxiety.

He rescues us! At the very end of this psalm, David—who wrote this while being hunted down by his enemies—writes, "The Lord be exalted who delights in the well-being of his servant."

I seldom remember that God truly delights in our well-being. He is our Rescuer from whatever distresses and endangers us.

Praise Him. When I feel hunted down by anything at all, whether internally or externally, I appeal to my Rescuer.

100. Your Glorious Descent

It's time.

You lift off, send yourself into the glorious unknown, and let God carry you.

My children twirl about in this dance of falling leaves.

We'll crunch them underfoot and crush them in our hands. They'll go on to nourish the soil and let another generation of leaves rise up. As I think about getting older, about surrendering, about giving my life away to others, I realize it's a glorious descent.

I feel like that beautiful leaf against the brightest blue sky. My daughter reaches up and grabs it in her hand, delighted.

You let go, die to yourself every single day, and fall into the ancient pattern.

That's the only way to dance in the wind.

It's the only way to be free.

Notes and Permissions

Welcome

[1] William Wordsworth, "Lines Composed a Few Miles Above Tintern Abbey, On Revisiting the Banks of the Wye During a Tour, July 13,1978," originally printed in *Lyrical Ballads with other Poems. In Two Volumes* (London: Longman and Rees, 1800) found in *The Norton Anthology of English Literature,* Vol. 22, ed. 6 (London: W.W. Norton & Company, 1993) 137.

[2] © 2014 Monique Duval. All rights reserved. Used with permission from Compendium, Inc.

Winter

[1] Mary Pipher, *Writing to Change the World* (New York: Riverhead, 2006) 63. © 2006 Mary Pipher. All rights reserved. Used with permission.

[2] Ernest Hemingway qtd in Pipher, 78.

[3] A. H. Maslow, "A Theory of Human Motivation," *Psychological Review* (1943): 370–96. Retrieved from http://psychclassics.yorku.ca/Maslow/motivation.htm.

[4] Wikipedia contributors, "Late Bloomer," *Wikipedia, The Free Encyclopedia*, 30 Aug. 2014. Web. 6 Nov. 2014.

[5] Carson Creagh, "Taking Off," *Things with Wings* (Alexandria: Time-Life, 1996) 18-19.

[6] E. Stanley Jones, *Abundant Living: 365 Daily Devotions* (New York: Abingdon-Cokesbury, 1946) Week 17, Sunday.

[7] Walter A. Henrichsen and Howard G. Hendricks, *Disciples are Made Not Born: Helping Others Grow to Maturity in Christ* (Colorado Springs: David C. Cook, 1988) 47. © 2002 Walter A Henrichsen and Howard G Hendricks. *Disciples are Made Not Born: Helping Others Grow To Maturity in Christ* is published by David C Cook. All rights reserved. Used with permission.

[8] Henry David Thoreau, *Walden, Or Life in the Woods* (Radford: Wilder Publications, 2008) 54.

[9] E. Stanley Jones, *The Way* (New York: Abingdon-Cokesbury, 1946) 98.

[10] Jens Peter Jacobsen, *Mogens, and Other Stories* (Denmark: N.L. Brown, 1921) 9.

[11] Rainer Maria Rilke, *Letters to a Young Poet,* Trans. M.D. Herter Norton (New York: W.W. Norton & Company, 1954) 18-19.

[12] E. Jean Carroll in "Ask E. Jean," *Elle Magazine* (January 2012). ©2012 E. Jean Carroll. All rights reserved. Used with permission.

[13] Jorge Luis Borges, trans. Norman Thomas di Giovanni, "The Life of Tadeo Isidoro," *The Aleph and Other Stories* (New York: Dutton, 1970) as quoted by Javier Cercas, trans. Anne McClean, *The Anatomy of a Moment* (London: Bloomsbury, 2009) 8.

[14] Henri Nouwen, *Return of the Prodigal Son* (New York: Doubleday, 1992) 33, 18.

[15] Jones, *The Way*, 345.

[16] Pipher 106.

[17] Pipher 106.

[18] Interview recounted by Brad Bright in his introduction, "Serving is a Lifestyle" in Dr. Bill Bright's book, *My Life is Not My Own: Following God No Matter What the Cost* (Ventura: Gospel Light and Bright Media Foundation, 2010) vi.

[19] Hippocrates, *The Hippocratic Oath*, Late 5th century BC. Full translation appears in the National Library of Medicine (National Institutes of Health) http://www.nlm.nih.gov/hmd/greek/greek_oath.html.

[20] According to the Boy Scouts of America ®, the Scout Oath (or Promise) originally written by Robert Baden-Powell in 1908, states, "On my honor I will do my best, to do my duty to God and my country and to obey the Scout Law; To help other people at all times; To keep myself physically strong, mentally awake, and morally straight." The Scout Law states, "A Scout is trustworthy, loyal, helpful, friendly, courteous, kind, obedient, cheerful, thrifty, brave, clean, and reverent." http://www.scouting.org/scoutsource/BoyScouts.aspx.

[21] Parker J. Palmer, "Good Talk about Good Teaching," *Change: The Magazine of Higher Learning* 25.6 (1993): 8-13. Web. ©1993 Parker Palmer. All rights reserved. Used with permission.

[22] Robert Wilkinson, *The Saints travel to the land of Canaan Wherein is discovered seventeen false rests below the spiritual coming of Christ in the Saints. Together with a brief discovery of what the coming of Christ in the spirit is; who is the alone rest and center of spirits. By R. Wilkinson. A member of the army.* (London: printed for Giles Calvert, at the black spread-Eagle at the west end of Pauls, 1648).

[23] Quoted in Pipher, 13.

[24] Pipher 208

Spring

[1] Michael Jackson, "Beat It," *Thriller* (Epic, 1983).

[2] Hayden Planetarium Guide, as quoted by Lorrie Moore in the front matter of her book, *A Gate at the Stairs* (New York: Vintage, 2010). To confirm this quote, I contacted the Hayden Planetarium staff. While they could not direct me to the source of this quote, they claimed, "[The quote] is factually correct. The planetarium is a spherical space, with the floor mildly sloping upward. The images projected onto the domed ceiling and upper part of the wall can be seen equally well by everyone."

[3] Alicia Britt Chole, in the prologue to *Anonymous: Jesus' Hidden Years. . .and Yours* (Nashville: Thomas Nelson, 2006) 2.

[4] Jonathan Swift, as attributed in *Escape the Pace: 100 Fun and Easy Ways to Slow Down and Enjoy Your Life* (2004) by Lisa Rickwood, no earlier source yet located.

[5] Daniel Defoe, *Robinson Crusoe, 1719* (Oxford: Oxford UP, 2008) 14.

[6] J.I. Packer, *Knowing God* (Downers Grove: InterVarsity Press, 1993) 34.

[7] Larry Crabb, "Living the New Way" presented by Colorado Christian University, New Way Ministries & Dr. Larry Crabb, Radio Audio Cuts on K-Love.

[8] From the sermon by Tim Keller, "Made for Stewardship," preached October 22, 2000, downloaded from http://sermons2.redeemer.com/sermons/sermonlist/265. Accessed 29 August 2011.

[9] Jones, *The Way*, 119.

[10] Sue Monk Kidd, *The Secret Life of Bees* (New York: Penguin, 2002) 63. © 2002 Sue Monk Kidd Ltd. All rights reserved. Used with permission.

[11] Dr. Bill Bright, *How You Can Love by Faith* (Peachtree City: New Life Publications, 2002). ©2002 Bright Media Foundation and Campus Crusade for Christ International (CCCI). Used with permission. http://www.cru.org/train-and-grow/classics/transferable-concepts/love-by-faith.4.html.

[12] Patricia J. Ruta McGhan for the US Forest Service, "Pink Ladies Slipper (Cypridedium acuale Ait.)" http://www.fs.fed.us/wildflowers/plant-of-the-week/cypripedium_acaule.shtml and "Meet the Ladies: The Slipper Orchids," http://www.fs.fed.us/wildflowers/beauty/cypripedium/.

[13] Joseph Campbell's monomyth—or the Hero's Journey—was a pattern he articulates in *The Hero with a Thousand Faces* (Princeton: Princeton UP, 1949).

[14] Taken from *My Utmost for His Highest*® by Oswald Chambers, edited by James Reimann, ©1992 by Oswald Chambers Publications Assn., Ltd., and used by permission of Discovery House Publishers, Grand Rapids MI 49501. All rights reserved.

[15] Walt Whitman, "A Backward Glance O'er Travel'd Roads," *The Complete Poems* (New York: Penguin, 2005) 582.

[16] --The Preface to the 1855 edition of *Leaves of Grass* (New York: Penguin, 1961).

[17] Roy and Revel Hession, *We Would See Jesus, 1958* (Philadelphia: CLC Ministries, 2005).

[18] Timothy Keller, *The Freedom of Self-Forgetfulness: The Path to True Christian Joy* (Nashville: Thomas Nelson, 1982) 31.

[19] Keller 35.

[20] Keller 32.

[21] Susannah Meadows, "Meet the Gamma Girls," *Newsweek* 139.22 (June 3, 2002): 44-50.

[22] Michael Crawley, "Cynicism" http://michaelmfc.wordpress.com/2011/01/30/cynicism/ © 2011 Michael Crawley. Used with permission.

[23] E.O. Wilson, "The Naturalist," *Being Human: Core Readings in the Humanities* (New York: W.W. Norton, 2004) 90-91.

[24] C.S. Lewis, *Surprised by Joy: The Shape of My Early Life* (Orlando: Harcourt Books, 1955) 220.

Summer

[1] A.R. Ammons, "Loss," *The Selected Poems of A.R. Ammons* (New York: Norton, 1987): 56. ©1987 A.R. Ammons. All rights reserved. Used with permission from Writer's Representatives LLC.

[2] Frederick Buechner, *Longing for Home: Reflections at Mid Life* (New York: HarperCollins, 1996). © 1996 Frederick Buechner. All rights reserved. Used with permission from Frederick Buechner Literary Asssets, LLC.

[3] Hannah Whitall Smith, *The Christian Secret of a Happy Life, Complete and Unabridged*, 1870 (Urichsville: Barbour, 1985).

[4] Lewis Carroll, *Alice in Wonderland and Through the Looking Glass*, 1865 (New York: Bantam, 1984) Chapter 5, "Wool and Water" in *Through the Looking Glass*.

[5] See slowmovement.com to learn more about the Slow Movement. I first heard about Slow Food in *The Telling Room: A Tale of Love, Betrayal, Revenge, and the World's Greatest Piece of Cheese*, by Michael Paterniti (New York: Random House, 2013).

[6] Roy and Revel Hession, preface.

[7] Elizabeth Goudge, *The Scent of Water, 1963* (Peabody: Hendrickson, 2012) 93.

[8] Charlotte Bronte, *Jane Eyre, 1847* (Radford: Wilder Publications, 2008) 255.

[9] Dr. Alice Russell "Poisonous Plants of North Carolina." North Carolina State University http://plants.ces.ncsu.edu/plants/category/poisonous-plants/.

[10] Hannah Whitall Smith from July 21 "Consecrating or Surrendering" in *God is Enough* (Grand Rapids: Zondervan, 1986) 148.

[11] Pipher 45.

[12] Hayden Planetarium Guide. See note 2 in Spring.

[13] Dr. Wayne Dyer in the forward to *Left to Tell* by Immaculee Ilibagiza (New York: Hay House, Inc. 2014) xiv. ©21014 Hay House, Inc. All rights reserved. Used by permission from Hay House, Inc.

[14] Paige Benton Brown, "In the Temple: The Glorious and Forgiving God." Plenary address on 1 Kings 8 at the Gospel Coalition 2012 National Women's Conference. thegospelcoalition.org/resources/a/in_the_temple_the_glorious_and_forgiving_god_1_kings_8.

[15] Margaret Silf, *Inner Compass: An Invitation to Ignatian Spirituality* (Chicago: Loyola Press, 1999) 218. © Margaret Silf. All rights reserved. Used with permission from both US and UK publishers. In the UK, this book is called *Landmarks: An Ignatian Journey* (London: Darton, Longman & Todd, 1998).

[16] Silf 63.

[17] Smith, *The God of All Comfort*, 121.

[18] Jamie Zeppa, *Beyond the Sky and Earth: A Journey into Bhutan* (New York: Penguin, 1999).

[19] Corrie Ten Boom, *The Hiding Place* (Grand Rapids: Chosen, 1984) 60.

[20] Thomas a Kempis, *The Imitation of Christ*, 1418 (New York: Dover, 2003).

[21] Judy Douglass in "What I Learned from My Children: Go Low—A Path of Selflessness," July 13, 2012. http://inkindle.wordpress.com/tag/unselfishness/.

[22] For the full transcript of The Declaration of Independence (July 4, 1776), visit the US government archives: http://www.archives.gov/exhibits/charters/declaration_transcript.html.

[23] Ruth Haley Barton, *Longing for More: A Woman's Path to Spiritual Transformation in Christ* (Downers Grove, InterVaristy Press Books, 2007) 14.

[24] Barton 14-15.

[25] Transcript of Oprah Winfrey's speech, delivered May 30, 2013, in *Harvard Gazette online*, May 31, 2013 paragraph 11 http://news.harvard.edu/gazette/story/2013/05/winfreys-commencement-address/.

Autumn

[1] Chamberlain, recalling Little Round Top and the Civil War. Speech on the Dedication of the Maine monuments at Gettysburg, October 3, 1889. To explore speeches and documents, visit the digital archive prepared by Bowdoin College. http://learn.bowdoin.edu/joshua-lawrence-chamberlain/.

[2] Parker Palmer, *To Know As We Are Known* (HarperCollins, 1993) ©1993 Parker Palmer. All rights reserved. Used with permission.

[3] Tina Seelig, *InGenius: A Crash Course on Creativity* (New York: HarperCollins, 2012) 105.

[4] Smith, *The God of All Comfort*, 159.

[5] Smith 159.

[6] Paul Miller, *A Praying Life* (Colorado Springs, Nav Press: 2009) 73.

[7] Miller 73.

[8] Jones 234.

[9] A.W. Tozer, *The Pursuit of God* (St. Joseph: Green Acres, 2014) 97.

[10] Smith 43.

[11] Timothy Lane and Paul David Tripp, *Study Guide: How People Change: How Christ Changes Us By His Grace* (Greensboro: New Growth Press, 2005) 4-5.

Bibliography

Ammons, A.R. "Loss." *The Selected Poems of A.R. Ammons.* New York: Norton, 1987.

Barton, Ruth Haley. *Longing for More: A Woman's Path to Spiritual Transformation in Christ.* Downers Grove: InterVarsity, 2007.

Borges, Jorge Luis. Trans. Norman Thomas di Giovanni. "The Life of Tadeo Isidoro." *The Aleph and Other Stories.* New York: Dutton, 1970.

Bright, Bill. *My Life is Not My Own: Following God No Matter What the Cost.* Ventura: Gospel Light and Bright Media Foundation, 2010.

--*How You Can Love by Faith.* Peachtree City: New Life Publications, 2002.

Bronte, Charlotte. *Jane Eyre*, 1847. Radford: Wilder Publications, 2008.

Brown, Paige Benton. "In the Temple: The Glorious and Forgiving God." Plenary address on 1 Kings 8 at the Gospel Coalition 2012 National Women's Conference. thegospelcoalition.org/resources/a/in_the_temple_the_glorious_and_forgiving_god_1_kings_8.

Buechner, Frederick. *Longing for Home: Reflections at Mid Life.* New York: HarperCollins, 1996.

Campbell, Joseph. *The Hero with a Thousand Faces.* Princeton: Princeton UP, 1949.

Carroll, E. Jean. "Ask E. Jean." *Elle Magazine* (January 2012). Web.

Carroll, Lewis. *Alice in Wonderland and Through the Looking Glass*, 1865. New York: Bantam, 1984.

Cercas, Javier. Trans. Anne McClean. *The Anatomy of a Moment.* London: Bloomsbury, 2009.

Chamberlain, Joshua Lawrence. "Speech on the Dedication of the Maine Monuments." Gettysburg, October 3, 1889.

Chambers, Oswald and James Reimann, ed. *My Utmost for His Highest.* Grand Rapids: Discovery House Publishers, 1992.

Chole, Alicia Britt. *Anonymous: Jesus' Hidden Years. . .and Yours.* Nashville: Thomas Nelson, 2006.

Crabb, Larry. "Living the New Way." Presented by Colorado Christian University, New Way Ministries & Dr. Larry Crabb. Radio Audio Cuts on K-Love.

Crawley, Michael. "Cynicism." 30 January 2001. http://michaelmfc.wordpress.com/2011/01/30/cynicism/.

Creagh, Carson. "Taking Off." *Things with Wings.* Alexandria: Time-Life, 1996.

Defoe, Daniel. *Robinson Crusoe*, 1719. Oxford: Oxford UP, 2008.

Douglass, Judy. "What I Learned from My Children: Go Low—A Path of Selflessness." July 13, 2012. http://inkindle.wordpress.com/tag/unselfishness/.

Duvall, Monique. Compendium, Inc. 2014.

Goudge, Elizabeth. *The Scent of Water*, 1963. Peabody: Hendrickson, 2012.

Henrichsen, Walter and Howard G. Hendricks. *Disciples are Made Not Born; Helping Others Grow to Maturity in Christ*. Colorado Springs: David C. Cook, 1988.

Hession, Roy and Revel. *We Would See Jesus, 1958*. Philadelphia: CLC Ministries, 2005.

Ilibagiza, Immaculee. *Left to Tell*. New York: Hay House, Inc. 2014.

Jackson, Michael. "Beat It." *Thriller*. Epic, 1983.

Jacobsen, Jens Peter. *Mogens, and Other Stories*. Denmark: N.L. Brown, 1921.

Jones, E. Stanley. *Abundant Living: 365 Daily Devotions*. New York: Abingdon-Cokesbury, 1946.

-- *The Way*. New York: Abingdon-Cokesbury, 1946.

Keller, Timothy. "Made for Stewardship." Preached October 22, 2000, downloaded from http://sermons2.redeemer.com/sermons/sermonlist/265. Accessed 29 August 2011.

-- *The Freedom of Self-Forgetfulness: The Path to True Christian Joy*. Nashville: Thomas Nelson, 1982.

Kempis, Thomas à. *The Imitation of Christ*, 1418. New York: Dover, 2003.

Kidd, Sue Monk. *The Secret Life of Bees*. New York: Penguin, 2002.

Lane, Timothy and Paul David Tripp. *Study Guide: How People Change: How Christ Changes Us By His Grace*. Greensboro: New Growth Press, 2005.

Lewis, C.S. *Mere Christianity*. New York: Macmillan, 1952.

-- *Surprised by Joy: The Shape of My Early Life*. Orlando: Harcourt Books, 1955.

Maslow, A.H. "A Theory of Human Motivation." *Psychological Review* (1943): 370–96.

Meadows, Susannah. "Meet the Gamma Girls." *Newsweek* 139.22 (June 3, 2002): 44-50.

Miller, Paul. *A Praying Life*. Colorado Springs: Nav Press, 2009.

Nouwen, Henri. *Return of the Prodigal Son*. New York: Doubleday, 1992.

Packer, J.I. *Knowing God*. Downers Grove: InterVarsity Press, 1993.

Palmer, Parker J, "Good Talk about Good Teaching." *Change: The Magazine of Higher Learning* 25.6 (1993): 8-13.

-- *To Know As We Are Known*. New York: HarperCollins, 1993.

Paterniti, Michael. *The Telling Room: A Tale of Love, Betrayal, Revenge, and the World's Greatest Piece of Cheese*. New York: Random House, 2013.

Pipher, Mary. *Writing to Change the World*. New York: Riverhead, 2006.

Rilke, Rainer Maria. *Letters to a Young Poet*. Trans. M.D. Herter Norton. New York: W.W. Norton & Company, 1954.

Seelig, Tina. *InGenius: A Crash Course on Creativity*. New York: HarperCollins, 2012.

Silf, Margaret. *Inner Compass: An Invitation to Ignatian Spirituality*. Chicago: Loyola Press, 1999.

--*Landmarks: An Ignatian Journey*. London: Darton, Longman & Todd, 1998.

Smith, Hannah Whitall. *The Christian Secret of a Happy Life, Complete and Unabridged*, 1870. Urichsville: Barbour, 1985.

-- *God is Enough*. Grand Rapids: Zondervan, 1986.

Ten Boom, Corrie. *The Hiding Place*. Grand Rapids: Chosen, 1984.

Thoreau, Henry David. *Walden, Or Life in the Woods*. Radford: Wilder Publications, 2008.

Tozer, A. W. *The Pursuit of God*. St. Joseph: Green Acres, 2014.

Whitman, Walt. "Preface." *Leaves of Grass, 1855*. New York: Penguin, 1961.

-- "A Backward Glance O'er Travel'd Roads." *The Complete Poems*. New York: Penguin, 2005.

Wikipedia contributors. "Late bloomer." *Wikipedia, The Free Encyclopedia*. 30 Aug. 2014. Web. 6 Nov. 2014.

Wilkinson, Robert. *The Saints travel to the land of Canaan Wherein is discovered seventeen false rests below the spiritual coming of Christ in the Saints. Together with a brief discovery of what the coming of Christ in the spirit is; who is the alone rest and center of spirits*. London: Printed for Giles Calvert, at the black spread-Eagle at the west end of Pauls, 1648.

Wilson, E.O. "The Naturalist." *Being Human: Core Readings in the Humanities*. New York: W.W. Norton, 2004.

Winfrey, Oprah. "Winfrey's Commencement Address." *Harvard Gazette online*. May 31, 2013. Par 11. Commencement Address. http://news.harvard.edu/gazette/story/2013/05/winfreys-commencement-address/.

Wordsworth, William. "Lines Composed a Few Miles Above Tintern Abbey, On Revisiting the Banks of the Wye During a Tour, July 13,1978." *Lyrical Ballads with other Poems. In Two Volumes*. London: Longman and Rees, 1800.

Zeppa, Jamie. *Beyond the Sky and Earth: A Journey into Bhutan*. New York: Penguin, 1999.

I invite you to visit www.livewithflair.blogspot.com to enjoy original photography, free summer devotions for children, recipes, and daily reflections.

Many of your favorite entries over the years may not have been selected for this collection, but they too remain on the blog.

Special thanks to Rachel Schrock for her cover design and to Denise Haley for offering her editorial expertise.

Thank you for your faithful readership over the years.

May you live with flair today and every day.

Made in the USA
Charleston, SC
20 July 2016